Elections in Hard Times

Why are "free and fair" elections so often followed by democratic backsliding? *Elections in Hard Times* answers this critical question, showing why even clean elections fail to advance democracy when held amidst challenging structural conditions. The book opens with a comprehensive, accessible synthesis of fifty years of research on elections and democratization, a resource for experts, policymakers, and students. It then develops a new theory of why elections fail in countries with little democratic history or fiscal resources, and a history of violent conflict. In a series of five empirical chapters, the book leverages an eclectic mix of cross-national data, short case studies, and surveys of voters to support this theory. It closes with a careful examination of popular strategies of democracy promotion, evaluating steps designed to support elections. This book will attract academic experts on democratization and elections, students, and policymakers.

THOMAS EDWARD FLORES is Associate Professor in George Mason University's School for Conflict Analysis and Resolution. His research has been published in the *Journal of Politics, Journal of Conflict Resolution,* and *Review of International Organizations,* among others.

IRFAN NOORUDDIN is the Al-Thani Chair in Indian Politics and Professor in the School of Foreign Service at Georgetown University. He is the author of over twenty scholarly publications including *Coalition Politics and Economic Development* (Cambridge, 2011).

Elections in Hard Times

Building Stronger Democracies
in the 21st Century

THOMAS EDWARD FLORES

AND

IRFAN NOORUDDIN

CAMBRIDGE
UNIVERSITY PRESS

published in association with Wilson Center Press,
Washington, DC

CAMBRIDGE
UNIVERSITY PRESS

University Printing House, Cambridge CB2 8BS, United Kingdom

Cambridge University Press is part of the University of Cambridge.

It furthers the University's mission by disseminating knowledge in the pursuit of education, learning and research at the highest international levels of excellence.

www.cambridge.org
Information on this title: www.cambridge.org/9781107584631

© Thomas Edward Flores and Irfan Nooruddin 2016

First published 2016

Published in association with Woodrow Wilson Center Press, Washington, DC

Printed in the United Kingdom by Clays, St Ives plc.

A catalogue record for this publication is available from the British Library

Library of Congress Cataloguing in Publication data
Names: Flores, Thomas Edward, author. | Nooruddin, Irfan.
Title: Elections in hard times : building stronger democracies in the 21st century / Thomas Edward Flores, Irfan Nooruddin.
Description: Cambridge; New York, NY : Cambridge University Press; Washington, DC : Woodrow Wilson Center Press, 2015. |
Includes bibliographical references and index.
Identifiers: LCCN 2016004912 | ISBN 9781107132139 (hardback)
Subjects: LCSH: Elections–Cross-cultural studies. |
Voting–Cross-cultural studies. | Democracy–Cross-cultural studies.
Classification: LCC JF1001.F56 2016 | DDC 324.9–dc23
LC record available at http://lccn.loc.gov/2016004912

ISBN 978-1-107-13213-9 Hardback
ISBN 978-1-107-58463-1 Paperback

Wilson Center

The Wilson Center, chartered by Congress as the official memorial to President Woodrow Wilson, is the nation's key nonpartisan policy forum for tackling global issues through independent research and open dialogue to inform actionable ideas for Congress, the Administration, and the broader policy community.

Conclusions or opinions expressed in Center publications and programs are those of the authors and speakers and do not necessarily reflect the views of the Center staff, fellows, trustees, advisory groups, or any individuals or organizations that provide financial support to the Center.

Please visit us online at www.wilsoncenter.org.

Jane Harman, Director, President, and CEO

To our parents

Ernesto Javier and Lillian Belle Flores

and

Noëlle Marie Vaz and Irshad Ali Nooruddin

Because, ah them that's got are them that gets
And I ain't got nothin yet
That old sayin them that's got are them that gets
Is somethin I can't see
If ya gotta have somethin
Before you can get somethin
How do ya get your first is still a mystery to me

Ray Charles and Ricca Z. Harper, "I Ain't Got Nothing Yet
(Them That Got)"

*(Lyrics reproduced with permission)**

Contents

Figures

Tables

Preface

Democracy is in global retreat forty years after the Third Wave of Democracy began. The Arab Spring has ended in reinforced authoritarianism in Egypt, civil war in Libya, and the most fragile of democratic politics in Tunisia. Turkey's Recep Tayyip Erdoğan continues to crack down on the press and punish dissent, firing or reassigning thousands of police officers and judges. Elections in Sub-Saharan Africa are followed by violence as often as peace. The likes of Paul Kagame, Vladimir Putin, Robert Mugabe, and Hun Sen, meanwhile, continue in power as they "win" tarnished elections. In Hungary, Prime Minister Viktor Orbán openly advocates abandoning liberal democracy in favor of an "illiberal state." Even in Western Europe, a supposed bastion of electoral democracy, confidence in democracy seems to be declining amid high unemployment and hostility towards migrants.

Democracy promoters have reacted to their cause's perceived global decay with public alarm and despondence. Freedom House's *Freedom in the World 2015* report is sub-titled "Discarding Democracy: Return to the Iron Fist," betraying its gloomy outlook. The National Endowment for Democracy, meanwhile, recently published a new volume titled *Democracy in Decline?*, which includes an entry from Francis Fukuyama, who famously predicted in the heady days of the early 1990s that liberal democracy would be the endpoint of history. If an organization whose entire mission centers on supporting democratic change questions whether democracy is in decline, the answer almost certainly would seem to be yes. Even *The Economist*, the classically liberal news magazine, dedicated a special issue in 2014 to this democratic malaise, asking, "What's gone wrong with democracy?"

For many, the answer to this question is elections themselves. Rather than seeds of democratic change, elections have become a veritable scapegoat, blamed for everything from entrenching autocrats to causing civil war. Preeminent scholars in political science have painstakingly shown how incumbents cheat to win elections, even as

Western monitoring organizations try to stop them. Bad elections, they argue, yield bad democracy. *The Economist* itself blames elections when it contends that, "One reason why so many democratic experiments have failed recently is that they put too much emphasis on elections and too little on the other essential features of democracy."

In this book, we offer a different interpretation of elections' role in democratic change. Elections rapidly spread to every corner of the globe after about 1988 in what we call the "electoral boom." They also became dramatically more competitive, despite claims to the contrary, as international pressure forced incumbents to eschew many forms of manipulation. Yet elections since 1988 have been followed by little democratic change; in fact, they have been as likely to be followed by authoritarian reversal as democratic progress.

Why did elections lose their democratizing power just as they spread globally and improved in transparency? Our answer centers on the political-economic context in which elections take place. When election winners take power, voters demand performance, particularly economic growth. True, an election winner does enjoy some degree of *contingent legitimacy,* that democratic honeymoon period that comes with winning a clean election. Yet voters are impatient for results and that places politicians in a bind, since they often inherit low stocks of what we call *performance legitimacy* – that is, the ability to generate public goods. What is a rational incumbent to do? An obvious re-election strategy is to buy off some voters with bribes and suppress dissent among others. This, however, is harder to do when a deep stock of *democratic-institutional legitimacy* constrains the incumbent from subverting democratic rule. Elections, then, are more likely to end in disappointment when held in places with shallower stocks of legitimacy. Elections in these circumstances more likely begin the low-legitimacy trap that so worries democracy promoters – elections, poor government performance, democratic erosion, voter disillusionment with democracy, and then more elections.

The core of this book is dedicated to testing these arguments. We show that the electoral boom's very success contained the seed of its disappointment: as elections inexorably spread the world over, they arrived in countries with daunting challenges to democratization. The electoral boom undoubtedly represented a democratic triumph, yet came on the heels of the international upheavals of decolonization, the global debt crisis of the 1980s, and the collapse of Communism and economic contraction of Eastern Europe. It is precisely these countries where elections arrived: younger, poorer, and more ethnically divided societies with a history of foreign domination. We present robust evidence that elections disappoint when they are held in countries with little democratic experience, scant fiscal space, and a history of civil war. Elections in these circumstances are followed by democratic stasis, voter disillusionment, opposition complaints, worse elections in the future, and entrenched incumbents. Even the more competitive elections in these settings yield no additional democratic dividend. This is our main finding: electoral seeds fail to bear democratic fruit not because they are poor quality, but because of the inhospitable terrain in which they are sown.

What does this mean for democracy promotion in the twenty-first century? There is much room for pessimism, we admit. Any "easy" cases for democracy have already democratized and the countries left – the places where we most dearly wish for democracy's success – suffer from precisely the challenges we identify here. Nor can democracy promotion succeed merely by improving the quality and integrity of elections. Instead we argue that democracy promoters must seek to supplement depleted stocks of performance and democratic-institutional legitimacy if they are to succeed. The evidence here is not unrelentingly bleak, however. We show that some efforts at democracy promotion do succeed in specific low-legitimacy contexts, especially election observation, democracy aid, and peacekeeping missions that make electoral support an explicit part of their mandate.

The origins of this book date to a late night at the annual meetings of the Midwest Political Science Association (MPSA), as we scribbled on a cocktail napkin in the lobby of the Palmer House Hilton in Chicago, Illinois. That was over ten years ago. Since then, we have accumulated intellectual debts at a rate that would make us blush if we had any shame about such things. Our deepest debt is to three academic giants on whose shoulders we stand. Since we were undergraduates, we have been awed by the intellectual contributions of Robert Dahl, Samuel Huntington, and Adam Przeworski. Their thinking about democracy influences every page of this book. In writing it, we aspire to produce the kind of book they did (and do) – bursting with "big" ideas but grounded in reality. We also owe a deep debt to the members of our dissertation committees at the University of Michigan (go blue!):

Pradeep Chhibber, William Clark, Rob Franzese, John Jackson, Jim Morrow, and Michael Ross. Though they did not technically advise this project, the lessons they imparted as advisors continue to shape our thinking.

What began as an analysis of post-conflict elections evolved into this book. That metamorphosis was encouraged and enabled by the wise counsel and support of our colleagues. Gaby Lloyd edited, indexed, and improved the entire manuscript. She, Alex Castillo, and Susan Guarda provided research assistance at an early stage of the project. Susan Hyde, Emily Beaulieu, and Daniela Donno generously shared their data and offered useful comments on the whole book. In addition, Carew Boulding, Daniel Corstange, Jennifer Raymond Dresden, Thad Dunning, Terrence Lyons, Niki Marinov, Porter McConnell, Tess McEnery, Will Moore, Agnieszka Paczynska, Heidi Sherman, Joel Simmons, Alberto Simpser, and Lauren Young offered advice at various stages of the book's development. Audiences at Columbia University, Florida State University, the Free University of Berlin, George Mason University, Georgia State University, the International Studies Association, the University of Arizona, the V-DEM Institute at the University of Gothenburg, the University of Michigan, the Woodrow Wilson International Center for Scholars, and Yale University also improved this work through their generous comments.

The support of various institutions merits acknowledgement. A fellowship for Irfan at the Wilson Center came at an ideal time in the development of our thinking. Tom thanks his colleagues at the School of Conflict Analysis and Resolution at George Mason University and the Center for Global Affairs at New York University for their support of this research. Our editors, John Haslam, David McKenzie, and Carrie Parkinson at Cambridge University Press, and Joe Brinley at the Wilson Center Press, have been supportive throughout. We thank also Dave McBride at Oxford University Press for the two excellent reviews he secured. More mundanely, this book would not exist without plentiful supplies of caffeine, so we thank a different set of institutions for keeping us awake, mostly alert, and writing: Flying Fish, Tryst, Big Bear, and Potter's House in Washington, DC; Northside Social in Arlington, VA; and Grandview Grind and Impero Coffee in Columbus, OH. We'll have two large coffees with a little room for cream, please.

We thank each day what God may exist for our children – Charles Ernest Flores-McConnell and Esme Alice and Emil Francis Nooruddin. Together, they are the most adorable (and adept) writing blocks known to humankind. We especially thank Charlie for being a good sleeper, given that he was born only nine months before this book was submitted to Cambridge, and Emil for being a lousy one since it helped Irfan get some writing done in the middle of the night. The single most trenchant criticism of this book came from Esme, who expressed utter chagrin at its length. She suggested condensing it to two pages – a step we have failed to accomplish by two orders of magnitude, though we assure her we tried.

Thanking our spouses, Porter McConnell and Heidi Sherman, adequately is impossible. We could praise their steadfast support, frequent counsel, and occasional proofreading. We could detail how Porter's work on illicit financial flows or Heidi's sociological imagination directly influenced our ideas. We could thank them for bringing us children we adore. We could thank them for the dozens of times they cared for those same children alone while we presented our work at conferences. We could even appreciate their frequent, though gentle, jibes at our geeky academic selves. They deserve all that and more. But we most deeply thank Porter and Heidi for infusing our lives with a happiness, joy, and purpose that far exceeds anything either of us have ever known.

Our parents, and our brothers and their families, laid the foundation of support upon which all our accomplishments are predicated. To our parents, Ernesto Javier and Lillian Belle Flores and Irshad Ali Nooruddin and Noëlle Marie Vaz, we gratefully dedicate this book. You continue to be our wisest teachers and our truest guides and it is our dearest hope that we make you proud.

Despite the sincere efforts of all named above, errors and omissions remain and we each remind our readers that all mistakes are the fault of the other guy.

PART I

From Elections to Democracy: Theory and Evidence

1 | Introduction

The largest competitive election in world history took place in India during April and May 2014. It featured roughly 563 million voters (out of 815 million eligible citizens), choosing from among 8,251 candidates, representing nearly three dozen political parties, competing for 543 seats in the Lok Sabha (the Indian Parliament's lower house), over thirty-five days and nine phases. The results, though anticipated in pre-election polls, sent shockwaves throughout India. The Indian National Congress party, led by Rahul Gandhi, scion of the Nehru-Gandhi family, suffered its worst loss since independence – it won only 44 seats, compared to the 206 seats won in the election five years earlier. The Bharatiya Janata Party (BJP) won enough seats to form the first majority government India had experienced since 1984. Its National Democratic Alliance, a coalition with 20 other parties, holds 336 seats. Sporadic violence did force the Election Commission to order re-polling in certain locales and allegations of vote-buying were common, if unverified. Yet few questioned the legitimacy of this complex vote. The BJP's leader Narendra Modi took power as the fifteenth Prime Minister of India on May 26, 2014 after Gandhi conceded Congress's crushing defeat and Prime Minister Manmohan Singh peacefully relinquished power.

India's 2014 elections extended a long legacy of competitive elections. India has held sixteen competitive national elections since its independence from Great Britain in 1947, beginning with the 1951–1952 elections that first brought the Congress party, led by Jawaharlal Nehru, to political power. Though the Congress party dominated Indian politics for several decades – hardly a surprise given the party's central role in the nation's struggle for independence – it has placed second or lower in four of the last seven general elections. Its first electoral loss in 1977 followed "the Emergency" in 1975, in which President Fakhruddin Ali Ahmed declared a state of emergency, allowing Prime Minister Indira Gandhi to suspend elections, imprison opposition leaders, and censor newspapers criticizing her rule. No government in India has attempted such an autocratic gambit since.

Just one year before India's 2014 election, Pakistan held elections on May 11, 2013. That two neighboring countries born in 1947 with a common history of British colonial rule held elections in consecutive years speaks to the potential for democratic hegemony in South Asia.[1] However, these similarities do not obscure the striking contrasts between elections in India and Pakistan. Violence marred the vote in Pakistan. Armed groups such as the Tehrik-i-Taliban Pakistan (TTP) attacked candidates and party headquarters in an effort to disrupt the election, causing dozens of deaths in the run-up to voting. Even so, the National Democratic Institute for International Affairs (NDI), an internationally recognized election monitor and democracy promotion organization, declared the election a success, noting its improved "legal and regulatory framework" and increasing participation by young people.[2] Nawaz Sharif of the Pakistan Muslim League (N), who had been prime minster twice before, won a convincing victory and formed a government by attracting independent candidates to his banner. Allegations of vote-rigging have haunted his government, and third-place candidate (and former star cricketer) Imran Khan has continually accused the government of vote-rigging, leading multiple protests against alleged corruption in the government. Beyond elections, Pakistan's domestic politics are roiled by extremist groups and the shadow of an extremely powerful military that has traditionally enjoyed outsized independence and influence over elected politicians.[3] Unhappily, the 2013 election in Pakistan appears unlikely to deepen democratic practice; violence, elite distrust, and political instability instead threaten to unravel the benefits of a relatively clean vote.[4]

Pakistan and India's democratic divergence in the sixty-nine years since their independence is striking. Each was born in 1947 as the sun set on the British Empire, could turn to remarkable founding fathers for political leadership in its early years, has held elections throughout its independent history, has struggled with poverty and internal violence, and has often voted for dynastic families in free elections. Yet India has steadily burnished its democratic credentials, while Pakistan had sadly endured four military coups by 2013 and has never before had one popularly elected administration hand power over to another, despite having held ten elections since 1970.

Elections have produced puzzlingly different consequences elsewhere, too. We might, for example, consider the cases of Tunisia and Egypt, each of which deposed entrenched autocrats in largely bloodless uprisings in early 2011. Yet their paths – and the repercussions of rapidly held elections – have diverged since. Tunisia held elections in 2011 to a constituent assembly charged with writing a new constitution and has held successful and peaceful parliamentary and presidential elections in the last few months of 2014. Challenges remain in the form of a collapsing regional neighborhood and increasingly outrageous forays by extremist groups. Nevertheless, hopes are understandably high that Tunisia's success will set an example for democratic accession to power in its region.[5] By contrast, the initial headiness from the protests in Egypt's Tahrir Square that led to the ouster of Hosni Mobarak have given way to grim cynicism. Competitive elections in 2011 brought to power a government led by Mohamed Morsi of the Muslim Brotherhood. Yet Morsi's government fell in a military coup in 2013 – only one year after taking office – after which General Abdel Fattah al-Sisi came to power, in part by winning a carefully choreographed election, the result of which was distinctly preordained. Egypt's courts have handed down mass death sentences, including to Morsi, and state repression of dissent is high.

We do not have to compare different countries to depict the puzzling consequences of competitive elections. Liberia's post-war history since 1995 also demonstrates how competitive elections can generate startlingly disparate consequences for democracy. Competitive elections in 1997 were held to fulfill the obligations of a 1996 peace agreement ending seven years of civil war following the end of Samuel Doe's repressive rule, which itself had followed decades of domination by Americo-Liberians. Voters swept Charles Taylor – the former leader of the National Patriotic Front, a guerrilla group, who campaigned on the slogan "He killed my ma, he killed my pa, but I will vote for him" – into office over Ellen Johnson Sirleaf, a World Bank economist.[6] The results were perhaps predictably catastrophic. Taylor ruled with an iron fist and fomented civil war in neighboring Sierra Leone. After the dawn of the Second Liberian Civil War in 1999, multiple insurgent groups marched on Monrovia, ending Taylor's reign in 2003. Liberia's second post-war election in a decade, however, thus far seems to have ended far more happily. The 2005 general elections brought Sirleaf to power. Upon assuming control, Sirleaf quickly sought loan forgiveness, pursued foreign aid in foreign capitals, and won the Nobel Prize for Peace. Liberians re-elected her in 2011.

These anecdotes highlight an electoral paradox familiar to those working to promote democracy around the world. Elections in post-independence India, Tunisia since the Arab Spring, and Liberia in 2003 were followed by democratic progress, however halting. Elections in Pakistan since its independence, Egypt since 2011, and Liberia in 1997, in contrast, were followed by political violence, instability, and authoritarian rule. Explaining this variation in the democratic dividend of elections is our goal.

The Triumph and Failure of the Electoral Boom

The period since 1988, which we label the "electoral boom," witnessed the spread of elections to every corner of the globe. Many of these were opportunities for opposition parties to contest elections that were supervised by international monitors. Yet the apparent triumph of the electoral boom was accompanied simultaneously by failure; elections after 1990 typically yielded little-to-no democratic change. Just as elections became freer and more frequent, they seemingly lost their power to propel long-lasting political change.

Figure 1.1 illustrates the dramatic political change wrought by the electoral boom. It displays the percentage of sovereign countries holding any elections in each year since 1946. It also shows the percentage of countries holding competitive executive elections in those years, thus imposing a higher threshold on what constitutes an election.[7]

The late 1940s represented the previous peak of elections. During this peak, European countries, including Eastern European countries before the Communist takeover of the late 1940s, held relatively free elections in the wake of World War II. Just over a third of sovereign countries held an election, and more than a fifth of countries held a competitive executive election, in 1946. These proportions halved over the next thirty years, falling to about 17 percent and 8 percent, respectively, by 1977. The reasons for this long decline in election-holding are numerous. The geo-political pressures of the Cold War led the Soviet Union and the United States to bolster "friendly" authoritarians around the globe. Colonialism also ended during this time period, substantially expanding the state system, but birthing countries that

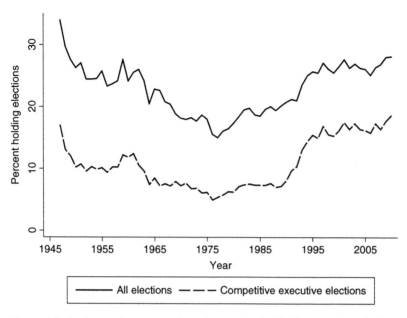

Figure 1.1 An increasing proportion of countries held elections after the late 1980s

avoided elections for years. The late 1970s witnessed the global nadir of elections.

The electoral boom reshaped this state of affairs. The change is most noticeable for competitive executive elections. Until the mid-1980s, fewer than one-tenth of countries held a competitive executive election in any given year. However, with the fall of the Soviet Union and the end of the Cold War, societies turned (or returned) to electoral competition to choose their political leaders. The percentage of countries holding competitive executive elections nearly doubled in just ten years between 1988 and 1997. The same trend holds if we consider the wider population of all elections. The proportion of countries holding elections has remained highly stable since the electoral boom's initial surge ended in the mid-1990s, running between 25 and 30 percent since about 1995. To state it plainly, in any year in the past three decades, one out of every four countries has held an election of some kind, and three out of every four were within a year of doing so.

The electoral boom particularly transformed politics in the developing world. Developing countries held more elections between 1988 and 2010 (544 competitive executive, 889 total) than in the forty-one years between 1946 and 1987 (332 competitive executive, 866 total). Another indicator of the ubiquity of elections is the number of countries in a given year that are electoral exceptionalists. This group of dubious exclusivity includes countries that have not yet held a national competitive executive election since the conclusion of World War II. Membership in this group is dwindling rapidly. As of 1987, more than 57 of 135 developing countries had yet to hold an election; by the end of 2015, just thirteen countries remain on the list of states yet to hold a national competitive executive election. This set of "election hold-outs" are dominated by Middle Eastern monarchies.[8]

A tempered response to the triumphalist "end of history" narrative of the electoral boom might be that these elections were only nominally free and fair but were de facto uncompetitive. As democracy activists and journalists – not to mention putative opposition candidates – would attest, printing an opposition candidate's name on the ballot is not the same as allowing that candidate to compete on an even playing field. Morgan Tsvangirai of Zimbabwe, for example, was arrested and beaten in 2007 for daring to oppose President Robert Mugabe in the upcoming elections, and Viktor Yushchenko was poisoned as he contested the presidency of Ukraine in 2004. Corrupt autocrats have held nominally competitive elections while stealing them through other means, such as harassing the opposition. Did the electoral boom only reshape autocratic rule, or did it actually represent meaningful political change?

Figure 1.2 divides all elections held since 1946 into three categories: uncompetitive; nominally competitive, but featuring harassment of the opposition; and competitive without such harassment. It then plots the proportion of elections in each category by decade. The electoral boom not only increased the number of elections held, but also improved their quality. For the first time since the 1940s, the majority of elections (more than 60 percent in the 1990s and 2000s) are competitive without harassment of the opposition. The proportion of elections deemed uncompetitive, meanwhile, plummeted to less than 10 percent after remaining stable at around 30 percent for more than thirty years between the 1960s and 1990s. Nominally competitive elections have also become more common; they comprised more than a quarter of all elections in the 1990s and 2000s. The rise of nominally competitive elections has come mainly at the expense of

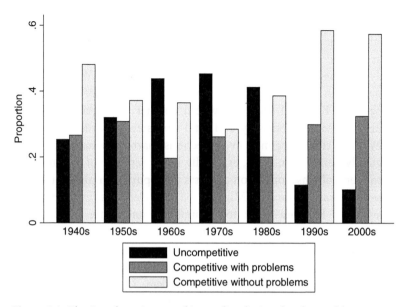

Figure 1.2 Elections have increased in quality during the electoral boom

uncompetitive elections – the share of elections rated uncompetitive by National Elections across Democracy and Autocracy (NELDA) dropped by roughly 25 percent between the 1980s and the 2000s, while the share of nominally competitive elections with harassment of the opposition increased by about 12 percent and the share of clean competitive elections increased by about 14 percent. The trend over the last three decades has been inexorably towards cleaner elections, especially when we consider just how many more elections were held in the 1990s and 2000s. The elections of the electoral boom, then, have been the cleanest in post-war history, a claim which has been verified by the scores of electoral monitors attending such elections in recent years.

Thus far, we have told a rather happy democratic story: the electoral boom not only spread elections to every corner of the globe, but elevated standards of electoral integrity as well. These gains seem permanent – the proportion of countries holding competitive executive elections has remained stable, and even slightly increased, since the heady days of the mid-1990s. Electoral cynics might point to the stubbornly high percentage of elections that adhere to only minimal norms of open competition. Citing unhappy cases such as Egypt since the Arab Spring or Zimbabwe in the past few decades, they might argue that a wide proportion of elections in developing countries remain only nominally competitive. This amounts to a claim that such elections will do little to improve democratic practice in the medium and long runs. Electoral optimists would counter by arguing that elections represent a necessary and vital first step towards opening up previously closed regimes; even elections marred by malpractice are arguably better than none, especially if the scrutiny of international actors emboldens opposition activists and spurs incumbents to enact pro-democratic reforms.[9] Might it be that elections, even imperfect ones, open Pandora's box for incumbents and begin an inevitable process of genuine democratization?

The claim of "democratization by elections" is intuitive and normatively attractive. Elections, in this telling, do more than merely provide a mechanism to choose new political leaders. They also create spaces for political oppositions to organize, alter the expectations of political representation among voters, and reveal the true popularity of incumbent regimes. Even when these incumbents – nervous about their prospects – resort to fraud and intimidation to secure victory, merely having to do so exposes their vulnerability and inspires domestic outrage and international condemnation.[10] In a sense, this is precisely the history of the established democracies of the West, whose early efforts at elections would scarcely have passed muster with election observers from the Carter Center or the European Union.

Has the electoral boom improved the prospects for democracy globally? Figure 1.3 suggests not. For every developing country holding a competitive executive election, we calculate the change in its democracy score two and five years into the future.[11] We call this the "democratic dividend" of elections. A positive democratic dividend means that the election yielded further democratic progress, while a negative democratic dividend means that democracy deteriorated following the election.

Figure 1.3 plots the average democratic dividend by decade, yielding several lessons about the capacity of elections to foment democratic change. The first trend should distress the electoral optimist: elections since World War II generally have not yielded a democratic dividend, but rather incurred a democratic debt. The average election in the thirty-four years from 1946 until 1980 actually precipitated a

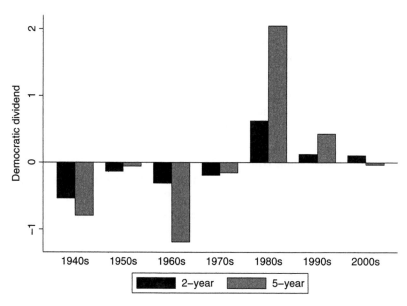

Figure 1.3 Elections during the electoral boom have yielded little democratic change

reduction in the country's democracy score. The five-year democratic debt was deeper than its two-year counterpart in each of these decades but the 1950s (though it remained negative even then), implying that democratic deterioration usually worsened with time. For instance, out of seventy-six competitive executive elections held in the 1970s, twenty-three (30 percent) were followed by democratic backsliding within five years with only thirteen (17 percent) witnessing democratic progress. All this would change in the 1980s; finally, elections were typically followed by a democratic dividend. The average developing country gained more than half a point on its democracy score within two years following competitive executive elections and almost two points within five years of the election. Thirty-two election-holding countries saw democratic progress within five years, versus only thirteen that witnessed democratic regression. Elections in the 1980s were also associated with more sustained democratic momentum; the five-year democratic dividend was actually positive and greater than the two-year dividend for the first time since World War II. This peak led to democratic triumphalism in the academy with the publication of

Huntington's *Third Wave* and Fukuyama's *End of History*. However, this victory was temporary.

In the 1990s, the average democratic dividend from elections plunged to a fraction of its 1980s peak. The change remained positive, which still differentiates the 1990s from the dark days of the 1960s and 1970s, but the return from competitive executive elections clearly had entered a slump. That slump continued into the 2000s, when the average two-year democratic dividend was nearly nil; on average, a developing country holding a competitive executive election experienced no democratic change. The 2000s also witnessed an important change from the 1980s and 1990s: the five-year democratic dividend once again turned negative.[12] Sixty years of elections had yielded little democratic fruit; elections in the developing world were associated with democratic change for only a brief shining period during the 1980s, just before the electoral boom of the late 1980s and early 1990s. The global spread of elections following the end of the Cold War, however, did not produce a healthy democratic dividend.

Perhaps we judge elections' success in encouraging democratic change too harshly. It is entirely possible that the countries holding elections democratized so quickly and completely before they held elections that little work remained to be done after elections. There is some truth to this objection; the typical developing country holding a competitive executive election in the 2000s was already quite democratic, suggesting that it was reaching a kind of democratic ceiling in which further democratic change was less possible.

Yet this objection does not undermine the core empirical point at issue for two reasons. First, election-holding countries have hardly reached their democratic ceiling; by any accepted measure of democracy, nearly one-third of countries holding competitive executive elections are non-democratic. Indeed, this trend of authoritarian governments calling elections has led to a proliferation of labels such as "hybrid regimes," "electoral autocracies," and "competitive authoritarianism." Further democratic change certainly remains possible after elections. Second, the poor democratic performance of elections is evident even if we consider only those countries holding their first multiparty elections. By definition, such countries have healthy room for democratic improvement. The comparison of the 1980s and 1990s is again telling. Countries holding their first elections in the 1980s harvested a bumper democratic crop; however, by the 2000s, the democratic dividend had again turned to a deficit as the average country holding its first multiparty elections lost ground on its overall level of democracy.

We can now more fully describe both the unprecedented triumph and the ultimate frustrations of the electoral boom. The several years following 1988 witnessed not only the fall of the Berlin Wall and the collapse of Communism, but also the global spread of competitive elections. Nearly one in five countries around the world holds a competitive election for the office of head of government every year. The developing world held more competitive executive elections in the thirteen years after 1987 than it did in the forty-one years before. Nor was the sudden shift towards electoral competition mere autocratic window-dressing – elections since 1988 have been the most free of the post–World War II period. Yet these electoral feats also gave way to democratic disappointment. For just as the electoral boom took shape, elections' ability to foment democratic change dissipated. The 1980s represent the only decade in which elections were associated with sustained post-election democratic change, even though the electoral boom did not commence until 1988. The elections of the electoral boom, meanwhile, were followed by little, if any, democratic change.

We are left with a puzzle: why did elections lose their democratizing power soon after the beginning of the electoral boom, during which they spread globally and improved in quality? We sketch our answer below, but defer a fuller elucidation of our logic and of our evidence to subsequent chapters.

Electoral Seeds and Democratic Fruit

We propose a new theory of elections that explains why elections advance democratization in some times and places but not others. This effort places us in the debt of a long line of scholars who have studied the dynamics of elections and democracy, though with varying emphases. Two earlier generations of political scientists minimized the role of elections in fomenting meaningful political change. Classical theories of modernization, such as those enunciated by Karl Deutsch and Seymour Martin Lipset, argued that slow-moving structural changes (e.g., urbanization, economic growth, mass communications) held the key to understanding democratization.[13] Subsequent scholars studying democratic transition and consolidation, such as Dankwart

Rustow, and Guillermo O'Donnell and Philippe Schmitter, instead proposed that political elites drove political change, with the actual path depending on idiosyncratic factors.[14] Elections represented the denouement, rather than a driver, of political liberalization. Neither of these classic accounts of democratization attributed much theoretical power to elections as agents of change.

The theoretical field shifted in the twenty-first century as political scientists – no doubt inspired by the electoral boom of the 1990s – placed elections squarely in the center of theories of democratic change. Yet profound disagreements persist. One group of scholars propose that elections tend to yield democratic change, even when they fail basic standards of openness.[15] Such theories of democratization by elections envision elections as incubators of democratic change, creating new avenues for dissent in closed regimes. These scholars focus on how differences in the conduct of elections might affect the subsequent democratic dividend, eschewing the more structural bent of other approaches to comparative democratization. Students of authoritarian resilience have offered a powerful rejoinder to this narrative.[16] These scholars recognize that the international political zeitgeist certainly tilted towards liberalism after 1990. Yet they describe in great detail how autocrats have responded to this pressure by creating quasi-democratic institutions – including holding nominally competitive elections – to supply a democratic veneer to their otherwise closed regimes.

The relationship between elections and processes of democratization therefore remains theoretically ambiguous, or in Jan Teorell's more colorful phrase, the study of comparative democratization is "inchoate, diversified and incoherent."[17] Previous scholars have claimed variously that elections trigger democratization, bolster authoritarianism, and do neither. One might point to cases to support any of these perspectives: the controversial presidential elections held in Afghanistan in 2009 and 2014; the relatively successful 2012 by-elections in Burma, which furthered a slow process of political reform; and the cases of Tunisia, Egypt, Pakistan, India, and Liberia, which we discussed earlier in this chapter. Yet we lack clear theoretical guidance regarding why some elections yield a positive democratic dividend and others do not.

Our answer unites two previously disjointed approaches to understanding political change: an older approach dating back to modernization theory, which emphasizes the structural prerequisites of democracy, and the newer electoral approach, which instead concentrates on the nature of elections themselves as a predictor of democratic change. We argue that the democratizing power of elections depends crucially on the structural circumstances in which they are held. Elections do represent windows of opportunity for political change, but the width and height of the window – to torture the metaphor – is contingent on other factors. Such a simple answer begs the obvious question: which factors? We define three stocks of political legitimacy that support the process of democratic change after elections: contingent legitimacy, performance legitimacy, and democratic-institutional legitimacy. Each of these stocks vary in their depth. First, contingent legitimacy, or the legitimacy conferred on an election winner solely by virtue of the manner of her election victory, deepens with the integrity of the preceding election. Thus, the stock of contingent legitimacy inherited by an election winner is shallower when she has clearly rigged or otherwise dramatically manipulated the election. Second, performance legitimacy deepens in the success of previous governments, and the state as a whole, in providing public goods that support economic development. Third, a deeper democratic-institutional legitimacy cloaks a leader in a well-defined set of rules and norms of democratic governance, including rules constraining her power. Thus, stocks of performance and democratic-institutional legitimacy are shallower when the state has generally failed to provide public goods and when democratic rules and practices remain poorly defined and unpredictable.

Variation in the size and type of the democratic dividend – or the improvement or deterioration in democratic practice after elections – can be predicted by the depth of performance and democratic-institutional legitimacy. Newly elected leaders assume power with drastically different stocks of legitimacy at their disposal. Luckier election winners take charge of a political system with comparatively deeper wells of contingent, performance, and democratic-institutional legitimacy. For these fortunate winners, the benefits of contingent legitimacy are short-lived, even when they have inherited a great deal of it, as newly minted chief executives cannot bask in the warm afterglow of an election win forever but must instead take on the challenging business of governing. When it comes to governing, however, these leaders recognize the relatively well-defined rules of the democratic political game and can take credit for continuing public-good provision begun by past political leaders. Their less fortunate counterparts, by contrast, assume control of states with little success in public-good provision and play a political game with only ill-defined democratic rules.

New incumbents everywhere wish to retain power in future elections, but how they do so is conditioned by the depth of performance and democratic-institutional stocks. Where stocks are relatively deeper, new leaders are more likely to generate electoral support through new forms of public-good provision, confident that such steps are politically beneficial. Such leaders might try to cheat when these new policies fail, but will be constrained from doing so by the relatively deep democratic stock. Where stocks are shallower, incumbents must resort to more nefarious means to secure their hold on power. They cannot easily provide new forms of public goods, given the scant performance legitimacy they inherit. Instead, they take two steps to secure support for their re-election. They deliver private goods to key constituencies, using a combination of clientelism and corruption. Yet private goods cannot earn a leader broad public support for re-election, since they only reach a minority of citizens. Thus, leaders also exploit the relatively shallow stock of democratic practice to cheat at the next election. The result is the erosion of democratic practice.

This theoretical approach yields a clear empirical prediction: elections generate a larger democratic dividend when election winners can access deeper stocks of performance and/or democratic-institutional legitimacy, all else equal. Where these stocks are more developed, election winners can bet on running for re-election on their policy record. Where such stocks are diminished, leaders are more likely to undermine democratic practice to retain power. Unfortunately, these stocks exhibit a kind of increasing marginal return; incumbents will find it difficult to build democratic practice where previous democratic institution stocks are shallow. Likewise, election winners will find it difficult to build a capacity for public-good provision where little already exists, precisely because the onset of future elections necessitates showing shorter-term results.

Our argument yields three observable indicators of the depth of performance and democratic-institutional legitimacy. First, democratic-institutional stock is deeper the longer a country's previous democratic experience. Institutions require years to coalesce, as actors come to recognize the new rules of the political game. The stock of formal rules and informal norms deepens in the length of previous democratic experience, magnifying the democratic dividend from elections. When politicians have little experience governing according to democratic rules, they are less constrained by these rules after they win elections. Elections more likely succeed in countries with a longer past experience with democracy.

Second, performance legitimacy is deeper the larger the fiscal space available to politicians. Politicians must collect taxes or sell debt to fund the investments citizens demand in highways, bridges, schools, clinics, and communications networks. We define this ability to generate revenue from taxation, state-owned enterprises (SOEs), natural resources, debt, and foreign aid as a state's fiscal space. Leaders with access to relatively ample fiscal space are more likely to have success generating performance legitimacy through public-good provision. A tighter fiscal space, in contrast, limits the ability of leaders to invest in large public goods. With such paltry resources at their disposal, leaders will instead turn to providing private goods to co-ethnics, which require fewer fiscal resources to supply. Their over-reliance on private and club goods, in turn, necessitates the kinds of electoral shenanigans we described earlier, which erode democratic rule. Thus, elections are more likely to succeed when election winners enjoy greater fiscal space.

Third, we posit that violent civil conflict erodes performance and democratic-institutional legitimacy. Physical security is the ultimate public good, and leaders lose their ability to generate support through public-good provision once the state has lost its monopoly on legitimate violence. Election winners during civil war can more easily generate performance legitimacy by punishing their enemies militarily than by improving the lives of citizens. Violent civil conflict also creates new non-democratic avenues to power for incumbents, as election winners more likely can suspend elections, ban parties, or cancel inauspicious election results in the name of national security. Elections held during civil conflict, therefore, will generate smaller democratic dividends than those held during peacetime.

Our theoretical framework predicts that elections generate positive democratic change when a country has a longer experience of democratic rule, election winners can access a wider fiscal space, and everyone enjoys the benefits of civil peace. To test our argument, we rely on statistical tests of elections and democratic change based on data from 1,755 elections in the developing world between 1946 and 2010. Our analysis concentrates on how the size of the democratic dividend depends on stocks of performance and democratic-institutional legitimacy, even after controlling for other factors that are known to affect democratization in the developing world. This cross-national strategy merges a detailed analysis of elections as discrete political events with a recognition of the heterogeneous structural circumstances in which they are held. We complement this election analysis with survey data from nearly every region in the world. Analysis of the Comparative Study of Electoral Systems (CSES) data indicates, for instance, that citizens express more confidence in the workings of democracy when their governments have access to wider fiscal space.

The preponderance of the evidence presented in this book supports our argument regarding the contingent effect of elections on political liberalization. Four main findings are worth highlighting here. First, the electoral boom sowed the seeds of elections in increasingly infertile ground. Elections quickly spread after 1988 to younger, poorer, and more ethnically fractionalized countries with long histories of foreign domination through either colonialism or Communism. The electoral surge also arrived in countries with depleted stocks of legitimacy. The countries of the electoral boom had little previous experience with democracy. They were also in the midst of aggressive economic liberalization, willingly cutting their own fiscal space after the debt crisis of the 1980s. Finally, many new election-holding countries were emerging from civil war. This evidence strongly suggests an answer to our empirical puzzle of declining democratic dividends during the electoral boom: the only countries left to democratize by the late 1980s were more difficult cases. Democratization should never be described as an "easy" process. Yet by 1988, few countries like Chile – a relatively prosperous country with recent experience with democracy – remained to return to elections. The majority of countries turning (or returning) to electoral rule more closely resembled Sierra Leone, a country with a history of violence, authoritarianism, and a weak state.

Second, past democratic experience magnifies the political benefits of elections today. Chapter 5 shows how the democratic dividend from elections increases the longer the country's past experience with formal democratic rule. Our model shows that elections in sub-Saharan Africa lacking at least six years of democratic experience yielded no perceptible democratic dividend. Countries with longer democratic experience, in contrast, tended to hold freer and more stable elections that expanded civil liberties. Our analysis also shows that a history of executive constraints is an especially important component of democratic experience. These findings raise a critical question for policy, which we confront in Part III of the book: if elections fail to promote democracy in the absence of past democratic experience and elections themselves are an important aspect of democratic practice, how can countries with little democratic experience escape the gravitational pull of their own inexperience?

Third, elections promote faster democratic change when election winners can access wider fiscal space. Chapter 6 shows how the democratic dividend from elections is positively correlated with fiscal space at the time an election is held, even when controlling for income per capita, the rate of economic growth, and a host of other factors. Our findings support the causal mechanism we suggest: fiscal space improves politicians' provision of public goods and good governance, reducing the odds that incumbents will harass opposition groups ahead of elections. We also show that voters themselves report much higher satisfaction with democracy when governments have access to ampler tax revenues. Taken together, these findings suggest that the decline in fiscal space in the developing world since the 1980s has endangered democratic progress after elections. Too often, such issues are treated as the domain of the international financial institutions; democracy promotion actors must engage the prescriptions of economists with a critical eye by considering their unintended consequences for democratic consolidation.

Fourth, civil conflict hampers democratic momentum after elections. Chapter 7 shows that elections held during civil conflict have a significantly negative effect on democracy. This is especially true when conflicts are the result of ethnic secessionist motivations and where low-level violence is allowed to persist for extended periods of time. Post-conflict elections held in the first year after conflict ends do nothing to further the cause of democracy but the data indicate that waiting even an extra year can generate positive dividends for democracy. This is consistent with our prior research on post-conflict elections. We also show that conflictual elections are more likely to be followed by future elections that experience opposition boycotts and post-election violence. We offer a partial explanation for these findings through an examination of post-war Guatemala. Guatemala returned to democracy just as its civil war ended, yet only a minority of Guatemalans today report confidence in the state of their democracy. Elections have built a stable de jure democracy, but one that has not gained the confidence of Guatemalans themselves. We suggest that high post-war crime rates explain continuing democratic stasis; the inability of successive governments to promote security has damaged citizens' faith in democracy twenty years after civil war ended. These findings suggest that scholars should broaden their understanding of the impact of conflict on democratic change.

Finally, we find that the international community can help countries sustain democratic change after elections in difficult circumstances; however, we argue that successful democracy promotion requires a rethinking of accepted practice. Specifically, Chapter 8 argues that international interventions must address the structural challenge of low legitimacy if they are to promote successful elections. We therefore analyze how international interventions soften the constraints of democratic inexperience, fiscal straitjackets, and violent civil conflict. Our results should encourage democracy promoters: we find that election monitors, democracy and governance aid, threats to cut off foreign aid following electoral malfeasance, and United Nations (UN) peacekeeping missions with a mandate to administer elections all enlarge the democratic dividend from elections held in challenging contexts.

Academic Contributions and Policy Implications

The argument and findings in this book occupy a middle ground between democratic optimism and pessimism. On one hand, we find that many of the countries of the electoral boom confront serious obstacles on the path to democratization by elections. On the other hand, we also find that international support can help them along the way by addressing their dearth of democratic experience and building fiscal space. These lessons contribute to three important scholarly literatures.

Our research most deeply contributes to the study of comparative democratization by clarifying the theoretical and empirical link between elections and subsequent political change. This field has been polarized along both theoretical and empirical lines. A theoretical gap has emerged in the last twenty years between what we refer to as structural and electoral approaches to democratization. Each of these theoretical traditions has contributed much to our knowledge. Structural accounts have highlighted the importance of economic and social change to the process of democratization, while electoral accounts have refined our understanding of elections as agents – rather than mere reflections – of political change. Yet each of these schools has tended to disregard the other, regrettably fracturing the field and hampering further advances in our understanding of democratization. Our core theoretical claim that the impact of elections on democratization hinges on structural circumstances intuitively merges these disparate insights. This fusion yields powerful insights into the diverse structural circumstances in which elections have been held since 1988, shining new light on the challenges facing electoral competition in developing countries. Most importantly, the theoretical and empirical synthesis offered here produces our clearest understanding to date of the contingent impact of elections.

This book also yields insights into two other fields from which it draws. Chapter 6's discussion of fiscal space contributes to longstanding debates in political economy and international development on the relationship between economic and political liberalism. Political economists have long understood democratization as a battle over redistribution between elites and masses.[18] In this reckoning, democracy threatens elites by raising the level of taxation, which in turn funds the provision of public goods that promote human development.[19] We enrich these debates by showing that election winners are more likely to respect democratic norms if they can access wide fiscal space. These findings suggest a thorny puzzle: democracy might produce more fiscal space, but an already ample fiscal space might itself be important to the survival of democracy in its early stages. We therefore question whether economic liberalism – particularly fiscal orthodoxy – might undermine the cause of political liberalism.

Finally, we contribute to an ongoing debate on the link between conflict and elections within the larger field of security studies. Scholarship surrounding these questions has flourished over the last fifteen years. Our own research suggests that elections held in new democracies shortly after the conclusion of conflict threaten the peace.[20]

We turn to a different question here: do elections held during conflict promote democracy? Our findings are unequivocal in their pessimism about the effect of such "conflictual" elections. Post-conflict elections do appear to do better but only if the country can wait at least two years after the conflict ends before going to the polls. Our discussion of Guatemala's post-war history suggests that scholars would do well to consider post-war physical insecurity's impact on democratic legitimacy.

This book's primary ambition is scholarly. Thus, it concentrates on deepening our understanding of elections as agents of political change. Yet our research also generates insights for advocates of democracy who feel discouraged by military coups in Thailand and Egypt or continuing electoral authoritarianism in Russia or Venezuela. Our research design allows us to predict the democratic dividend from elections, provided we know the circumstances in which the elections are held, and verify how certain those predictions are. We can therefore identify electoral trouble spots in which structural conditions at election-time augur post-election complications. Our predictions are probabilistic, not deterministic, and the confidence intervals around these predictions are necessarily wide. Yet the "uncertain certainties" generated by this research still provide important guidance to policymakers assessing the potential ramifications of elections in uncertain places. We ignore such real-world messiness at democracy's peril.

Our second contribution to policy debates arises from our ability to identify electoral trouble spots, since that predictive power contains the seeds of a dispiriting point: elections are subject to a vicious cycle. The democratic dividend from elections increases a country's institutional legitimacy because election winners are more likely to eschew public-good provision and violate democratic rules in low-stock environments. In other words, individual politicians are more likely to take steps that erode institutional legitimacy where it is already depleted, while they are more likely to bolster legitimacy when it is already relatively deep. This is most recognizable in our discussion of democratic experience, which shows how elections in countries with little democratic experience tend not to produce democratic change. Our book thus predicts that countries holding elections with meager stocks of institutional legitimacy can become ensnared in a vicious cycle of elections, poor public-good provision, and democratic backsliding. We therefore pinpoint an important conundrum for democracy promoters: elections are more likely to produce harm where democratic change is most sorely needed.

Our book illuminates a source of hope in this otherwise discouraging schema: external assistance can help soften this vicious cycle. Our theoretical framework hints that steps to bolster otherwise shallow pools of legitimacy might also bolster the impact of elections. This logic in turn suggests that efforts to build trust in democratic rules and norms, expand fiscal space, and bring peace to otherwise conflictual societies might end vicious cycles and even commence virtuous ones. Our results on this score are encouraging: democracy assistance, foreign aid, and UN peacekeeping operations help counter the negative repercussions of scant democratic experience, constrained fiscal space, and civil conflict. We cannot prove causality with the observational data used here; yet our findings do suggest that outsiders can magnify the democratic impact of elections in low-stock countries using policy instruments already at their disposal, though at a much higher level of investment than is currently in vogue.

The Way Forward

The remainder of this book proceeds as follows. Part I develops the broad outline of our answers to the questions posed here. Chapter 2 develops the theoretical framework sketched earlier in this chapter. We begin with a history of political thought on the origins of democratic change, emphasizing how, until the last fifteen years, scholars frequently relegated elections to the fringes of their theoretical efforts. We highlight a continuing weakness of this broader literature: with some important exceptions, structural accounts of democratic change have generally remained divorced from accounts that emphasize electoral approaches to democratization. The result has been an unfortunate neglect of the structural circumstances under which elections are held and a concomitant emphasis on whether, as opposed to when, elections contribute to democratic change. The second half of Chapter 2 details our theory of elections, stocks of institutional legitimacy, and the democratic dividend. We highlight our three main hypotheses regarding democratic experience, fiscal space, and civil conflict.

We commence the empirical portion of the book in Chapter 3, which paints a detailed portrait of election-holding since 1946. We argue that the famed Third Wave of democracy actually consisted of three sub-waves: Wave 3.0, which originated in Iberia in the mid-1970s and spread to South America by the mid-1980s; Wave 3.1, which began in Eastern Europe just as the Berlin Wall fell; and Wave 3.2, which began in 1999 and has heavily featured countries in Sub-Saharan Africa. We then follow past scholars in demonstrating the origins of the electoral boom, which coincided with the dawn of Wave 3.1 in the late 1980s. We show how the countries of the electoral boom faced challenges that would shape their subsequent experience with elections and democracy. Crucially, the electoral boom brought elections to poorer, more ethnically fragmented countries with long histories of colonial and Communist rule. Elections thus spread to countries predicted by our theory to face serious roadblocks on the road to democratization, including little democratic experience, fiscal spaces sharply constrained by the neoliberal turn in economic policymaking, and long histories of violent civil conflict.

Part II is comprised of four chapters that analyze the effects of better election quality and of founding elections (Chapter 4), and the challenge posed by democratic inexperience (Chapter 5), constrained fiscal space (Chapter 6), and political violence (Chapter 7), on elections in the developing world. Part III explores the role of international interventions in supporting elections and concludes the book. Chapter 8 argues that external efforts to support elections must attend to the massive structural challenges facing developing countries. It identifies policies that address democratic inexperience, a lack of fiscal space, and violent conflict. We return to our data to assess these efforts. We find that democracy and governance aid, threats to cut aid, and election monitors are particularly helpful for very young democracies, a finding that should encourage democracy promoters. However, we find little evidence that foreign aid can mitigate the challenge of tight fiscal resources – it is given in amounts far too small to do so. Efforts to bypass governments entirely in favor of non-governmental organizations (NGOs) may also be counter-productive. Finally, we find that United Nations Peacekeeping Operations (UNPKOs) with a mandate to administer and monitor elections improve electoral success in conflictual societies. Chapter 9 concludes with a review of our main findings and a discussion of future research into elections and political change.

2 | *Why Have Elections Failed to Deliver? An Answer*

Chapter 1 describes a troubling trend: the democratizing power of elections rapidly deteriorated after the beginning of the electoral boom in the late 1980s. This electoral shortfall is no small cause for concern for political scientists and policymakers. One need look no further than Egypt's troubled recent history for an illustration. Democracy promoters cheered as Egyptians staged mass protests in Tahrir Square in 2011, leading to the overthrow of longtime dictator Hosni Mubarak. Elections followed about fifteen months later, bringing to power a government led by the Muslim Brotherhood's Mohamed Morsi. Yet the democratic momentum quickly reversed. Morsi soon issued a declaration prohibiting challenges to presidential decrees. Liberal groups abandoned the constituent assembly tasked with writing a new constitution, complaining that it intended to enshrine Islamic practice into law. Street protests demanding Morsi's resignation presaged a military coup in 2013, which ousted Morsi from power only one year after his election. A new, far less transparent election in May 2014 installed the architect of that coup, General Abdel Fattah al-Sisi as president, with a suspicious 97 percent of the vote.

Our cross-national evidence and Egypt's troubled post-Tahrir history force us to confront two difficult questions. First, why did elections yield smaller democratic dividends in the 1990s and 2000s? Second, why have some countries reaped the proposed benefits of elections, while others have not?

This chapter offers answers to these questions, beginning with a brief intellectual history of academic thought on democratization. Political scientists long relegated elections to the background of theories of democratic change, viewing them as ancillary to either a broad structural transformation or elite negotiations over the political future. This all changed in the 2000s, as scholars reimagined elections as flash points upon which the political future crucially depended. Advocates of democratization by elections found that repeated elections incubate democratic governance. Other scholars disagreed, however, finding that elections may cause political violence or serve as agents of authoritarian control. Still other scholars split the difference, contending that future democratic change hinges on the integrity of elections. Thus, the last fifteen years have yielded new understandings of how elections promote democracy. Yet many questions remain. A persistent and unfortunate isolation of electoral and structural approaches to understanding political change is the prime culprit.

We seek to integrate these approaches to understand electoral success and failure. The conceptual nucleus of our approach is the recognition that elections occur not in a vacuum, but in diverse structural contexts. We concentrate on three forms of legitimacy that politicians inherit when they win elections: contingent, performance, and democratic-institutional.[1] Politicians enjoy contingent legitimacy after winning elections, which increases with the authenticity of that election. Such legitimacy is short-lived, however, since self-interested voters demand economic growth as a price for their continued support. The depths of performance and democratic-institutional legitimacy condition politicians' paths to re-election. Where performance legitimacy already exists, incumbents provide public goods and run on their records. Similarly, when democratic-institutional legitimacy is deep, incumbents are constrained from manipulating rules to their advantage. The absence of performance and democratic-institutional legitimacy, however, necessitates a more cynical path to re-election: clientelism, corruption, and repression. The result is stalled democratization, where societies become caught in a low-legitimacy trap of increasingly problematic elections, poor state performance, and disaffected voters. This logic leads us to hypothesize that elections will be more likely to spur democratic change when a country has a longer and more recent experience with democracy, political leaders have access to more fiscal space, and national politics have been more peaceful.

Elections on the Road to Democracy?

The return of democracy to Southern Europe and Latin America in the 1970s and 1980s inaugurated an intellectually fertile period for the study of comparative democratization, which the liberalization of Eastern Europe at the end of the Cold War only intensified. One consequence of this interrelationship between world events and scholarly inquiry has been the redefinition of elections from the conclusion of democratic transitions to the impetus for these transitions. Yet Jan Teorell characterizes the study of comparative democratization as "inchoate, diversified and incoherent."[2] Our own view of the field is more sanguine, but we concur that scholars continue to disagree profoundly not only over the role of elections in democratization, but also on the more fundamental question of the role of elections versus political structures in political change. We review this debate here. To accompany our discussion, we sketch the development of the field in Figure 2.1, which shows how different lines of inquiry have developed over time.

Democratization by (Legitimate) Elections

For thirty years between the early 1970s and early 2000s, political scientists seeking to uncover the causes of democratization regarded elections as the culmination, rather than the stimulus, of a process of democratization. Dankwart Rustow, for instance, envisioned a three-phase transition from dictatorship to democracy.[3] First, a preparatory phase would begin with struggles between competing societal groups, perhaps along class lines. Second, these struggles would create a decision phase in which political elites resolve conflicts between hard- and soft-liners and opt for democratic change. Third, a habituation phase would witness deepening acceptance and support for the new democratic regime. Only in this last phase would regular elections commence. To illustrate the insignificance of elections to Rustow, the word "election" appears in his article only three times, compared to roughly twenty times in the introduction to this chapter.

Rustow's theory of democratic transitions represented a dramatic departure from modernization theory, which had emphasized how major socioeconomic changes would presage democratization. Karl Deutsch, for instance, proposed that rising incomes, the expansion of exposure to mass media, and urbanization would culminate in a widening of political participation.[4] Economic development played a special role in such theories, as modernization theorists hypothesized

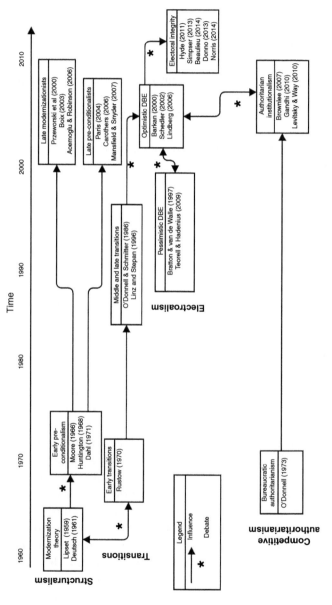

Figure 2.1 Electoral and structural accounts of democratic change have tended to develop separately

that economic growth, relative equality, and the creation of a middle class would create propitious conditions for democracy.[5] Despite these differences, however, modernization theory and the incipient democratic transitions literature had one important aspect in common: neither envisioned elections as progenitors of democratization. Modernization theory did concentrate on expansions of what Deutsch called the "politically relevant strata of society," but saw democracy as the natural outgrowth of important structural changes and thought little of elections at all.

Rustow's understanding of democratic transitions soon became synonymous with the study of comparative democratization as the Third Wave of democracy gained momentum, a trend which we depict in Figure 2.1. "Transition-ologists" defined democratization as a dynamic process with two main phases: transition and consolidation. The timing and length of these phases depended on peculiarities of the society, regime, and transition, while the kinds of systemic factors emphasized by modernization theory played little role. Scholars theorized that regular competitive elections would only begin once elites had resolved the difficult questions of democratic transitions in intensive bargaining. A "founding election" – the first competitive, post-authoritarian elections that brings to power a government with policymaking power[6] – would conclude the transition and initiate the process of consolidation. Guillermo O'Donnell and Philippe Schmitter, for example, discussed founding elections as occurring only after the first tentative autocratic opening; the conclusion of "pacts" among regime hard-liners, soft-liners, and opposition groups; the establishment of new rules for the political game; and the regeneration of civil society.[7]

The prevailing intellectual winds soon shifted, again in reaction to world events. The transitions literature had taken shape partially in response to events in Southern Europe and Latin America, as long-standing dictatorships gradually negotiated their removal from power with pro-democracy elites. The new electoral literature, which we depict in Figure 2.1, recognized two new patterns in international politics. First, a new norm had taken shape, one that insisted that new governments should be chosen through free and fair elections. Second, there was a new democratizing pattern, one in which elections themselves initiated processes of democratization, even in otherwise authoritarian regimes holding nominally competitive elections.

Andreas Schedler argued that de jure competitive elections in non-democratic societies represent a kind of two-level game. The formal game pits an autocrat against an opposition in a contest for popular support. Yet elections also create a forum for these same contestants to re-define the rules of political competition; this is the "meta-game." Autocrats' continued attempts to rig this meta-game may further erode popular support and risk electoral loss, encouraging opponents and protesters.[8] Elections themselves create avenues for political change, rather than merely signaling the conclusion of a democratic transition.

Scholars of what came to be known as "democratization by elections" proposed that elections erode autocracy and incubate democratic institutions. Joel Barkan placed elections at the center of a "protracted transition" towards democracy in Sub-Saharan Africa. Competitive elections, he argued, are very much like a mouse nibbling at cheese, allowing opposition parties and new electoral rules to develop slowly over successive elections, eventually leading to regime collapse.[9] Jan Teorell and Axel Hadenius proposed a different metaphor – that of a pressure chamber. Successive elections increase the pressure for democratization and hence the probability that a complete transition occurs, rather than incrementally augmenting democratic attributes.[10] Staffan Lindberg contended that elections expand media freedom, establish self-fulfilling democratic norms, and create new cadres of democracy promoters.[11]

Empirical research soon followed these theoretical contributions and yielded new evidence in favor of the democratization-by-elections thesis. Hadenius and Teorell, for example, found that authoritarian regimes that allow even limited multiparty competition tend to transition to more democratic governance. Marc Howard and Philip Roessler agreed, finding that elections in certain authoritarian regimes can lead to a "liberalizing electoral outcome," in which an autocratic incumbent is replaced by a more democratic government. Lindberg's studies of elections in Sub-Saharan Africa found that democratic qualities improved with repeated elections and the risk of democratic collapse diminished after the second consecutive election. Lindberg concluded that elections, even when flawed, remained the best means of hurdling difficult obstacles to democracy in Sub-Saharan Africa.[12]

Yet not all scholars agreed. Michael Bratton and Nicolas van de Walle's examination of democratic transitions in Africa had already found that elections had done little to transform authoritarianism. The contributions to Lindberg's own 2009 edited volume on democratization by elections also cast empirical doubt on the democratization-by-elections thesis. Jan Teorell and Axel Hadenius found little evidence of democratization by elections in a global sample, while Jennifer McCoy and Jonathan Hartlyn reported the same null finding in a Latin American sample. Roessler and Howard found that 32 percent of elections in competitive authoritarian regimes promote democracy, but 19 percent lead to more restrictive forms of authoritarianism, hardly evidence that elections are a democratic linchpin.[13] Jason Brownlee agreed, arguing that while elections in competitive authoritarian regimes more likely lead to democracy, they may alternatively create a result in which "one hegemonic electoral autocracy is likely to be replaced with another," as illustrated by Egypt's experience since the Arab uprisings.[14]

A different group of scholars proposed a new explanation of elections' heterogeneous impact on democratic change. These researchers broadly contended that the democratizing power of elections depends on their integrity; not all elections are created equal. In many elections, incumbents and their political parties muzzle the independent media, harass opposition parties, and falsify the final vote count. In other elections, they are prevented from doing so. This heterogeneity holds the key to understanding why elections sometimes fail to promote democratic change. Scholars again cited a momentous shift in international norms: the international community had come to insist not only that elections occur, but also that they be free and fair. Incumbents could no longer simply manipulate elections without risking international condemnation and a loss of financial assistance from Western governments.[15] Norms of electoral integrity, Pippa Norris argues, do not merely reflect a strategic alignment with globally important actors, but also an ethos of fairness shared between elites and common citizens in diverse contexts. Scholars have also investigated why regimes still choose to violate the norm. Alberto Simpser, echoing Andreas Schedler, contended that autocrats manipulate elections not to win them, but to frustrate any future challenges to their power. Susan Hyde contends that observers constrain incumbents' capacity to manipulate elections. Judith Kelley generally concurs, arguing that monitored elections are higher quality and more likely replace incumbents. Jessica Gottlieb, meanwhile, suggests that better informed voters hold local politicians more accountable and hence enhance electoral integrity.[16]

Authors studying electoral integrity do more than study the development of this norm and ask why it is sometimes violated. They also argue that electoral integrity holds the key to understanding whether elections succeed or fail: manipulated elections are unlikely to contribute democratic reform, while honestly administered elections make democratic change possible. Simpser found that electoral manipulation lengthens autocrats' duration in office, and hence constrains elections' power to foment democracy. Electoral manipulation also depresses political participation by creating disillusioned voters. Norris argues that illegitimate elections have serious consequences for democratic practice, since they weaken voter confidence not only in the election process, but also in democracy itself, depressing turnouts and increasing the risk of protests and political violence. Emily Beaulieu, meanwhile, explores a specific mechanism determining electoral illegitimacy and its impact on democratic practice: electoral protest. She finds that opposition protests of election results occur mainly because an incumbent and opposition cannot agree on what constitutes an acceptable election. Election protests, in turn, only lead to improved democratic practice where they garner substantial international support. Daniela Donno concurs, finding that international actors can heighten democratic change after imperfect elections by promoting institutional changes that raise the costs of electoral manipulation and make incumbent replacement more likely.[17]

Over the past fifteen years, scholars have entirely reimagined the role of elections in democratization, placing them front-and-center. Electoral scholars disagree about the relative importance of integrity in democratic change after elections, but agree on one foundational premise: the electoral cycle, from voter registration to the inauguration of new officeholders, holds the key to understanding subsequent democratization. As in the transitions literature initiated by Rustow forty-five years ago, these theories leave little theoretical room for how structural factors drive electoral integrity or the future path of democratization. As we shall argue, however, structural approaches must continue to have a say in this debate.[18]

Electoral Pessimism

Even as electoralism gained momentum in the pages of prestigious academic journals and book presses, two far more pessimistic accounts of the impact of elections on political development also gained credence. This literature emphasized that efforts to expand political participation tend to lead to endemic political instability, political violence, or strengthened authoritarian control. Two lines of research, which we label "pre-conditionalism" and "competitive authoritarianism" in Figure 2.1, are particularly instructive.

Pre-Conditionalism

The notion that particular political-economic conditions are necessary for stable democratic change pre-dates both the transitions and electoral literatures. Instead, it originated in debates over political modernization in the 1960s. We have already seen how Lipset and Deutsch, among others, argued that democratization represents a culmination of a long process of socioeconomic transformation that includes urbanization, industrialization, and the development of mass communications.[19] We term this broad approach "structuralism" in Figure 2.1. The converse of the modernization thesis also remained true, however: if mass political participation surged before these structural changes, democracy would prove brittle. Socioeconomic change, then, formed a kind of pre-condition for successful mass elections. Subsequent theory-building and research would identify four such pre-conditions: economic development, strong administrative institutions, democratic institutions enshrining contestation, and national unity.

First, economic pre-conditionalists argued that democracy cannot take root in poor, unequal economies reliant on mineral and oil production or a large landowning class. Adam Przeworski and his colleagues favor an "exogenous" version of the modernization thesis: democratic transitions are equally likely in poor and rich countries, but democracies born into poverty are more likely to revert to authoritarianism.[20] Other economic pre-conditionalists have focused not on the level of income, but on its distribution, following Barrington Moore's famous aphorism, "No bourgeoisie, no democracy."[21] Carles Boix claims that relative economic equality and capital mobility reduce pressures for redistribution and, with them, elite opposition to democracy. Michael Ross provides another perspective, showing persuasively that economies dominated by oil and mineral production tend not to democratize.[22]

Second, administrative-institutional pre-conditionalists follow Huntington in arguing that only strong institutions preserving law and order could stop rapid expansions of political participation from devolving into chronic instability. Richard Rose and Doh Shin adroitly summarize this perspective, arguing that the Third Wave featured "democratization backwards," holding competitive elections before creating a modern state, hence placing fragile new democracies at risk of democratic reversals. Jessica Fortin echoes their argument, contending that state capacity has been a necessary condition for successful democratization in post-Communist Europe. Roland Paris proposes delaying elections after civil war to allow rule of law to coalesce.[23] Perhaps the clearest articulation of this position comes from Francis Fukuyama, who admits that "in today's world the only serious source of legitimacy is democracy," but counters that building strong institutions in failing states is the single most pressing – and difficult – task facing the world today.[24]

Third, democratic-institutional pre-conditionalists also focus on the power of institutions, but look instead to the pre-existing strength of democratic institutions. Robert Dahl stressed the importance of a long period where only a small set of citizens participate in democratic politics. Such a period would allow the incubation of institutions governing how citizens formulate preferences and compete for power. Mass political participation would come later, when institutions governing contention are sufficiently strong. The simultaneous expansion of both competition and participation would lead to unstable democracy. Bratton and van de Walle agree in their treatment of transitions in sub-Saharan Africa, concluding that democratization "is easier from a regime in which competition is encouraged and the main challenge is to broaden participation."[25] Democratic-institutional pre-conditionalists especially focus on political parties and judiciaries as institutions that undergird successful elections. Others find that an established, independent judiciary can prevent democratic reversals.[26]

Fourth, identity pre-conditionalists underline the importance of a common national identity for political liberalization. Eric Nordlinger argues that stable, democratic governance depends on its presence before universal-suffrage elections.[27] Barry Weingast finds that societal divisions create an environment conducive to the violation of citizens' economic and political rights. Paul Collier worries about the spread of elections to "dangerous places," such as those riven by ethnic hatred, arguing that elections in such places fail to engender legitimate, accountable governments and instead raise the risk of civil violence.[28]

Edward Mansfield and Jack Snyder have developed an influential marriage of these lines of thought.[29] Autocrats prefer to rule without popular political participation, yet international pressures have created incentives for them to seek such support through elections. They therefore devise mechanisms to show popular support, while limiting popular demands. Inciting nationalism represents an especially efficient means of doing so by allowing elites to win electoral support through sentiment, rather than performance.[30] The unfortunate consequence is incomplete democratic rule and a higher risk of violent political conflict. They follow others in contending that economic development, democratic institutions, and the rule of law form effective bulwarks against this violent nationalist spiral.

Pre-conditionalism thus diverges dramatically from the electoral literature we outlined earlier. Scholars in this tradition obviously view with great suspicion the thesis that rapid democratization through successive elections can build democratic governance. Yet their intellectual dispute with electoralism runs still deeper, for pre-conditionalists are inheritors of a structural approach in which elections matter little compared to the political-economic context in which they occur. We will return to this theme, but first turn to another group of scholars who advance a still more pessimistic rendering of the democratizing power of elections.

Competitive authoritariansim

Competitive authoritarians view elections not as agents of liberalization or even political instability, but as part and parcel of a dictator's efforts to remain in power. In this respect, they echo concerns raised by the electoral-integrity literature, which sees great danger in low-integrity elections. Competitive authoritarians owe their deepest intellectual debt, however, to theories of bureaucratic authoritarianism originating with O'Donnell. O'Donnell dissented from early forms of modernization theory, suspecting that socioeconomic transformation would more likely lead to new forms of authoritarianism, rather than democracy.[31] Subsequent scholars have expanded upon his central insight by defining specific quasi-democratic institutions that support authoritarianism and adapting the narrative to a post–Cold War world. This literature challenges both electoral and structural accounts of democratization in two ways. First, it contends that the West's stubborn insistence on elections has encouraged only the illusion of democracy, while leaving autocrats firmly in power. Second, it insists that many of the same institutions so important to pre-conditionalists, especially political parties, are more likely to reinforce authoritarianism than encourage political liberalization.

This literature begins from similar bases as scholars of electoral integrity: the challenge of autocratic governance in the post–Cold War world, or what Susan Hyde dubs the "pseudo-democrat's dilemma." As we have seen, the spread of the norm of regular, competitive elections during the Third Wave substantially raised the international political costs of maintaining a completely closed regime.[32] At risk were autocrats' access to the financial and political benefits of friendly relations with the West. Hyde describes how the burgeoning norm of election observation placed "pseudo-democrats" in a quandary – invite international scrutiny of their elections and risk losing power, or refuse observers and face international isolation.[33] They also faced the perennial quandaries facing all autocrats: forestalling rebellion and mass protests and preventing cracks within their regimes.[34]

How can autocrats simultaneously maintain their political hegemony, while at least superficially adhering to the international political zeitgeist? The solution, competitive authoritarians suggest, lies in designing institutions that present a veneer of democracy while quietly subverting any real political competition. Steven Levitsky and Lucan Way, for example, stress how robust ruling parties help forestall intra-elite rifts, galvanize public support for incumbents competing in limited elections, and facilitate control of legislatures. Brownlee emphasizes the ability of ruling parties to regulate competition among elites, preventing their defection to the opposition – a crucial step in theories of democratic transition. Dan Slater's theory of authoritarian durability imagines elites building strong ruling parties in reaction to enduring urban-based movements demanding a far-reaching redistribution of wealth.[35]

Jennifer Gandhi concurs that authoritarian leaders can co-opt otherwise democratic institutions to render an electoral loss effectively impossible, but focuses instead on legislatures and opposition parties. Nominally democratic institutions, she reasons, allow dictators to make policy concessions to new opposition groups, particularly when such groups pose a credible threat of rebellion and dictators lack independent sources of revenue (e.g., from natural resources). Political parties and legislatures in non-democracies thus represent a dictator's best political response when she requires cooperation from relatively powerful opposition groups to strengthen her grip on power.[36]

Competitive authoritarians, therefore, offer an account of elections and democratization that is far more pessimistic than even pre-conditionalists. They find that elections and the institutions surrounding them can actually serve to preserve dictators' hold on power, even in places where the cause of democracy has ostensibly advanced.

Outstanding Questions

The brief intellectual history presented here reveals a rapid revision of scholars' thinking on elections and democratization. In it, we see how academic thinking has co-evolved with world events. Scholars quickly noted how the end of the Cold War opened a new path to democracy through international expectations that regimes would hold regular, competitive elections. Scholars contended that these developments presaged more democratic rule in Sub-Saharan Africa, Eastern Europe, and East Asia. As a question of policy, they suggested that improving electoral administration and monitoring electoral malfeasance could also help galvanize democratic rule. Yet pre-conditionalists saw danger; they maintained that these same elections risk political instability and authoritarian backsliding in societies lacking key economic and political structures. Competitive authoritarians proposed a still more dismal outlook, seeing in elections a means for dictators to co-opt democratic trappings and extend their rule.

We have thus seen scholarly dynamism, as well as continuing confusion. Researchers still lack unanimity on the question that inspires this book: what is the lasting political impact of elections? The field regards them as vehicles for democratization, agents of political instability, or chimeras that reinforce authoritarianism, depending on whom one asks. Each of these perspectives is supported by distinguished scholars. Each has marshaled strong evidence in its support and engaged in impressive data collection.[37] Each has found support among policymakers.

The field's ongoing confusion regarding the democratizing properties of elections originates in part in its tendency to ask whether elections foment democratic change, rather than when and where they are most likely to do so. Only students of electoral integrity have consistently attended to the latter questions, proposing that only elections free of manipulation stand a chance to promote democracy. Yet these statements are, of course, probabilistic – even the most free elections sometimes set the stage for democratic backsliding, as in Egypt, and some manipulated elections provide a focal point for democratic reforms.

We propose that a deeper, long-standing tension within the field is partly to blame for this thick tangle of conflicting theories and inconsistent findings: the continuing divide between structural and electoral approaches to understanding political change. Note the relative isolation of these two intellectual families in Figure 2.1. Structuralists have built a sophisticated understanding of the political-economic pre-conditions for democracy, while electoralists have done the same for the relationship between elections and democracy. Yet they have tended to say little to each other. Structuralists, on one hand, have neglected elections themselves as political events with meaningful consequences. Instead, they focus on how the timing and success of episodes of democratization depend on the slow evolution of economies and societies. Electoralists, in contrast, have tended to ignore how elections are embedded in deeper historical, political, and economic contexts that may condition their democratizing capacity. What matters instead are processes internal to electoral competition. In this view, democratic failures can be fixed, mostly by holding more and better elections.

A better bridge between structural and electoral accounts is yet to be devised. However, such a bridge promises to be intellectually fruitful. We turn to that task next.

A Theoretical Synthesis

Our theory of elections synthesizes the structural and electoral approaches to democratic change. We propose that higher-integrity elections do indeed endow election winners with greater legitimacy.

Yet that legitimacy remains contingent on incumbents' subsequent performance. Where incumbents can generate performance legitimacy and are constrained by deep stocks of democratic legitimacy, elections will help motivate further democratic reform. Where stocks of performance and democratic legitimacy remain low, however, elections more likely result in democratic stasis.

We define three desiderata for our own theory of elections. First, we prefer a theory that predicts why some elections succeed in promoting democracy and others fail to do so. We especially desire a theory that links the political-economic context in which elections occur to their success. We do not deny the importance of electoral integrity; it plays an important role in our theory. Yet our main goal is to integrate electoral and structural models of political change by thinking of elections as important political events that place election winners in strikingly disparate settings.

Second, our theory commences with an odd point of departure for a theory of elections: the moment when an election ends and an election winner takes office. In fact, relative to much of electoral scholarship discussed earlier, we will spend relatively little energy on elections themselves. We do not do so because these details are unimportant; they most certainly are. We instead propose that democratic change after elections depends crucially on the choices politicians – and especially incumbent chief executives – make in-between elections. Some take steps that deepen democracy, while others take steps that weaken it. Explaining why some newly minted chief executives choose the former versus the latter path is a prime goal of our theory. Our theory follows past scholars in contending that political-economic structures condition these choices in important ways that extant scholarship on elections neglects.

Third, we prefer a theory of incumbent behavior that avoids leaning too heavily on a typology of politicians. The literature on elections often implicitly or explicitly makes assumptions of politicians' underlying types. Susan Hyde, for example, defines two types of incumbents seeking re-election: "true democrats" and "pseudo-democrats."[38] These labels are not merely semantic; our academic and practical understanding of the impact of elections relies heavily on them. If politicians are of several types, some of which are better for democracy than others, the challenge for theorists, not to mention international policymakers, is to divine their types. It seems clear in retrospect that Charles Taylor, the victor in Liberia's 1997 post-war presidential elections, was an autocrat in democrat's clothing, while Liberia's current elected president, Nobel Prize-winner Ellen Johnson Sirleaf, is a true(r) democrat. Yet such distinctions are rarely obvious ex ante. President George W. Bush of the United States, for example, famously declared of President Vladimir Putin of Russia that, "I looked the man in the eye. I found him to be very straight forward and trustworthy ...I was able to get a sense of his soul."[39] Putin, of course, subsequently cracked down on political dissent and invaded Ukraine. We prefer a theoretical model that relies on process rather than types.[40]

We commence our theory-building with two basic assumptions regarding politicians and voters. We assume that politicians are rational and wish to win and retain political office. This minimalist assumption implies a skepticism regarding their commitments to democracy. All leaders exploit levers of power in an attempt to retain office. How they do so is precisely what we wish to explain. The primary difference between Prime Minister Hun Sen of Cambodia, frequently accused of despotism, and Prime Minister Manmohan Singh of India, who peacefully relinquished power in May 2014, lies less in their personal honesty and more in the structural contexts in which they took power. We therefore find ourselves agreeing with Nikita Khrushchev, who quipped that, "Politicians are the same all over. They promise to build a bridge even where there is no river."[41]

What of the citizens who participate in these elections by voting, joining political parties, and protesting? We begin by assuming that voters are rational, just like politicians. Yet we assume a slightly more complex set of motivations for citizens than for politicians. Citizens first choose politicians to support according to how they will affect their income. On this point, we side with Christopher Achen and Larry Bartels, who argue that voters exhibit "blind retrospection," either embracing or blaming politicians for events beyond their control.[42] We assume that voters benefit from their consumption of three streams of goods offered by politicians: public, club, and private. Citizens benefit from inexhaustible and non-excludable public goods (e.g., roads) that expand their earning potential. They also benefit, however, from club goods directed only at their home region or identity group. Finally, politicians can offer private goods, such as when Mexico's Institutionalized Revolutionary Party (PRI) allegedly gave out gift cards for use at local grocery stores during Mexico's 2012 presidential elections. We do not assume that voters intrinsically prefer public, club, or private goods to the others, but do assume that they are risk-averse, in that they resist changes to pre-existing streams of benefits.

Finally, we assume that voters value political, as well as economic, goods. They prefer expansions of their political and civil rights (e.g., free speech) and security (e.g., low crime), all else equal. Therefore, citizens must balance competing motivations in our theory. They prefer combinations of public and private goods that expand their income, but also seek an expansion of security and civil rights. We do not assume that voters prefer political over economic goods or vice versa, but that they evaluate politicians by their impact on each.

We begin to define the component parts of our model, which is summarized in Figure 2.2, with an election. We imagine an election that establishes a new chief executive in office. Election winners inherit three stocks of legitimacy when they take office: contingent, performance, and democratic-institutional. The depth of each stock depends on the actions of past governments, and politicians cannot immediately alter them. We propose that the choices an election winner makes while in office – whether or not to provide public goods and respect democratic norms – depend crucially on the depth of these stocks.

Let us begin with contingent legitimacy, which we define as the legitimacy conferred on an election winner solely by virtue of the manner of her election victory. Political victory in elections should endow leaders with a kind of temporary democratic halo, during which they likely enjoy the support, even if begrudgingly, from a relatively large proportion of the electorate. This support may also be global in scope when newly elected leaders receive international praise from journalists, human rights activists, and other heads of government. Newly elected leaders sensibly often seek to exploit this halo by introducing dramatic reforms.

Yet election winners inherit differing levels of contingent legitimacy, depending on at least two factors. First, contingent legitimacy increases with the integrity of the preceding election. Election winners who rigged or otherwise manipulated an election will enjoy few benefits of their victories. They are more likely to inherit disillusioned voters, an angry opposition bent on protests and disruption, and a distrustful international community. Winners of free and fair elections, in contrast, are more likely to inherit the benefits of an electoral after-glow. Second, winners of founding elections are likely to enjoy deeper contingent legitimacy. The winner of a founding election is likely to inherit not only the legitimacy of a clean election, but also the hope for a return to democracy itself. In many cases, the winners of founding elections are political giants who have helped lead their people to free-dom, such as Nelson Mandela of South Africa. They do not always fulfill these hopes, however; two other winners of founding elections are Hamid Karzai of Afghanistan and Jean-Bertrand Aristide of Haiti. Yet each came to power imbued with the natural democratic optimism that comes with a return to regular, clean elections.[43]

Contingent legitimacy is by definition short-lived, even when an election leader inherits a great deal of it. There is a reason why pun-dits typically refer to a chief executive's first several months in office as a "honeymoon." A newly married couple may take a romantic trip after their wedding, but eventually must return to their normal lives. Likewise, newly minted chief executives cannot simply bask in the warm afterglow of an election win; they must confront the business of governing. And this is a serious business, indeed, for voters expect politicians to perform while in office. An election winner's ability to win re-election depends on her ability to increase the incomes and political rights of voters. Consider the example of Barack Obama, who easily won election as president of the United States in late 2008. Obama succeeded a historically unpopular president in George W. Bush, who was widely blamed for a poor economy and two pro-tracted wars. Obama also became the first African American to win the presidency. If ever a politician enjoyed contingent legitimacy, it was Obama. This adulation, however, could not last. Within two years, Obama's Democratic Party lost control of the House of Rep-resentatives and Obama himself was blamed for the same stubborn recession he inherited.

Politicians cannot coast on the goodwill generated by winning an election. They must take steps that expand the economic and polit-ical well-being of their citizens to ensure their survival in office. How they do so depends on two types of legitimacy, which we envi-sion as stocks that vary in their depth. Unlike contingent legitimacy, these stocks are rather durable. They depend on the accumulated record of past governments – their accomplishments, failures, and actions. Some politicians inherit deep stocks of legitimacy, while others find themselves inheriting little legitimacy outside of the contingent kind generated by their election. Politicians likewise can take actions that deplete, preserve, or bolster the stocks of legitimacy they inherit.

An elected leader comes to power inheriting a stock of performance legitimacy, based on the achievements of past governments. She in essence takes responsibility for her predecessors' performance; as a sign on US President Harry Truman's desk famously said, "The buck stops here." A newly elected executive inherits a deeper stock where past governments successfully provided public goods that expanded human development; she alternatively inherits a shallower stock where previous leaders failed to do so. A leader likewise can generate flows and leaks into and out of the stock of performance legitimacy. She can enact policies that expand the incomes of citizens. Doing so generates performance legitimacy by creating a flow into the pre-existing stock. It also solidifies her chances of retaining power in the next election, all else equal. A leader may also oversee economic collapse or otherwise fail to generate improvements in citizens' well-being. Such a performance creates a leak from performance legitimacy and makes it more difficult for the incumbent to win another election, all else equal.

Why do some elected leaders succeed in improving the socioeconomic welfare of citizens while others do not? This is no small question, but the logic of stocks and flows suggests an answer. We claim that a newly elected executive more easily generates performance legitimacy where previous governments have left behind more abundant stocks. In other words, performance legitimacy exhibits increasing returns to scale. Consider Brazil's well-known Bolsa Família. The program, introduced during Luiz Inácio Lula da Silva's presidency, transfers cash directly to poor families, conditional on families sending their children to school and keeping their vaccinations up to date. The program undoubtedly contributed to Lula's popularity and re-election and has been credited with reducing poverty. Yet Bolsa Família would not have been possible without the existence of schools and clinics, not to mention previous experiments with similar schemes at the state level in Brazil's federal system. Lula won credit for Bolsa Família, but that credit depended on the relatively deep stock of performance legitimacy he inherited upon taking office. It is easier to generate performance legitimacy where a deep well already exists.

Leaders who inherit a deep stock of performance legitimacy are more likely to generate new flows and secure the support of voters for re-election. An election winner in a system with little prior performance legitimacy faces a far more vexing dilemma – she must generate performance legitimacy to win re-election yet must do so from a very low base, given the failures and ineptitude of past governments. All else equal, however, the voters who elected her care little for her troubles, or that performance legitimacy is difficult to generate, and will turn on her if she fails to do so.[44]

We identify a third and final stock, democratic-institutional legitimacy, which also varies in its depth. We define democratic-institutional legitimacy as the total strength of the formal rules, norms and practices, and organizations that collectively define democracy. These norms and practices are often informal, as illustrated by American history. The United States' first president, George Washington, originated a tradition of stepping down from power after only two terms in office. The norm was respected until President Franklin Roosevelt ran for a third term in 1940, which in time inspired the passage of the 22nd Amendment to the US Constitution. This case shows how a norm endured 150 years, after which it became formalized into law.[45] Democratic-institutional legitimacy deepens in the predictability of democratic competition and governance; where politicians clearly recognize the rules of the political game and expect their enforcement, the stock is deep. A newly elected leader who inherits a deep stock of democratic-institutional legitimacy inherits a well-defined and broadly understood set of prerogatives and constraints. A shallow stock, however, confers far deeper uncertainty regarding the rules of the political game; their enforcement is likely to remain dependent on personal relationships among politicians.

Another example from the United States involving the relationship between the executive and judiciary illustrates how democratic-institutional stock can deepen over time. In 1832, the Supreme Court ruled in *Worcester* v. *Georgia* that Georgia had no constitutional authority over lands legally held by the Cherokee people. President Andrew Jackson responded by writing in a letter that, "the decision of the Supreme Court has fell still born, and they find that they cannot coerce Georgia to yield to its mandate." The Supreme Court's inability to enforce its own ruling, according to Jackson, meant that he could ignore it. A different president's attempt to bend the Supreme Court to his will a hundred years later would come to a very different end. President Franklin Delano Roosevelt (FDR), rebuffed by the Supreme Court's invalidation of key elements of the New Deal, introduced legislation that would increase the number of Supreme Court justices, a ploy frequently referred to as "packing the Court." He argued that the number of justices was determined by acts of Congress, not the Constitution. The United States Senate rebuffed Roosevelt's plan, preserving the Court's independence. The century separating Jackson and FDR had solidified the United States' system of checks and balances.

This example also highlights how elected leaders can bolster or deplete democratic-institutional stock, just as they can with performance legitimacy. A leader may take steps that expand the rights of women, strengthen civilian control over the military, or preserve the rights of journalists. Merely respecting democratic norms also augments democratic-institutional stock. A leader who acknowledges an electoral loss and peacefully steps down creates or extends a tradition of doing so. On the other hand, leaders may disenfranchise minorities or weaken judicial and legislative checks on their power; such actions erode democratic-institutional legitimacy. Why might leaders willingly enfeeble democratic practice? After all, we have presumed that voters prefer expanding political rights, all else equal. Our answer echoes our discussion of performance legitimacy – elected leaders' capacity to build democratic-institutional legitimacy increases with the depth of the pre-existing stock. A shallower pool places fewer constraints on an incumbent's capacity to reshape the rules of electoral competition to her advantage. All politicians might fancy an ability to manipulate democratic rules, but only low-stock systems allow it.

An example from a democratizing country provides a potentially positive portrait of deepening democratic-institutional legitimacy in real-time. President Mathieu Kérékou of Benin seized power in a military coup and then maintained power for nineteen years through force and uncompetitive elections. Yet he stepped down after losing an election under a new constitution in 1991. He won the presidency back in a free election in 1996, won re-election under controversial circumstances in 2001, and then refrained from changing the constitution in 2006 to run for another term. Kérékou could hardly be described as an unstinting democrat, but his actions set an example that his successors will hopefully emulate. Indeed, Benin's current president, Yayi Boni,

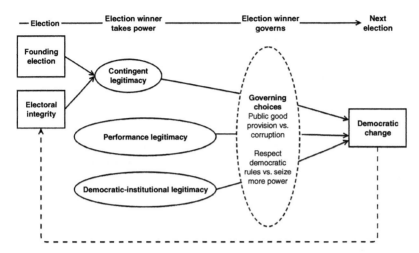

Figure 2.2 The democratizing impact of elections depends on stocks of democratic-institutional and performance legitimacy

has already committed to step down from power when his second term elapses in 2016.

With these theoretical pieces in place, we can now explain why only some elections advance democratic change: in the face of shallow stocks of democratic-institutional and performance legitimacy, new incumbents are more likely to choose courses of action that end in democratic reversal or stagnation. Figure 2.2 illustrates our argument.

Imagine the challenges facing a newly elected executive. She has won a free election and enjoys the benefits of the contingent legitimacy that come with her victory, including supportive phone calls from international leaders, a public inauguration, and the grudging admiration of the opposition. However, our chief executive knows that this will all soon change; if she is to remain in power, she must take steps that will build performance and democratic-institutional legitimacy. Now let us vary just one detail – the inherited depth of these two stocks. A more fortunate leader comes to power with deeper stocks of each. She leans on her relatively deep stock of performance legitimacy to enact policies that enhance human development. Her new policies may succeed or fail, bolstering or diminishing her chances of re-election, respectively. Either way, she could decide to cheat by limiting the opposition's access to government-run media and stuffing ballot boxes. Yet the relatively deep democratic-institutional stock stops her from doing so. Perhaps our fortunate incumbent wins re-election, perhaps she loses. But democratic change during her term will likely be positive.

Now consider her less fortunate counterpart who takes office in a country with relatively lean stocks of performance and democratic-institutional legitimacy. This leader also wishes to encourage economic development to earn re-election. Yet he relies on far weaker accumulated stocks of performance legitimacy. He may, for example, preside over a corrupt bureaucracy maintained by his predecessor or, even worse, a weak state with barely a bureaucracy at all. This ill-starred leader faces a quandary; as his contingent legitimacy quickly wanes, so does his likelihood of remaining in office.

What is a self-interested politician to do? Our framework avails him of two avenues to retaining power. He can deliver benefits directly to key constituencies without the headache of building public goods programs. Our leader can create a clientelistic or neo-patrimonial system that directly provides consumer goods to key constituencies. Barkan discusses the importance of such forms of authority in Sub-Saharan Africa, in which a "big man" uses an otherwise weak bureaucracy to deliver patronage, particularly jobs, directly to citizens.[46] Clientelism holds a key advantage for elected leaders – less extant performance legitimacy is needed to deliver goods. Therefore, our leader will substitute private and club goods for public investment, eroding what little performance legitimacy already exists. That decision, however, fails to solve our leader's dilemma entirely, since clientelism will likely fail to please enough voters to ensure his re-election. Leaders of a democratic system are unlikely to remain in power offering mostly club goods, since they cost too much per head to offer to a majority of the population. Yet elected leaders have another option to retain political power – subverting the democratic process. They can manipulate the rules of the political game – what Schedler calls the "meta-game" – to secure their political survival. They can disband newspapers and radio stations that voice dissent, disenfranchise groups of voters who do not benefit from private goods, and stuff ballot boxes. This is more possible where the pre-existing democratic-institutional stock is so shallow. Democratic backsliding is far more likely in this instance.

This is the central theoretical claim of this book: the democratic dividend from elections is smaller in countries with lower stocks of performance and democratic-institutional legitimacy, all else equal.[47] Our theory predicts that executives who inherit paltry stocks of these resources are more likely to engage in a host of activities (e.g., loosening executive constraints, clamping down on opposition groups) that undermine democratic practice during their terms in office. Two additional testable implications are worth noting. First, we expect that voters will report far less satisfaction with democracy in these circumstances. Second, we should see lower-integrity elections in the future. Many of the steps incumbents take that either support or injure democratic practice should be felt during the next election, in which we presume they will run for re-election. Electoral integrity therefore will worsen over time in low-legitimacy contexts and improve in high-legitimacy contexts.

More broadly, our theory implies the existence of low-legitimacy traps. Our theory assumes rather sticky stocks of performance and democratic-institutional legitimacy; politicians will find it easier to generate more of each if extant stocks are already relatively deep. When elections occur in a relatively low-legitimacy setting, our theory predicts that politicians will be more likely to eschew building either stock. In fact, they will tend to take steps that further deplete both performance and democratic-institutional legitimacy, meaning that they will tend to cloak their successors in even weaker legitimacy. Elections, then, can be caught in a low-legitimacy trap, in which successive election winners are placed in a context where they are unlikely to win re-election by furthering democracy's cause and respond by further weakening stocks of legitimacy.

Understanding Stocks of Legitimacy

Our next task is to identify observable factors that define the depth of these stocks. We have already argued that contingent legitimacy deepens when the preceding election was a founding election or otherwise high-integrity. We define three factors that influence the depth of performance and democratic-institutional legitimacy: democratic experience, fiscal space, and violent civil conflict. This effort deserves special attention, since measuring these three factors will be the focus of Chapters 5, 6, and 7. In addition to completing our theoretical framework, this discussion allows us to contemplate the heterogeneity of countries holding elections during the electoral boom; each of these factors varies greatly among that set of countries.

Democratic Experience

The Third Wave of democracy brought elections to societies with very different historical experiences with democracy. By one measure, Spain had experienced over thirty years of intermittent democratic rule during its long history as a sovereign country when democracy returned after the death of Francisco Franco. Russia, in contrast, had virtually no prior democratic experience in 1990. The end of the Cold War in the late 1980s also birthed new sovereign countries, many of which immediately held elections. Armenia, for example, was born in 1991 as a former Soviet republic, and it promptly held an election in October of that year. By definition, countries like Armenia lacked a history of democratic, sovereign rule.

Past experience with democracy, particularly as captured by the age of democratic institutions, is an excellent measure of democratic-institutional stock. Institutions of any kind require long periods of time to coalesce. David Lake, for example, emphasizes that authority stems not from a legal framework, but from demonstrated performance.[48] New democratic institutions confer less legitimacy on elected leaders. Such leaders take charge of a system whose rules remain unclear to politicians and voters alike. This is the very definition of low democratic-institutional legitimacy. Politicians gradually refine the meta-game of politics as they govern, redefining through practice the rules and norms of the democratic system. This slow process of refinement builds democratic-institutional stock. Another example from the political history of the United States illustrates this process. The United States Constitution does not clearly state whether the Supreme Court may rightfully review acts of Congress. The matter remained a subject of debate until the Court, in its famous *Marbury v. Madison* decision in 1803, declared an act of Congress unconstitutional, establishing the precedent of judicial review. Thus, a key check of the judicial branch over the legislative branch of government remained undefined for fourteen years. This seems a short period indeed in the nearly 240-year history of the United States. Yet it is a time period longer than the existence of democracy in many countries of the Third Wave.

Even when new democratic rules clearly preclude certain acts, it often remains unclear who will enforce the rules when they are broken and how they will do so. Will checks on the chief executive be respected? Will the army stay out of politics? Will courts be independent of political influence? It may take years or decades for politicians to develop confidence that their peers will respect the rules. David Lake argues that political actors must make large compact-specific investments for a political order to become self-reinforcing.[49] Another way of emphasizing this point lies in our definition of democratic-institutional stock, which includes norms of behavior. These norms and expectations are likely to require years if not decades to coalesce. While they do so, self-interested executives can exploit their pliancy to twist rules of political competition and reinforce their hold on power.

The stock of democratic institutions deepens in their age. Each successful election, session of parliament, year without a coup, and graceful exit by a defeated incumbent adds to the democratic stock. Countries in their first few years of democratic rule simply lack this depth of experience. What of countries returning to democracy after years of non-democratic rule, however? Certainly such countries retain some democratic-institutional stock from previous experience. We argue that democratic-institutional stock deepens with the length of the previous democratic experience and lessens with the length of the authoritarian interlude. Chile's return to democracy exemplifies this pattern. Between the conclusion of World War II and General Augusto Pinochet's seizure of power in 1973, Chile held three competitive executive elections. These elections featured programmatic political parties, which debated economic issues, among others. When democracy returned to Chile in 1989, the country's party infrastructure sprang back to life. These elections were held only nineteen years after the last presidential elections in 1970. Chile's democratic stock might have paled next to a more established democracy, but a relatively recent history of electoral competition featuring programmatic political parties helped support a relatively smooth transition to democracy.

We contend, then, that the democratic dividend from an election will be larger the lengthier the country's previous experience with democracy. We cannot predict with certainty the length or recentness of previous democratic experience sufficient to support democracy. In other research, for example, we find that just a three-year delay in the timing of post-conflict elections in new democracies improves their impact on the potential for economic recovery.[50] Yet the anecdotal evidence discussed in this chapter suggests that significantly more time may be needed. We leave these questions to empirical testing in Chapter 5.

Fiscal Space

Our second contention is that greater fiscal space allows leaders to generate performance legitimacy more easily. We define fiscal space as the ability of the state to collect taxes, generate debt, and spend revenues efficiently. Revenues consist of taxes on income, consumption, trade, and other economic activities; non-tax revenues, such as revenues from the sale of natural resources; and foreign aid. Fiscal space is constrained by large sovereign debt owed to creditors, both foreign and domestic. When a government confronts large debts and meager revenues, its fiscal space is smaller; conversely, when debt is manageable and revenues stronger, its fiscal space is larger.

More fiscal space places a newly elected leader in an excellent position to generate performance legitimacy. She can dedicate the resources at her disposal to an array of public policies designed to demonstrate credibly her competence to voters. These policies may include building roads and schools, subsidizing fertilizer for farmers, or establishing a new pension system. The choices are nearly infinite, but their intent remains the same – to generate performance legitimacy in order to win re-election. Our logic is consistent with a long-standing argument in political economy that democracy improves public-good provision and redistributes income downward.[51]

Limited fiscal space spells trouble for newly elected leaders, for it limits their ability to invest in the kinds of public goods that will improve voters' lives. Leaders in these situations turn to providing private and club goods to favored allies – a strategy that costs more per head but less overall – and manipulating democratic rules to retain power. Such actions erode voters' faith in democracy as they observe continuing economic stagnation, eroding public integrity, and politicians' failure to redistribute income. Ted Robert Gurr's theory of relative deprivation emphasizes the danger of raising expectations and then failing to meet them.[52] Scholars of Sub-Saharan Africa, for instance, have noted the continuing neo-patrimonialism linking political parties and voters.[53] Lindberg also notes how geographically based political parties have developed patron–client relationships, with voters lacking access to public goods from the state.[54] Risk-averse voters, therefore, will choose private goods provided by an incumbent's political party, even though such benefits may do little to improve the general welfare.

Overall, this logic strongly suggests that elections held in countries with more fiscal space will result in larger democratic dividends. We will test this claim in Chapter 6.

Civil Conflict

Civil conflict impairs both performance and democratic-institutional legitimacy. A rather long literature has documented civil conflict's devastating impact on investment and economic growth; health outcomes; and politicians' incentives to invest in public goods.[55] These effects tend to reverberate years after the signing of a peace agreement, creating the spectre of countries caught in a "conflict trap," a vicious cycle of conflict in which post-war economic malaise only makes future war more likely. Researchers also doubt that democracy easily blooms in conflictual countries. Our own research finds that post-conflict democratization is fraught, especially when a new democracy holds elections within the first two years after the civil war.[56] These findings are consonant with the work of Roland Paris, who warned of the dangers of rapid liberalization when civil wars end.[57]

These literatures strongly hint at a simple claim – violent civil conflict hinders elected leaders in generating performance legitimacy and protecting democratic-institutional legitimacy. A newly elected leader in a peaceful country may face other obstacles, but can rest assured that armed factions will not obstruct her from building roads and clinics. She also has access to the performance legitimacy garnered from basic security. Her counterpart in a conflictual country is far less fortunate. He confronts violent opposition to public-good provision the moment he assumes office. He cannot provide the decisive public good for any leader – a monopoly on the legitimate use of physical force. Such a leader can only generate performance legitimacy through punishing his enemies on the battlefield and in the streets. He will tend to divert funds away from butter and towards guns, seeking to demonstrate his competence through military victory. Ethnic conflict may exacerbate this pattern, as the hardening of ethnic or sectarian lines incentivizes the provision of private and club goods.[58] Our less fortunate leader will also benefit from eroding democratic-institutional stock, forming alliances with the military that subvert civil authority, using violence as an excuse to disenfranchise certain groups or regions, and eliminating checks and balances on his power.

The rule of President Álvaro Uribe in Colombia provides a rich example of these dynamics. His predecessor's failed attempts to end the war through negotiation led to Uribe's electoral victory in 2002. He quickly raised military spending in an attempt to take the fight to the Fuerzas Armadas Revolucionarias de Colombia (FARC or Revolutionary Armed Forces of Colombia), which had access to revenues from drug trafficking.[59] Military personnel rose from 158,000 to 209,000. In an interview with the BBC, Uribe argued that, "Of course we need to eliminate social injustice in Colombia ... but what is first? Peace. Without peace, there is no investment. Without investment, there are no fiscal resources for the government to invest in the welfare of the people," echoing our theme that elected leaders during conflict will unrelentingly focus on military spending instead of public-good provision.[60] Uribe weakened checks on the executive, encouraging his supporters to amend the constitution to allow him to run for re-election. Uribe's administration also wiretapped opposition activists, politicians, and journalists in 2009. The early years of his presidency also saw a surge in extra-judicial killings by security forces. Colombia has a long tradition of democracy, but these changes are consistent with a weakening of the country's democratic-institutional stock.

This discussion suggests that civil conflict weakens both performance and democratic-institutional legitimacy. Elections held in civil conflict will be far less likely to promote democratic change. We provide evidence for this claim in Chapter 7.

Discussion

In Chapter 1, we asked a seemingly simple question: do elections advance the cause of democracy? As we have shown, this question's simplicity belies enduring academic disagreement on the fundamental question of how political change happens. Scholars have viewed elections in startlingly different ways: spurs of democratization to some, harbingers of instability and violence for others, and means of authoritarian retrenchment for still more. Our intellectual history of comparative democratization portrayed an energetic research agenda over the last fifteen years, but one that remains bifurcated. Electoralists, on one hand, neglect the political-economic context in which elections occur, insisting that bolstering the integrity of repeated elections is the key to achieving the democratic dividend. Structuralists, meanwhile, focus precisely on the political-economic prerequisites of successful democratization, yet ignore elections as meaningful political events.

We offer a theoretical synthesis of these accounts; this allows us to predict when elections will succeed in promoting democracy and when they will fail. We agree with scholars of electoral integrity that freer and fairer elections, as well as founding elections, tend to grant election winners broad legitimacy. Yet such legitimacy is temporary and contingent on the ability of elected executives to perform well while in office. Their ability to provide public goods and extend democratic norms depends on the performance and democratic-institutional legitimacy they inherit from past governments. Where these stocks of legitimacy already run deep, they will take steps that support democratic change. Where these stocks are shallow, they will opt for corruption and democratic shenanigans. Leaders certainly vary in their honesty and political talent, but this variation matters less than the political-economic context they inherit. In turn, we hypothesize that elections will do more to further the democratic cause where countries have a longer history of democratic rule, executives have access to larger fiscal space, and countries are relatively peaceful. As we shall see in Chapter 3, election winners during the electoral boom inherited dramatically different degrees of each.

Our main predictions focus on democratic change after elections. We also predict that elections can become ensnared in a low-legitimacy trap. An election winner in a low-legitimacy system will be more likely to weaken democratic practice, leaving voters disillusioned with democracy itself, weakening the integrity of the next election, and further diminishing the already paltry stocks of performance and democratic-institutional legitimacy. Her actions, therefore, will place the next election winner in equally bad or even worse straits. A low-legitimacy trap becomes highly likely, then, unless a highly unlikely set of circumstances occurs, such as the election of a transformational figure or a dramatic change in a country's fortunes. In contrast, an election winner in a relatively high-legitimacy system is more likely to augment democratic practice, enhancing future electoral integrity and adding to the already deep stocks of legitimacy, creating a high-legitimacy cycle.

These predictions will focus our empirical attention over the next five chapters. It is now time to add statistical flesh to these theoretical bones.

3 | The Third Wave(s) and the Electoral Boom

We are confronted with a troubling fact: the democratic dividend from elections declined just as they became globally de rigueur and improved dramatically in competitiveness. Our explanation for this democratic decline relies heavily on the differing structural contexts in which elections take place. Some election winners inherit relatively deep stocks of what we call performance and democratic-institutional legitimacy from their predecessors; others do not. Leaders are more likely to perform in office in a manner that promotes democratic change when they inherit relatively deeper stocks. Countries run the risk of becoming entangled in a low-legitimacy trap, in which even transparent elections yield governments whose road to re-election relies on corruption and weakening democratic rule, thus disillusioning voters and lowering the integrity of future elections. We theorize that elections are more likely to promote democracy where there is a previous history of democratic rule, fiscal space is relatively ample, and the country is at peace.

Our theory operates at the election level, predicting which elections will be more successful in promoting democracy. If the theory holds water, we should observe that the global decline in the democratic dividend from elections after 1988 coincided with a similar decline in the structural circumstances in which the elections took place. That is, our theory makes predictions not only about particular elections, but also about time. If elections have generated virtually no democratic dividend since the dawn of the electoral boom, it is because those elections have been held in countries with less democratic experience, less fiscal space, and a more recent history of violent conflict than the countries in which elections were held before the electoral boom.

In this chapter, we unfold a short history of elections since 1946 that confirms this expectation. At first glance, this explanation seems unbelievable. After all, have we not witnessed major development gains from Latin America to South Asia over the last sixty years? The answer to this puzzle lies in examining which countries have begun to hold elections. Three major geopolitical and economic shocks that pre-dated the electoral boom played an important role in defining the structural context in which elections took place: decolonization between 1946 and 1977, the global debt crisis of the 1970s and 1980s, and the denouement of the Cold War in the late 1980s and early 1990s. The coincidence of these major political and economic upheavals with the electoral boom created a new, daunting challenge for democracy promotion: elections spread to younger, poorer, and more ethnically divided countries with less democratic experience and fiscal space and a longer history of violent civil conflict. As the Third Wave spread, the only countries left to democratize were the difficult cases. Gone are the days when relatively stable, rich countries – such as Chile or Poland – returned to free elections. Instead, new election-holding countries today look more like Afghanistan or Sierra Leone. This chapter offers the first evidence in favor of the theory of elections presented in Chapter 2.

Elections in the Third Wave(s) of Democracy

Figure 3.1 shows the number of democratic countries and competitive executive elections in each year between 1946 and 2010.[1]

Several trends visible in Figure 3.1 deserve special attention. The Second Wave of Democracy began in 1946, as Western Europe returned to democracy from the ashes of World War II. During this time, the number of democracies nearly doubled, from a post-war low of about twenty to about forty by the early 1960s. The Second Wave was quickly succeeded by a counter-wave that lasted for nearly fifteen years, during which the global number of democracies remained roughly the same.

After 1974, it would be more proper to talk about the Third Waves of Democracy, rather than of a single Third Wave. The Third Wave commenced in 1974 with the Carnation Revolution in Portugal, initiating what we call Wave 3.0, which increased the number of democracies from thirty-eight in 1974 to fifty-two in 1989. This wave saw the return to democracy in Latin America as the worldwide debt crisis, human rights abuses, and Argentina's disastrous war for the Falklands discredited military regimes and brought presidential democracy back to the region. Wave 3.1 began with the end of

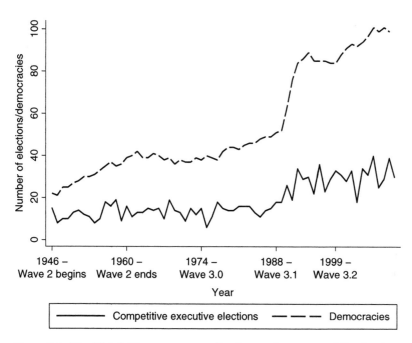

Figure 3.1 The Third Wave was actually three sub-waves, while elections expanded in one burst

the Cold War and spread democracy to Eastern European post-Soviet states. Figure 3.1 shows how Wave 3.1 dramatically accelerated liberal expansion – by 1994, eighty-nine countries counted as democracies. Yet Wave 3.1 stalled within several years of the breakup of the Soviet Union and the number of democracies fell back to eighty-four between 1994 and 1999. Wave 3.2 reignited the spread of democracy, however, pushing the number of democracies to roughly one hundred for the first time in world history. This sub-wave was more spread out geographically than previous sub-waves, but many of the Wave 3.2 countries could be found in Sub-Saharan Africa.

The growth in competitive executive elections, however, did not expand in tandem with our three sub-waves. Instead, Figure 3.1 shows an electoral boom that occurred virtually overnight after the mid-1980s. Between 1946 and 1987, the number of competitive executive elections per year averaged about thirteen and ranged between six and nineteen. There was little growth during this period, even as the number of countries expanded with decolonization and the beginning of

Wave 3.0. The electoral boom instead occurred just before Wave 3.1. The average number of elections held more than doubled to twenty-nine per year and the minimum number of competitive executive elections held was eighteen during this period, which had been roughly the maximum number of such elections in 1946–1987. Neither did Wave 3.2 really increase the number of elections significantly, though it increased the number of democracies. There is significant volatility in the number of elections held from year-to-year, of course, since the number depends on the vagaries of countries' electoral calendars, but the sea change is rather clear.

Younger, Poorer, and More Fractionalized Elections

We know that the number of elections being held in a given year dramatically expanded with the advent of the electoral boom in 1988. But what do we know about the countries holding elections during the electoral boom? How were they different than countries holding elections between 1946 and 1987? Before we address the question of stocks of legitimacy, we offer three answers here: countries holding elections during the electoral boom were younger, poorer, and more ethnically fractionalized.

Two political earthquakes entirely reshaped the international system both before and during the electoral boom: decolonization and the breakup of the Soviet Union. At the conclusion of World War II, our data count only seventy-one sovereign countries.[2] By 1975, that number had more than doubled to 148 members. In other words, between two and three countries were born in the typical year between 1946 and 1975. In 1960 alone, eighteen new countries were born. Decolonization had mostly ended by about 1975, but the disintegration of the Soviet Union nearly instantly created twenty new sovereign states in the three years between 1990 and 1993. By the end of our data, we count 170 sovereign countries.

What were the implications of these two geopolitical upheavals for the conduct of elections? For an answer, consider Figure 3.2, which displays the number of competitive executive elections before and during the electoral boom, which we break down by whether they were held in an "old" state that existed in 1946 or in a "new" state formed since then. The pattern is striking. Before the electoral boom, competitive executive elections took place mainly in old states. Fewer

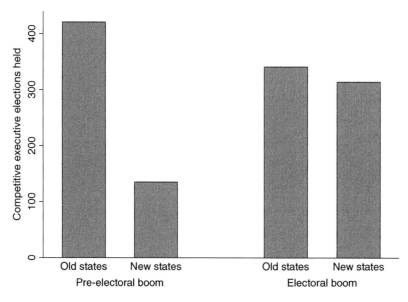

Figure 3.2 The electoral boom spread elections to younger countries

than one-quarter of competitive executive elections took place in new states, in fact. The picture changes dramatically during the electoral boom, when nearly half of all competitive executive elections took place in new states. We can make this point in still a different way. The median age of a country holding a competitive executive election before the electoral boom was roughly seventy-six years. The same figure during the electoral boom is seventy-two years – four years younger – despite the fact that countries have aged over this time period!

This, of course, reflects largely where elections took place. Before the electoral boom, only 7.5 percent of competitive executive elections took place in Sub-Saharan Africa, a share that nearly tripled to 21.8 percent during the electoral boom. Roughly two-thirds of elections took place in the Americas and Western Europe before the electoral boom; that proportion declined by nearly half during the electoral boom. The dramatic expansion of the state system meant that elections took place in starkly younger countries located outside of elections' previous home regions of Western Europe and the Americas.

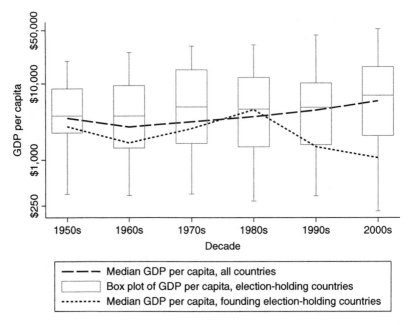

Figure 3.3 Election-holding countries have become poorer, even as the world has become richer

Elections not only arrived in younger countries; they also came to poorer countries. Figure 3.3 illustrates this surprisingly complex story. In it, we overlay three plots.[3] First, the box plots show per capita Gross Domestic Product (GDP) for election-holding countries only, by decade. The line within each box indicates the median GDP per capita for an election-holding country, while the box itself shows the distance between the 25th and 75th percentiles. The "whiskers" show the total length of the distribution of GDP per capita for election-holding countries.[4] Second, the dashed line shows the median GDP per capita for all countries, regardless of whether they held elections. Finally, the dotted line displays the median GDP per capita for countries holding founding elections.

Figure 3.3 recounts two competing stories in the post-war history of economic development and elections. The first story is a happy one: the typical country registered important developmental gains over our time period. The median country saw its GDP per capita more than double between the 1960s and 2000s, from roughly $2,700 to nearly $6,000. This rise came despite financial and economic tumult during the Latin American debt crisis, the end of the Cold War, and the East Asian financial crisis of the late 1990s. Our data concur with the accounts of economists such as Charles Kenny, who argues that a number of indicators of human development have dramatically improved, and Paul Collier, who argues that poverty has fallen in roughly 80 percent of the world, with the remaining 20 percent dubbed the "bottom billion."[5]

The second story is more ambivalent: elections have spread to progressively poorer countries, meaning that they are more often held in conditions of poverty. The typical election-holding country became richer between the 1950s and the 1970s. By the 1970s, the typical country holding an election had a GDP per capita of nearly $5,000. The typical election-holding country, in fact, was far richer than the typical country, which had a GDP per capita of only $3,200. However, over the next thirty years, the typical election-holding country actually got poorer, even as the world became richer. By the 1990s, the median GDP per capita of a country holding an election was still just below $5,000. During the 2000s, this situation improved and the typical election-holding country became richer. But elections had also spread to increasingly poorer countries. The lower whiskers show this trend most dramatically: the poorest countries holding elections in the 2000s had per capita income of about $214 – or only fifty-eight cents per day – while the poorest countries holding elections in the 1970s had a GDP per capita of $357.

These data reveal a clash between two major stories: although countries generally expanded their economies, election-holding countries became poorer in the period we study. Why? The answer lies in the nature of the electoral boom. Nearly every rich country had already held elections by the eve of the electoral boom, so the only places for elections to spread to were poorer countries. We show this in the dotted line in Figure 3.3, which displays the median GDP per capita for only those countries holding founding elections. In the 1980s, the typical Sub-Saharan African country holding an election had a GDP per capita that was slightly higher than the typical country and roughly equal to other election-holding countries. However, a great divergence occurred just as the electoral boom took shape in the 1990s. By the

2000s, the typical Sub-Saharan African country holding an election had a GDP per capita of only $1,074, compared to $4,560 during the 1980s.

We are left with a new understanding of the relationship between elections and economic development. Before the electoral boom, elections as an institution were mostly confined to rich societies. As the Third Wave slowly came to fruition in the early 1980s, countries returning to electoral rule remained relatively well-to-do. Yet once the electoral boom took off in the late 1980s and 1990s, the set of non-electoral countries grew progressively poorer. Founding elections overwhelmingly took place in far poorer societies than their predecessors from the 1980s and 1990s. The process of elections – registering voters, campaigning, counting votes, and beginning the process of governing – is now much more likely to take place in the midst of poverty.

As if the news was not bad enough, one other fact is worth understanding. Not only have elections spread to younger, poorer countries, they have also arrived in countries that are more fractionalized along ethnolinguistic lines. Competitive executive elections held before 1988 tended to be held in relatively unified societies, as the first panel of Figure 3.4 shows. Roughly 43 percent of such elections were held in countries with a fractionalization score of 0.20 or less, while only about 2 percent were held in countries with a score over 0.80. The flatter curve shown in the second panel demonstrates the dramatic change in election-holding after 1988 – the ethnic fractionalization in the typical election-holding country jumped to 0.41 from 0.26. Only 27 percent of elections were held in countries with a score of 0.20 or less and the proportion held in countries with a score of greater than 0.80 spiked to 6 percent.

Clearly, countries did not become ethnically fractionalized so quickly in the years we study! The explanation instead is similar to our explanation of the deterioration of income per capita in election-holding countries. Elections were largely the preserve of ethnically homogenous countries before the electoral boom. More ethnically diverse countries tended not to hold elections at all. The global spread of elections changed this entirely, as elections left the relatively safer grounds of ethnic homogeneity for more ethnically diverse destinations. We have already argued that elected leaders lacking performance legitimacy can exploit regional and ethnic divisions to provide club goods to co-ethnics while suppressing

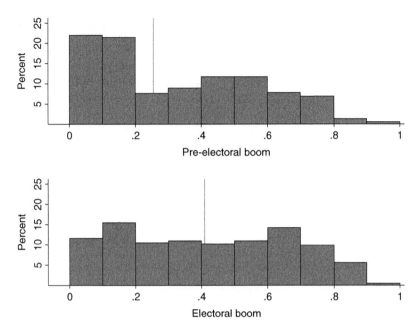

Figure 3.4 The electoral boom spread elections to more ethnically heterogeneous countries

electoral turnout among other groups. Figure 3.4 indicates that, at a minimum, such a strategy became easier after the electoral boom, as leaders had more divisions from which to choose.

When the Well Runs Dry: Stocks of Legitimacy During the Electoral Boom

We have already shown that the set of countries holding elections has become younger, poorer, and more ethnolinguistically fractionalized. But what of the stocks of performance and democratic-institutional legitimacy that we identified in Chapter 2? There, we hypothesized that elections do less to promote democracy when democratic institutions are young, fiscal space is constrained, and politics is violent. We also saw in Chapter 1 that elections in the 1990s and 2000s generated virtually no democratic dividend compared to elections in the 1980s. If our theory helps to explain this record, we should see that elections after 1988 have been more likely to take place in precisely these circumstances.

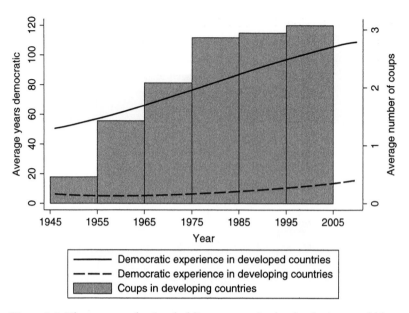

Figure 3.5 The average election-holding country in the developing world has little democratic experience

Democratic experience is an important marker of democratic-institutional legitimacy, which in turn supports further democratic change after elections. Democratic institutions require time to coalesce and function as credible constraints on election winners. In a happy world, we would observe elections being held in countries with deepening democratic experience over time. This would serve as evidence that democratizing countries had leapt into a virtuous cycle of democratic legitimacy.

Reality is not so happy. Election-holding countries in the developing world have accumulated democratic experience only slowly and haltingly since 1946. Figure 3.5 divides the countries of the world into two categories – developed and developing – and tracks the number of years countries in both categories have been democratic at the time they hold elections. The trend lines depict the average democratic experience on election day for each set of countries.[6]

Figure 3.5 reveals a large and steadily widening gap in democratic experience between the developed and developing worlds. In 1946, the average developed country holding a competitive executive election had sixty-four years of democratic experience, versus roughly ten years for the average developing country. This is no small difference, certainly, but it has only expanded over time. Developed countries have steadily accumulated democratic experience; after about 2000, the average developed country holding a competitive executive election typically had well over 100 years of democratic experience. The history outside of this select group is not nearly as happy, as indicated by the stark differences in the slopes of the trend lines. For most of the period 1946–2010, election-holding countries in this group barely accumulated any democratic experience at all. By the 2000s, the average developing country holding an election still had fewer than twenty years of democratic experience, accumulating just about ten more years of democratic experience in sixty-four years. Putting this differently, the gap between developed and developing countries had doubled since 1946 from roughly fifty to one hundred years. We can point to one more piece of evidence in this regard. During the electoral boom, about 41 percent of elections in the developing world took place in countries that had not spent even one year as a democracy.

This analysis confirms a rather pessimistic view that echoes what we have already seen: the electoral boom largely spread elections to countries with little or no democratic experience, since more experienced societies had already democratized before the late 1980s. Yet we know also that elections spread to younger countries born of decolonization between 1946 and 1975, and of the breakup of the Soviet Union after 1991. It may well be that slowly accumulating democratic experience is more a result of younger countries holding elections. It is hardly fair to blame newborn countries for lacking democratic experience. Cuba, for example, had enjoyed 113 years of formal sovereignty by 2016, but not one year as a democracy. It would be difficult to compare its experience with that of Azerbaijan, which did not become an independent state until 1991, before which it had been ruled from Moscow. Azerbaijan largely lacked democratic experience – despite a brief period in 1918–1920 as an independent democratic state that became the first Muslim-majority country to extend the franchise to women – but for far different reasons than Cuba. Figure 3.5 may overstate the problem of democratic experience if newly independent countries have pulled the average down.

We therefore examine a different indicator to corroborate our story – a history of military coups. Military coups are the quintessential "leak" out of democratic-institutional stock, since they subvert elections, interrupt the peaceful alternation of power, and either create or prolong military rule. An accumulating record of coups over time would present reasonable evidence that elections have increasingly spread to places with a history of frequent interruptions of their accumulation of democratic-institutional stock. On the other hand, as increasingly younger countries have begun to hold elections, we might expect the typical coup experience to decline, due to the same bias that might understate the accumulation of democratic experience. Figure 3.5 charts the average number of coups that election-holding developing countries have had in their history by decade.[7] The evidence is rather clear: at the dawn of the electoral boom, election-holding countries in the developing world had experienced, on average, three coups in their past. Coup experience rapidly accumulated beginning in the 1950s and extending to the mid-1970s. We should be thankful that this growth has slowed, even if the recent coup in Egypt reminds us that the danger is never past. During the electoral boom, however, fully 34 percent of elections have occurred in countries with more coup attempts than years of democratic rule! Haiti is a tragic example. In 2006, it held elections having spent only 6 of its 147 years as a democracy, yet having experienced twelve coups, eight of which were successful, in that same period. President Michael Martelly has repeatedly postponed elections that were supposed to have been held in 2011, and since January 2015 has ruled by decree after the parliament was dissolved, leaving Haiti with no functioning government. At the time of this writing, Haiti is again experiencing violence at the polls and is gearing up for what promise to be tumultuous run-off presidential elections in late April 2016. While we sincerely hope we are wrong, we do not expect these elections – if they happen – to bring deeper democracy to Haiti.

Haiti's problems, like those of its fellow developing countries, are not limited to a lack of mature democratic institutions. A more immediate issue is that its government lacks the resources and capacity to govern. We have argued that elections in countries with ampler fiscal space are more likely to yield democratic change. Our theory of performance legitimacy depends crucially on the election winners' capacity to supply public goods, which requires substantial funding. The spread

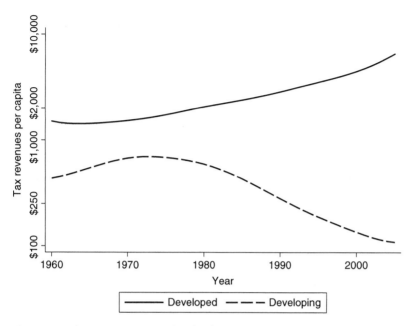

Figure 3.6 Election winners in the developing world have less access to fiscal space today than ever before

of elections to countries with little fiscal space should be a cause for worry, and evidence in favor of our explanation of the collapse of the democratic dividend during the electoral boom.

In Figure 3.6, we chart the median level of taxation per capita in constant dollars for countries holding competitive executive elections between 1960 and 2005.[8] We again divide our sample into groups of developing and developed countries and add a lowess-smoothed line to each series to show the broad trends in fiscal space over time.

Figure 3.6 shows that election winners have faced a deteriorating fiscal environment since the beginning of the Third Wave in the early 1970s. Before then, countries holding elections had been building their fiscal space. Taxes per capita between 1960, when the data series begins, and the early 1970s grew impressively, actually narrowing the gap with developed countries. Newly elected leaders of developing countries often had access to surprisingly robust tax revenues. This soon changed. The typical election winner in the developed world took power with increasing levels of taxes per capita at her disposal. The remainder of the election-holding world saw its fiscal space quickly decline after about the mid-1970s. At the dawn of the electoral boom in the late 1980s taxes per capita had fallen to about $250 – less than they had been in 1960. By the end of our data, the situation had worsened still: the average election winner took power with only about $100 per capita in tax revenues at her disposal.

These findings echo a constant refrain of this chapter's empirical history of elections since 1946: the electoral boom swept up countries with successively worse circumstances mostly because countries with better circumstances were already holding elections. At the advent of the electoral boom, elections had already spread to relatively old, rich countries with relatively deep democratic-institutional stock and ample fiscal space. The only countries left were younger, poorer, more ethnically fractionalized, and less democratically experienced. In that sense, the declining structural circumstances in which elections have taken place have everything to do with the changing set of countries holding elections, as opposed to collapsing indictors in the developing world at large.

The story of fiscal space is different, however. Figure 3.7 plots the median natural log of taxes per capita by region for all countries, not only those holding elections. It tells a startling story: fiscal space declined across time in nearly every region of the world, with the one exception of the West (i.e., North America and Western Europe). The decline is most pronounced for Latin America, which saw taxation decrease steadily from about 1980 until the end of our time series. That year nearly perfectly coincides with the onset of the worldwide debt crisis that saw Latin American countries lose a decade of economic growth. The same pattern is evident in Sub-Saharan Africa, though at a lower level; tax revenues per capita expanded in Sub-Saharan Africa until 1980 and steadily declined afterwards.

Thus, our evidence suggests not only that elections spread to countries with lower fiscal space, but also that developing countries generally lost fiscal space after about 1980, roughly a decade before the advent of the electoral boom. This pattern deserves more attention. Why did fiscal space decline so rapidly in the developing world after 1980? We argue that a neoliberal turn in economic governance explains this pattern. A series of major events preceded the electoral boom that irrevocably changed the policymaking environment in developing countries. The election of Ronald Reagan in the

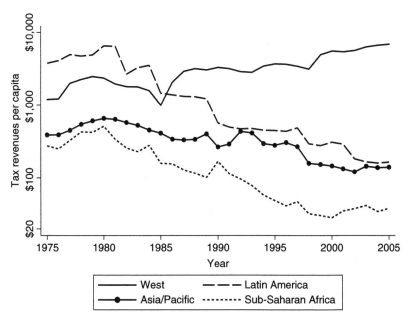

Figure 3.7 Fiscal space has declined in all regions but the West since the 1970s

United States and Margaret Thatcher in the United Kingdom signaled a shift away from Keynesianism and towards monetarism and an emphasis on economic freedom championed by Milton Friedman. The debt crisis in developing countries, which began in the early 1980s, forced major changes to microeconomic and macroeconomic policies, often through IMF structural adjustment programs.[9] Additionally, the collapse of the Soviet Union in 1991 forcefully discredited Communism, along with any other approach to development policymaking featuring heavy state intervention. By 1990, just two years into the electoral boom, economist John Williamson had described the "Washington Consensus," highlighting how US-based international institutions tended to promote a series of market-based reforms in developing countries, including deregulation, trade liberalization, and competitive exchange rates.[10]

These profound shifts had real effects on economic policymaking in election-holding countries, with the ultimate effect of shrinking their fiscal space. Figure 3.8 supports this contention. It charts the momentous shifts in economic policymaking before and after the

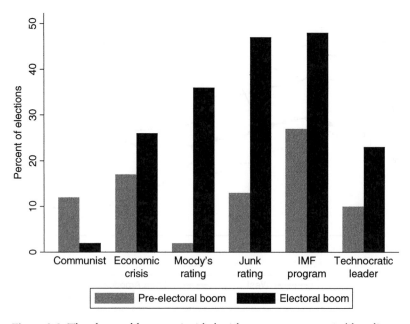

Figure 3.8 The electoral boom coincided with a turn to economic liberalism

electoral boom by capturing the proportion of elections in developing countries occurring in particular conditions. Predictably, far fewer elections during the electoral boom occurred in Communist countries; the proportion declined precipitously between the pre-electoral boom and electoral boom periods.[11] Countries holding elections during the electoral boom were more likely to find themselves in the midst of economic crisis, according to data from NELDA. We also examine whether these countries asked to have their sovereign debt rated by Moody's, a credit rating agency. Countries during the electoral boom were more than ten times more likely to do so, while nearly half of elections in this period occurred in countries with "junk" ratings. In other words, elections increasingly occurred in developing countries with only poor capacities to borrow on international markets. Elections were also more likely to occur in clients of the international financial institutions (IFIs) that were the braintrusts behind the so-called Washington consensus. Finally, we rate whether election-holding countries in the developing world were led by technocrats, or leaders with expertise in economics who are more likely to initiate neoliberal reforms.[12] During the electoral boom, this proportion doubled to over one-quarter.

This evidence supports a new understanding of the structural constraints on election winners in the developing world after 1988. Elections did increasingly spread to countries with limited fiscal space, but this dynamic was compounded by the general decline in tax revenues per capita across the developing world. The electoral boom may have advanced the cause of political liberalism, but it also took place during a turn towards economic liberalism. This ideological turn fundamentally shifted the policy levers at the disposal of election winners. Since this shift, election winners around the world have taken power with precious little fiscal space at their disposal, which we argue has placed them in more difficult political environments and has heightened the risk of post-election democratic stagnation.

Immature institutions and poor fiscal space are a recipe for social unrest and political conflict.[13] Such conflict threatens the ability of election winners to generate performance legitimacy through means other than violence. It also provides a ready pretense for limiting civil and political rights, stunting democratic-institutional stock. Unfortunately, here too the data warrant pessimism. Figure 3.9 shows the percentage of elections in developing countries held during civil conflict, in the first ten years after civil conflict ended, and in either condition between 1946 and 2010.[14] The proportion of elections held during organized civil conflict expanded steadily between 1946 and about 1985. By the early years of the electoral boom, roughly a fifth of elections still took place during civil conflict. Fortunately, that proportion soon declined and fewer elections were being held during civil conflict as the electoral boom progressed. Yet this still meant that a large proportion of elections were occurring soon after conflict ended. By the late-1990s, countries recovering from civil conflict comprised over 20 percent of election-holders. If we combine these two percentages, as we do in the solid line in Figure 3.9, roughly 40 percent of elections during the mid-1990s were being held in what we call conflictual societies. This proportion did decline as fewer civil wars erupted between 2000 and 2010 but it does not fall below 30 percent.

Quite clearly, civil conflict and the search for post-conflict peace have formed important backdrops for elections during the electoral boom. Even as the actual rate of civil conflict declined after the early 1990s, elections increasingly were held in its wake. We highlight one

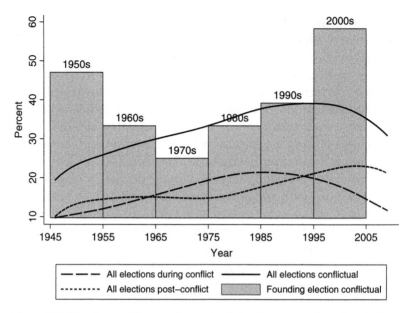

Figure 3.9 The electoral boom often spread elections to conflictual societies

particularly important piece of evidence in this regard in Figure 3.9. The bars capture the proportion of founding elections held in conflictual societies – that is, either during civil conflict or within ten years of its conclusion – by decade. The evidence is overwhelming: founding elections since the dawn of the electoral boom have increasingly been held in conflictual societies. The proportion has increased for three consecutive decades since the 1970s; during the 2000s, seven of twelve founding elections were held in conflictual societies. If we examine all founding elections during the electoral boom, we find that two out of every five have been held in conflictual societies. Of these, half were held during conflicts and the other half after conflict had ended (or during what we term "recovery"). This evidence supports the notion that the new entrants to the club of election-holders were often composed of countries seeking escape from cycles of political violence.

These trends again reflect major world events of the last thirty years, particularly the post–Cold War liberal euphoria. Scholars have long recognized that post-conflict democratization and elections have become standard peacebuilding practice in post-war countries from

Cambodia to El Salvador.[15] Our own work finds that post-conflict elections have been held more often and earlier since the 1980s.[16] The United Nations has tended to view elections not only as means to democratization, but also as tools of peacebuilding. Elections would signal agreement on the post-conflict political order and allow UN peacekeepers to return home, placing countries previously torn apart by violence on the road to peace and freedom. This emphasis on rapid democratization jibed well with the general turn towards liberalism in the post–Cold War era.

Discussion

The history of election-holding since 1946 begins in the ashes of World War II, continuing over seven eventful decades to the current era. The story we tell in nine pictures is at once triumphal and sobering. More optimistic is the rapid spread of elections and democracy. We contend that the Third Wave of democracy spanning thirty-five years between the mid-1970s and 2010 might better be thought of as consisting of three wavelets, rather than one continuous democratic expansion. Wave 3.0 began in Iberia in 1974 and spread to Latin America, ebbing by the mid-1980s. Wave 3.1 brought democracy to Eastern Europe after about 1988, but faded around 1999. Wave 3.2 reignited the spread of democracy to countries around the world, but principally in Sub-Saharan Africa. The growth in election-holding was more sudden than the spread of democracy, occurring in one quick jump – what we call the "electoral boom" – after 1988. In just a few years, the average number of competitive executive elections held globally more than doubled. The electoral boom raised the hopes of democrats around the world. Elections spread to societies with tragic histories of war, poverty, and dictatorship. Their specific histories might have differed, but democratic aspirations linked these societies. People in both tiny Haiti and vast Russia voted with the hope of launching a new path towards democracy.

This optimism is tempered by a cluster of structural barriers that complicate a smooth passage from elections to democracy. The electoral boom brought elections to younger, poorer, more ethnically divided countries with long histories of colonialism and, in the case of Eastern Europe and the post-Soviet states, Communism. At the dawn of the electoral boom, fewer older, richer countries remained non-democratic. Countries such as Chile – 150 years old, relatively rich, and ethnically homogenous when it returned to democracy in 1989 – became increasingly rare during Waves 3.1 and 3.2. The countries of the electoral boom instead came to resemble Sierra Leone – young, poor, and ethnically divided. Even as the world at large became richer, election-holding countries became poorer.

The structural challenges to democratization did not end there. We also saw that the electoral boom brought elections to countries with relatively emptier stocks of political legitimacy. New entrants to the elections club possessed little democratic experience or fiscal space. They did, however, have substantial experience with civil conflict and military coups. Again, reality is sobering: at the dawn of the electoral boom, the only countries left to begin regular competitive elections were those with shallow stocks of legitimacy.

This brief history recognizes that several momentous international events not only influenced the electoral boom's existence, but also fundamentally altered the world into which it was born. The first was decolonization, which began with the end of World War II and ended in the mid-1970s. The electoral boom overwhelmingly swept up the post-colonial world; over 70 percent of founding elections during the electoral boom happened there. The impact of decolonization can also be felt in the wave of civil conflicts that wracked the developing world after World War II. This violent tide ebbed after the early 1990s, but the fact remains that a large proportion of elections during the electoral boom – and especially founding elections – took place in countries on the precipice of violence. The second momentous event was the debt crisis of the early 1980s, which struck Latin America particularly hard, leading to the infamous "lost decade" of economic growth. Our analysis of fiscal space identifies 1980 as the point after which taxation per capita declined steadily around the globe. The debt crisis, we saw, was followed by fundamental changes in economic governance, most notably through a commitment to neoliberal economics. Finally, the end of the Cold War in the late 1980s and early 1990s presaged the electoral boom itself. It also further discredited heavy state intervention in the economy and set the stage for new UN efforts to curb civil conflict. The timing of the electoral boom must be considered in light of these seismic world events.

We return then to our motivating question: Why did the democratic dividend from elections collapse just as they surged in number and quality? Our answer is that, as elections diffused across the globe after 1988, the set of countries holding elections faced structural barriers not fully appreciated by democracy promoters. The analysis presented in this chapter supports this argument. Elections may have initiated and sustained democratization in the early and mid-1980s, when they occurred in societies with relatively deep stocks of legitimacy. However, the same could not be said of the electoral boom countries of the 1990s and 2000s, which were younger, poorer, more ethnically fractionalized, more riven by civil conflict, and lacking in democratic experience and fiscal space. In Part II of the book, we investigate the deleterious effects of these barriers on the democratic dividend of elections, before turning in Part III to how we might ameliorate them to improve the prospects for democracy in the twenty-first century.

Challenges Facing Elections in Developing Countries

4 | *The Ephemeral Power of Contingent Legitimacy*

The promise of elections is that they confer on the chosen a legitimacy that is denied to those who acquire power by other means. Short of a handful of states that still permit some form of hereditary rule, all modern states now use elections as the primary means of choosing rulers. The hope of democracy promoters is that legitimate elections will further consolidation in more experienced countries and jump-start transitions in nascent democracies. As we have seen, an influential literature argues that democratization by elections is a modern mode of democratic transition.

A primary question therefore is whether elections generate a positive democratic dividend in the developing world. Our answer is that they do, sometimes; yet, even when elections do generate a store of legitimacy for the victor, that legitimacy has an expiration date. We call this "contingent legitimacy" to emphasize the point that while elected leaders enjoy a governance advantage over their non-elected counterparts, they do so only temporarily. At some point, their democratic halo dissipates and they must perform and meet their citizens' lofty expectations or risk squandering their honeymoon period. The length of this post-election honeymoon period varies across countries because elections themselves differ in the contingent legitimacy they confer on their winners.

Over the past two decades, academic research has confirmed what journalists and civil society activists have long known – that many of the elections held across the developing world since the end of the Cold War were at best dubious in their commitment to the best practices for protecting electoral integrity. While some countries took great pains to ensure their elections met internationally promulgated standards and subjected their processes to external monitoring, many did not. Too many elections resembled instead the sham exercises conducted in Ethiopia in 2015, where the ruling party won all the seats in an overwhelming show of dominance secured by harassing opposition figures and suppressing independent civil society.[1] Common sense tells us that elections such as that of Ethiopia in 2015 will do little to further the cause of democracy in that country. By contrast, the same intuition tells us that clean elections should yield a greater store of contingent legitimacy, opening a larger window of opportunity for democratic change. And therefore cleaner elections should yield a greater democratic dividend, all else equal.

Similarly, while all elections are momentous, some are more so. Founding elections mark a historic departure from periods of dictatorship and authoritarian rule. The hope and global attention generated by a founding election is unique, and a country's first elected head of government occupies a special place in her state's history and imagination. Accordingly, founding elections should yield an especially large store of contingent legitimacy.

Our theory of contingent legitimacy stemming from elections is consistent with the democratization-by-elections and electoral integrity literatures, but our argument goes beyond those viewpoints. Cleaner elections are obviously intrinsically better than dirty elections, and founding elections are indubitably special occasions. But their potential to further democratic deepening, to yield a positive democratic dividend, is only realized if states possess the structural advantages that allow newly elected leaders to govern effectively. Otherwise the potential is wasted. Clean elections held in the absence of such favorable conditions should yield a short-run boost to democracy – a larger store of contingent legitimacy – but this dissipates quickly. Put differently, the window opened by founding or especially legitimate elections will shut quickly in countries lacking the right mix of structural conditions for democratic change. True democratic development requires more than clean or momentous elections.

We test these intuitions in this chapter by studying over 1,700 national elections in over 140 developing countries in the post–World War II era. We ask two questions. First, do cleaner elections result in greater gains for democracy? Second, are founding elections the fillip for democracy we hope they will be? Our analysis highlights two main findings. First, cleaner elections do not increase the democratic dividend from elections in the long-term. They do yield a larger short-term upswing in democratic practice, but this effect dissipates quickly – by our calculations, within two years. Cleaner elections do no better than elections with problems or even sham uncompetitive elections in the medium and longer term. Second, founding elections are special, yielding a statistically meaningful democratic dividend. But founding elections are rare (just 8 percent of all elections since 1945) and, by definition, not repeatable. Indeed subsequent analysis shows that this positive effect diminishes once we consider the country's first three elections instead of just its first.

The implications of these findings for theory and policy are provocative, but let's dive into the data before we discuss what they mean.

Contingent Legitimacy from Elections

Chapter 3 establishes that election-holding countries since 1988 are on average poorer, more ethnically divided, and more likely to be emerging from a recent colonial or Communist past. More worryingly, they also have less democratic experience, more limited fiscal space, and more often must confront a violent past. Yet we also see in Chapter 1 that elections improved in competitiveness during the electoral boom. The electoral seed has improved in quality, but the terrain has become less fertile. Unsurprisingly, the democratic dividend from elections collapsed just as the electoral boom took shape in the late 1980s and early 1990s. The circumstantial case is quite strong: the descriptive evidence suggests that the democratic dividend from elections declined in response to the spread of elections to countries with limited stocks of institutional legitimacy – even though elections in theory conferred greater contingent legitimacy on their winners.

We examine this question more systematically here. We built a dataset of elections in which each observation represents a country-election-year. The observations for the United States, for example, are for even-numbered years (e.g., 2000, 2002, 2004, and so on), since that is when that country held its national elections. But that is not the only way in which we could have proceeded. An alternate approach would be to build a dataset of each country-year for all countries for which we have data. We could then identify the years in which countries held elections and model democratic change as a function of whether or not an election was held in that year. This has largely been the approach taken by the literature on democratization by elections. We call the former approach the "elections-only" approach and the latter the "all-years" approach. Both approaches allow us to examine how the democratic dividend from elections depends on structural conditions, and happily both approaches yield the same conclusions. The elections-only approach simplifies the comparisons made, by testing how systematic differences in stocks of legitimacy condition the impact of elections, and so we adopt it throughout the book.[2]

The National Elections across Democracy and Autocracy (NELDA) project provides us our list of election-years.[3] NELDA's attractiveness stems from the exhaustive details it provides on elections, including elections' type and competitiveness, election observers' assessments of an election's quality, steps taken by incumbents to harass the opposition, election boycotts and violence, and the political aftermath. The investigators collect data only on national-level elections in which the general population votes, however constrained the franchise might be, as opposed to those in which a small junta or ruling committee makes the decision. Importantly, the dataset includes uncompetitive elections, which will prove useful as we move forward.[4] Three modifications to the original data are necessary for our purposes. First, we collapse multiround elections into a single observation using information on either the first or the last round of the election, depending on what we wish to know. For example, whether the incumbent lost power is determined by the last round, but whether the election permitted competition is indicated by its first round. Second, when legislative and presidential elections are coterminous (e.g., as they are every four years in the United States), we privilege the data from the presidential election. Finally, countries do hold multiple elections in the same year, though this is relatively rare (fewer than 10 percent of our cases). When it does happen, it is typically because a country held a legislative election a few months before the presidential election, as in Colombia. In these cases, we again privilege the information for the presidential election.[5]

One more housekeeping point is in order. We focus on the role of elections in democratic change in what we have frequently termed the "developing world." But what constitutes the developing world exactly? We might depend on region, analyzing only countries outside of Europe and North America. Doing so would exclude countries that returned to elections after a long autocratic period, as in Portugal or Greece. We might also invoke an income-based definition, but this would remove elections held in countries that grew rapidly and exceeded any such threshold over the past sixty years. We instead rely on a conceptual definition. For us, developing countries are those countries for whom a democratic system was not a certainty in 1946 or in the year of its birth as a sovereign country, whichever came second.[6] Our inquiry is into the political impact of elections in places where history has not already rendered democracy the only political game in town. We admit that this choice renders us vulnerable to charges of post hoc thinking, since we cannot know for certain whether democratic rule was in doubt in a certain time and place without observing its subsequent history. We therefore err on the side of including, rather than excluding, countries, eliminating elections in only nineteen countries from our analysis.[7] These choices generate a list of 1,755 elections in 144 developing countries between 1946 and 2010.[8]

Moving from "developing" to "consolidated" democracy requires that elections generate a positive democratic dividend so that each subsequent election starts at a higher point on the democratic scale. Measuring the democratic dividend first requires measuring democracy. For that, we use the Unified Democracy Scores (UDS), which incorporates ten separate democracy measures – including the popular Polity IV combined democracy score and Freedom House's ratings of civil and political liberties – to create a composite annual measure of democratic practice for a broad range of countries between 1946 and 2008.[9] This measure has several advantages relevant to our project. First, the inclusion of multiple measures reduces the sensitivity of our findings to the particular coding decisions of any one such measure. Second, the measure is continuous, which allows us to capture more incremental changes in democratic governance, whether towards democracy or dictatorship. Third, because of how it is constructed, the ceiling and floor effects in the UDS are less stringent than in conventional measures, therefore allowing even democratic countries to increase their score.[10]

We define the democratic dividend as the change in a country's democracy rating five years after a year in which the election is held. The choice of the five-year window over which to measure democratic change is driven by our focus on the dilemmas facing newly elected executives wishing to win re-election. We therefore think of a typical term in office – approximately five years – as appropriate. The longer period better corresponds to the full term of most elected executives,

Table 4.1 Elections are as likely to lead to authoritarian reversal as to democratization

Category	%	Examples
Major authoritarian reversal	9	Chile 1970; Thailand 2001
Minor authoritarian reversal	20	Russia 2000; Zimbabwe 1996, 2000
No change	39	Mexico 1976; India 2004
Minor democratization	22	Liberia 2005; Spain 1982
Major democratization	10	Poland 1985; Panama 1989

Note: 1,623 total elections.

though we acknowledge that elections can occur far more rapidly, particularly in parliamentary systems. Our data show that 91 percent of election-holding countries hold another election within five years. We will also examine whether our statistical results are robust to a shorter window for the democratic dividend.[11]

Most elections in the developing world do not lead to positive democratic change. Indeed, a plurality of elections result in no change at all (see Table 4.1).[12] A third of elections lead to some democratic development but just as many lead to democratic backsliding. While extreme political shifts following an election are rare, a small but important proportion of elections result in major change, both positive or negative. Our goal is to explain this variation in post-election democratic performance. Subsequent chapters will assess the effects of major structural factors, such as the length of a country's prior democratic experience, its fiscal space, and its conflict history, to explain variation in the size and direction of the electoral democratic dividend, but we start here by answering the other two questions posed at the start of this chapter: Do cleaner elections yield larger positive democratic dividends? And are founding elections good for future democracy?

Our approach to answering these questions is to estimate the average democratic change experienced by a country in the developing world five years after it held an election. To know if electoral integrity and founding election status matter, we need to estimate the conditional democratic change, which is easily done using regression analysis techniques.[13] Of course, we realize that a great many other factors also affect democratic development, some of which are plausibly correlated with electoral quality and whether a country is holding its first election. If we ignore these factors, we risk attributing to our key variables an explanatory power they do not deserve. To avoid such spurious conclusions, we include in our models these other factors, too (in the language of regression analysis, we control for them).

Prior scholarship indicates a plausible set of controls. The most important of these is the country's *current democracy score*. More consolidated democracies should expect a smaller democratic dividend from elections, as there is simply less democratic change possible than in a country with limited civil rights and suffrage. For example, Brazil today cannot likely experience the same democratic change as was possible during its long period of military dominance. Second, we control for *state age*, using data on countries' birth years from the Correlates of War (COW) project and the Uppsala Conflict Data Program (UCDP).[14] We know already that elections came to new and fragile countries born in the crucible of anti-colonial struggle or the collapse of Communism. Omitting state age from our analysis risks concluding that, for example, conflictual countries experience a smaller democratic dividend, when in fact young countries proved both less likely to gain from elections and more likely to experience conflict.[15] All models also incorporate a country's level of economic development, as proxied by its *GDP per capita*.[16] A long line of theory and research has established that democracy more likely survives in richer societies. Richer countries also may have greater fiscal space and a lower probability of civil conflict. Residing in a 'good neighborhood' has also been found to affect democratization, and so we control for *regional democracy*.[17] This allows us to assess if elections in countries surrounded by democracies are more likely succeed than those held in countries surrounded by dictatorships. Finally, we include *population size*; the *time period* in which the election was held, since historical geopolitical conditions affected the emphasis on holding elections and prospects for democratic progress; and *world geographic region*, both to improve our analysis of substantive trends and to consider region-specific factors not captured by the remainder of our variables.[18]

This set of controls is included in all models discussed in the book. Adding more variables to the set of controls comes at the steep price of a smaller sample due to missing data issues. Nonetheless, we did test whether our results are robust to the inclusion of several more control variables, including economic growth rates, ethnic fractionalization, whether or not the country is majority Muslim, protests in the years before the election, anti-government demonstrations, colonial history, trade openness, membership in democratic international organizations, oil exports, and inflation. Even when competing with this longer list of contenders, our results do not waver.[19]

Why Better Elections are not Always Better for Democracy

Do better elections lead to more positive democratic change? The jury is still out. One would certainly expect so given the intense focus on improving the quality of elections by democracy promotion practitioners and scholars alike. Pippa Norris titles the second volume of her important electoral integrity trilogy *Why Elections Fail*.[20] That volume examines the reasons many elections do not reach internationally accepted standards of electoral integrity. This is an important question but the title is especially revealing: elections "fail" when they do not meet our standards of integrity. "Dirty elections" are by this definition failed elections. We agree out of a *normative* desire for better elections. We wish to ask a more more provocative question about the *instrumental* benefit of electoral integrity: do more competitive elections more likely deepen democracy?

Scholars continue to disagree on the question of electoral legitimacy's democratizing impact. A group of scholars have made a strong case that electoral malfeasance may frustrate democratic change.[21] Norris herself, however, is more cautious, finding that while flawed elections can reduce voter turnout, delegitimize regimes, and spark violence, the ultimate effects for democratization depend on a host of contextual factors. Michael Miller, meanwhile, studies the effect of what he labels "autocratic elections."[22] Miller observes that until very recently few elections featured universal suffrage. Rather, the elections that laid the foundation for today's advanced industrial democracies would have been outright failures by Norris's (and our) standards. Yet these autocratic elections gave rise to stable democracies, while the democratic elections held by every developing country since 1950 have been more likely to give rise to electoral autocracies (sometimes called competitive authoritarian or hybrid regimes).

Our theoretical framework is relatively sanguine about the importance of good elections for the future of democracy. Cleaner elections
should generate greater legitimacy for the winner. This starting political
capital should generate real opportunities for election winners to enact
reforms, generating performance-based legitimacy and democratic-
institutional legitimacy. These legitimacy stocks give leaders the ability
to generate public policy records and are compounded by the development of ancillary public institutions that constrain executives and
promote the rule of law. By this reasoning, better elections give a young
democracy a window of opportunity. The more contingent legitimacy
generated by the election, the wider that window. Yet this window shuts
rather quickly, given the contingent nature of the legitimacy generated
by winning a clean and competitive election. Like all honeymoons, this
one too must end eventually, and if a government cannot deliver on its
promises to an expectant electorate, the tide turns quickly.

This fundamentally is the electoral paradox of our times: cleaner
elections that elect governments unable to govern effectively on
account of the structural deficiencies – limited institutional development, low fiscal space, civil conflict – their countries face. At that
point, facing a need for re-election, leaders make a Faustian bargain to
return to office by any means necessary. Elections "fail" not because
leaders are pseudo-democrats or because elections fail the integrity
test, but because politicians find it impossible to win clean elections
through legitimate means, given the daunting structural challenges
they face.

To evaluate our argument, we need first to identify which elections
are better than others. Our preference is to adopt a minimalist catego-
rization.[23] We combine two indicators to construct a three-category
measure. First, we separate elections that are prima facie uncompetitive from those that met minimal criteria for competitiveness, such as
permitting an opposition. That is, we separate elections that in theory
can be lost from those whose outcome is predetermined.[24] Second, for
the competitive subset, we further distinguish between those elections
in which there were credible allegations of government harassment
and intimidation of the opposition or other forms of malpractice and
those unsullied by such charges of electoral misconduct. We do not
bother doing the same for uncompetitive elections since an election
that does not permit an opposition scarcely merits points for not
harassing that opposition.

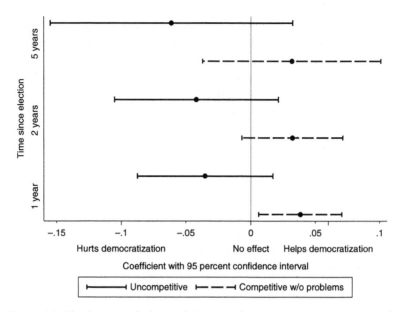

Figure 4.1 The impact of electoral integrity becomes more uncertain with time

We use regression analysis to estimate the effect of this measure of the quality and competitiveness of elections on the change in a country's democracy score five years after the election, using the modeling techniques described earlier.[25] Figure 4.1 presents our coefficients for electoral legitimacy by recording the coefficient and 95 percent confidence interval for our two indicator variables. Our base category is a competitive election with harassment of the opposition, so we might expect that the coefficients for uncompetitive elections and competitive elections without harassment of the opposition will be negatively and positively signed, respectively.

This is not the case, however. The first thing to notice is that the effect of uncompetitive elections is not statistically significant. Sham elections, perhaps surprisingly, do not lead to a lower democratic dividend than competitive elections. But neither does holding a clean competitive election lead to a larger democratic dividend, since the confidence interval for that effect also crosses zero. Better elections, therefore, do not bring about more democratic change, all else equal.[26] This finding runs counter to our gut intuitions. Surely better elections are better for democracy than those undermined by fraud, harassment, and violence? We would not expect uncompetitive elections to be good for democracy; why would we? But should not we expect better elections to be different?

The answer lies in thinking carefully about what is "contingent" in contingent legitimacy. Our theory states that especially legitimate elections do confer a brighter halo on election winners, but that halo slowly disintegrates as voters forget election day and turn back to their lives. This argument implies that we should see cleaner elections generate a larger democratic dividend in the short run, but not the long run. Do our tests support these intuitions? We re-estimate our model twice, reducing the window for democratic change to two years and then only one year, to answer this question. The effect over a two-year window remains statistically insignificant. Yet when we estimate a model of the one-year democratic dividend, we find that clean, competitive elections expand the democratic dividend from elections compared to ostensibly competitive elections with procedural problems. Electoral integrity has precisely the impact on democratic change that we would expect, but only in the short run. A cynical interpretation, which we cannot dismiss, is that the positive one-year effect is an artifact. Democracy scores are coded by researchers. Presumably among the coding rules used are whether the country held a competitive election and whether there was evidence of government harassment. Coders would observe these factors and dutifully increase the country's democracy score. This would generate the observed positive effect we estimated because it is tautological: cleaner elections result in higher democracy scores the year after the election because cleaner elections are evidence of more democracy in the eyes of coders. The power of this critique suggests that we should be skeptical of any analysis that uses a one-year change in democracy as the dependent variable and is a primary reason we use the far more conservative five-year window throughout the rest of the book.

A more substantive interpretation – and one consistent with our theory – is also worth considering. Electoral integrity matters, but only through its short-term impact on perceptions of politicians. For one year, winners of more competitive elections enjoy a political honeymoon by virtue of their victories. This impact fades, however, as politicians confront the real challenges of governing while voters expect results. The impact on democracy after this critical inflection point – where our theory picks up the theoretical narrative from theories of electoral integrity – is therefore negligible, as the shape of the governance challenge more heavily influences democratic change. We therefore see a one-year effect, but not one when we extend the window even one year further. Note one other feature of Figure 4.1. The point estimate of being in the "competitive without problems" category of elections is very stable. What really changes as we extend the window over which our dependent variable is calculated is the size of the confidence interval. As the window of time over which we estimate the effect of a clean election lengthens, so does our uncertainty about the actual effect of electoral integrity. We think this is because there is a divergence in the fates of nations. When clean elections occur in propitious circumstances, democracy can flourish. When they occur in difficult environments, democracy can suffer. The remainder of the book is tasked with identifying the specific contexts that shape this outcome, but we must first place one more building block before moving on.

Founding Elections Increase the Democratic Dividend

In 2014, India held its sixteenth national election. In 2015, South Sudan was to have held its first election as an independent nation but this was postponed to 2018 at least. Regardless of when that election actually occurs, the fact is it will be South Sudan's very first national election for executive office. First elections are very different from sixteenth elections, and arguably from the second or third ones, too. They represent a break from the past, and for the activists who fought for the right to vote for their leaders, and the millions who supported them, they are a watershed moment in a country's history. Do such elections yield a greater democratic dividend?

To answer this question, we re-estimate our baseline model six times. As mentioned earlier, we vary the length of the period over which we measure the change in the democracy score. We also use two different indicators for the sequencing of elections. The first codes what we term founding elections using the NELDA dataset.[27] The second takes a more expansive view and separates the first three elections in a country's democratic trajectory from the later ones.[28]

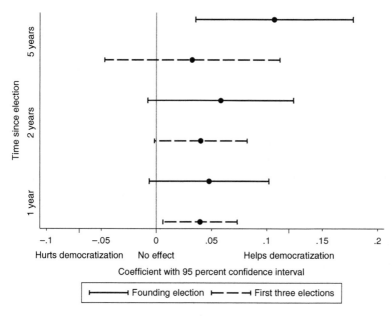

Figure 4.2 Founding elections, but only founding elections, enhance the democratic dividend

Figure 4.2 again plots both the coefficient and the 95 percent confidence interval from these six models. We highlight two take-aways from this analysis. First, founding elections do yield a greater democratic dividend than subsequent elections and this effect is more pronounced the longer the window of time that passes.[29] Our estimates of the impact of a founding election are always positive, but increase in both substantive and statistical significance as we lengthen the window for democratic change from one to five years. Note that we have controlled for the country's level of democracy in the year of the election, so these results are not an artifact of the fact that countries holding founding elections are generally less democratic than more established democracies. Founding elections are special events and a country's first elected executive occupies a special role in her nation's history. Second, when we consider a country's founding election together with the two elections that follow, we do not find a similar effect. As in our analysis of more competitive elections, the impact of the first three elections dissipates with time. We might have expected otherwise, assuming that even after a founding election, further electoral competition can prove to be a catalyst for democratic change. Our analysis suggests otherwise.

These results suggest even further support for our theory of contingent legitimacy. Founding elections are exceptional in the contingent legitimacy they confer on larger-than-life political figures. They represent sea changes in the political fortunes of nations for voters, politicians, and international observers. Yet after this moment, these transformational figures must turn to the mundane business of meeting with their ministers, negotiating with stakeholders over new policies, and generally facing the slings and arrows of outrageous political fortune – not to mention angry voters at the polls and on the streets. The next election, which may well return our political giant to power, offers no special democratic fillip. Founding elections may bring an increase in the level of democracy over five years, but the two elections after it fail to do so. And it is the very exceptionalism of founding elections that renders them an unsustainable means of promoting democracy. They are rare, representing only about 8 percent of elections in our sample. The key is to build on the head start they provide rather than squander the hard-won opportunity they represent.

Discussion

In any given year, one out of every five countries holds a national election to choose its leaders. By a more humbling (to us) metric, since we began work on this book, approximately 80 percent of countries will have held an election. Election holdouts are members of an increasingly exclusive and dubious club. Yet even as elections spread, and even as their quality improves, they remain a means to an end that increasingly is unrealized. We might have more elections and we might have better elections, but we do not have more or better democracies.

Over the next few chapters, we will build a case that the failure of elections to build democracies is due to the fact that elections are too often held in conditions that undermine democratic survival and consolidation. But does this mean the elections themselves are irrelevant to whether or not we get democracies in some places and not others? Of course not. Cleaner elections are justifiably valued for the national accomplishments they are, representing a break from a more repressive past. We value higher electoral integrity intrinsically. But the contribution of electoral integrity is contingent. By this, we mean that the effect of holding a clean competitive election is short-term. We liken it to a honeymoon period where the length of honeymoon is a function of the quality of the election. Dirty elections generate no honeymoon; good elections do. But honeymoons end and then leaders must govern. When conditions make it hard or even impossible for them to govern, they resort to electoral malpractice to secure re-election and democracy stagnates or suffers. We see this in our analysis too: better elections do yield a positive democratic dividend, but this effect dissipates more than a year out from the election. The only time this is not true is when elections are founding elections, in which case the effect lasts longer; but even here the positive effect is not sustained past this initial historic election.

Our results in this chapter speak directly to two influential literatures in political science. The first is the electoral integrity literature. We see our analysis as offering a sympathetic challenge to the focus of that body of work. We too value clean competitive elections and support efforts to improve the conduct of elections worldwide. But we take a longer-term view and argue that clean elections should be viewed as a means rather than an end in themselves. Democracy promotion must move past elections and must be linked to economic policymaking, conflict mediation, and institution building too. The second is the democratization-by-elections literature. Our analysis is more critical of this body of work. We find no evidence that holding elections has a long-term effect on democratic change, nor any evidence that the first three elections are particularly valuable for democracy. Yet, we agree wholeheartedly with the central insight of this literature, namely that elections represent a modern mode of democratic transition. Unlike earlier periods in which democracy followed years of holding autocratic elections, today's aspiring democracies are expected to hold high-quality elections before they have the other institutions we typically associate with established democracy. The hope today is that holding elections creates democracy in time, but our analysis makes clear that this has not been the case in the developing world. Rather, whether elections generate positive democratic change depends on the conditions under which they occur. Identifying the conditions that matter most is the task to which we now turn.

5 | *Experience Matters: Democratic Stock and Elections*

The electoral boom frequently brought elections to countries with little history of formal democratic governance. The average country holding its first multiparty elections during the earliest part of the Third Wave (1974–1987) did so with the benefit of seven and a half years of democratic experience – certainly not a long history, but one long enough to inform and educate politicians and citizens alike in the democratic process. The first multiparty elections in Greece at the dawn of the Third Wave are a good example. Despite military coups, autocratic rule since the 1960s, and a civil war in the late 1940s, Greece's 1974 elections were buttressed by nearly six decades of intermittent democratic rule in the nineteenth and twentieth centuries. Latin American countries holding founding elections during the 1980s shared Greece's history of intermittent democratic rule dating back over a century.

The countries of the electoral boom – largely concentrated in Sub-Saharan Africa and the former Soviet Union – often lacked the benefit of previous democratic rule. The average founding election during the electoral boom occurred in a country with only two and a half years of democratic experience, five years fewer than in 1974–1987. The countries of the Arab Spring are typical of this pattern. On the eve of the fall of authoritarian regimes in Tunisia, Egypt, and Libya, none had spent even a single year as a democracy; Libya, in fact, had experienced more military coups (three) than competitive elections (one)! Haiti also sadly exemplifies the challenge of elections in inexperienced countries. The Duvaliers, first François "Papa Doc" and then Jean Claude "Baby Doc," had ruled the country with an iron fist from 1957 until 1986. Haiti had never been consistently ruled as a democracy. Elections in 1990 promised a new day for the impoverished country. Jean-Bertrand Aristide, a Catholic priest and himself an opposition leader during the Duvalier dictatorship, won two-thirds of the vote. He was deposed in a military coup the following year, only returning to office in 1994 after intervention from the United States. Aristide won re-election in 2000, though opposition candidates boycotted the election amidst accusations of improprieties during parliamentary elections earlier that year. He was deposed in yet another coup in 2004.

Some countries hold elections with the benefit of a relatively recent – and sometimes long – political history of democracy, while others lack that experience. These differences are often rather subtle, but can exert a powerful effect. We argued in Chapter 2 that shallower stocks of democratic-institutional legitimacy more likely allow self-interested politicians to use political shenanigans to solidify their grip on power, while deeper stocks constrain them from doing so. We also contended that democratic stock deepens in the age of democratic institutions; each competitive election, parliamentary session, and peaceful transition of power adds to the stock.[1] In contrast, democratic stock withers under repressive rule. Elections held in the context of shallow democratic-institutional stock more likely are followed by democratic stagnation, lower-legitimacy elections in the future, and voter dissatisfaction.

In this chapter, we take the model developed in Chapter 4 and adapt it to assess these intuitions. After a brief theoretical review, we develop a new measure of democratic experience and then put it to the test. We find that longer democratic experience magnifies the democratic dividend of holding elections. In fact, our main model predicts that even clean competitive elections fail to promote democracy when they are held in countries with no democratic experience. We therefore ask why and how democratic experience matters for successful elections. Our main finding is that democratic experience helps elections through the incubation of constraints on executives, which is consistent with our theoretical emphasis on the role of election winners' choices while in office. Our analysis also shows that countries with more democratic experience today hold better elections in the future and also improve political and civil rights. We then turn to survey data from the Comparative Study of Electoral Systems (CSES) and find that voters in countries with longer democratic experience are more likely to voice satisfaction with democratic rule.

Prior Democratic-Institutional Stock Improves Elections

The notion that democratic traditions are an important pre-condition for a successful democratic transition has a long and distinguished lineage in political science. This literature's guiding light remains Robert Dahl's theory of polyarchy, which warned that expanding political participation in societies lacking a history of political competition placed democracy at risk.[2] Subsequent scholars have continued in Dahl's tradition, pointing to the importance of political parties and judiciaries for democratic transitions.[3] Our own theory of democratization clearly echoes this pre-conditionalist tradition while more clearly specifying how elections are buoyed by a stock of democratic institutions. Structuralist theories of democracy only rarely discuss elections, while electoral theories pay comparatively little attention to structural conditions.[4] Our theory of democratization and elections bridges this gap by clarifying how the stock of democratic institutions conditions the impact of elections.

We begin by establishing a clear definition of democratic-institutional stock as the total strength of the rules (e.g., constraints on the executive), practices (e.g., campaigns), and organizations (e.g., political parties) that collectively define national democracy. This is a systemic definition, envisioning a depth of democratic governance that encompasses all of national politics, as opposed to that of a specific organization or institution. Democratic-institutional stock deepens in the predictability of the rules of the political game. A deeper stock makes it more likely that politicians and voters clearly understand and are accustomed to the norms and rules governing their actions. Just as stocks of economic capital require investment to prevent depreciation, the stock of democratic institutions requires renewal through continued democratic governance. When an incumbent loses an election and peacefully cedes power, she invests in democracy. When she ignores the results and clings to power, she erodes democratic stock.

This definition of democratic-institutional stock has a clear temporal dimension: the stock deepens the longer democratic rules have functioned. A new democracy is characterized by younger, more poorly defined rules, norms, and practices. Politicians and voters doubt whether and how they might function. The slow maturation of democratic rule over time tends to resolve these uncertainties, as politicians learn from past iterations of the political game. A longer period of uninterrupted democratic rule deepens the stock. Similarly, democratic-institutional stock depreciates when it is not replenished, though it is also sticky; a dictatorial interruption of democratic rule does not immediately destroy the stock, but erodes it slowly. Our definition thus implies that democratic-institutional stock is shallower the less time a country has experienced continuous democratic governance and the longer ago such an episode occurred. We will return to this point later when we develop our measure of democratic-institutional stock.

This definition helps us understand why elections better promote democracy when held in more democratically experienced settings. Elections held in this circumstance embed politicians and voters in a system with rules they understand and expect will function as they represent organizations and groups whose interests are well-defined. The contrary is true of elections held in countries with little democratic experience. Here, a newly elected chief executive can more easily move to fix the rules of electoral competition in her favor by manipulating voter lists or harassing the opposition.

The principal implication of our argument is that the democratic dividend from elections will increase the longer a country's past experience with democracy. Our logic also suggests three other empirically verifiable hypotheses. First, the theory places the bulk of the blame for democratic backsliding on chief executives. It is their governing choices that erode democracy in low-stock settings. We expect, therefore, that a history of meaningful institutional constraints on the executive is an especially important aspect of democratic experience. Second, our theory suggests that election winners undermine democratic rule by manipulating the next election. They can limit campaigning by opposition parties or stack an electoral commission with cronies. If we are correct, we should see that elections in countries with little democratic experience are more likely to be succeeded by worse elections in the future. Third, our theory suggests voters will become disillusioned with democracy when they witness this kind of malfeasance.

Testing our argument requires a valid measure of democratic-institutional stock. This is no small task, as the pre-conditionalist literature has often stumbled in clearly defining a measure of the "maturity" or "strength" of democratic institutions. On one hand, France clearly seems to possess a deeper stock of democratic institutions than Cameroon, its former colony. Yet how are we to measure the more subtle difference between Cameroon, which has largely pre-served democratic institutions though it has been ruled by only two men since its independence in 1960, and its neighbor Nigeria, which has largely been ruled by military juntas since 1960 though it has tentatively practiced democracy since 1999?[5]

Huntington's definition of the degree of institutionalization pro-vides one answer. "The level of institutionalization of any particular organization or procedure," Huntington argues, "can be measured by its adaptability, complexity, autonomy, and coherence."[6] Measuring these concepts in a meaningful and reliable manner cross-nationally is challenging, but Huntington suggests a short-cut: "the longer an organization or procedure has been in existence, the higher the level of institutionalization. The older an organization is, the more likely it is to continue to exist through any specified future time period. The probability that an organization which is one hundred years old will survive one additional year, it might be hypothesized, is perhaps one hundred times greater than the probability that an organization one year old will survive one additional year."[7] We rely on the tempo-ral aspects of our conceptualization of democratic-institutional stock to define a measure: we contend that countries that have practiced democracy longer have a deeper stock. To construct our measure, we rely on the well-known Polity IV dataset, which provides a twenty-one point composite democracy score with an accepted threshold for being a "full democracy."[8] We define two versions of the mea-sure. The first is the natural logarithm of the number of years a country has been democratic since its political independence.[9] The measure increases with each year a country is democratic, in line with our expectation that each year of stable democratic practice represents a flow into the stock of democratic institutions. Yet the measure increases logarithmically, meaning that each added year of democratic governance adds slightly less to the stock than the year before it. A country's hundredth year of democratic governance, for example, adds comparatively less to its stock than its first even if, as Huntington suggests, the probability that a country adds to its democratic stock increase with each year. For each country hold-ing an election, we calculate its accumulated democratic-institutional stock.[10]

This measure has much to recommend it, not least of which is its simplicity, but it lacks one important attribute: it does not decrease during times of non-democratic rule. The number of years a country has been democratic obviously can only increase or stay the same; it cannot decrease. Our theory implies, however, that democratic-institutional stock erodes during periods of autocratic rule. A government that shutters an independent media, restricts electoral competition, and weakens checks on the executive gradually depletes democratic-institutional stock. We might prefer a measure that also erodes during periods of authoritarian rule. We therefore define a more complex measure that increases during periods of democratic rule and decreases during periods of autocratic rule, while also exhibiting the same diminishing returns as in our first measure.[11] The measure possesses the desirable attribute of assigning a lower score both to countries with shorter experience of democratic rule and to those whose democratic experience is farther in the past.

Consider India and Pakistan. Both former British colonies gained independence in 1947, but their political trajectories have since dramatically diverged. While India has remained a relatively stable democracy since its birth, Pakistan has oscillated between brief periods of tenuous democratic rule and military dictatorship. Figure 5.1 illustrates how each of our measures records the time path of democratic institutional stock in these two countries. The first panel is for our first, non-decaying measure, while the second records our second, decaying measure. Each captures India's process of slowly enriching its democratic-institutional stock over time. Similarly, each depicts Pakistan's more tortuous political history; in both panels, Pakistan is shown only slowly adding to its democratic stock. The two panels differ in one important respect, however. The simpler measure does not allow for the decay of Pakistan's stock during its frequent periods of military rule, while the second depicts a stock that ebbed and flowed for long periods of time.

All else equal, we prefer the simpler non-decaying measure since it makes interpreting the statistical results in substantive terms easier. Fortunately the two measures are highly correlated, since they only differ for those countries that had democratic interruptions. The correlation for our sample of elections is extremely high (0.9) and,

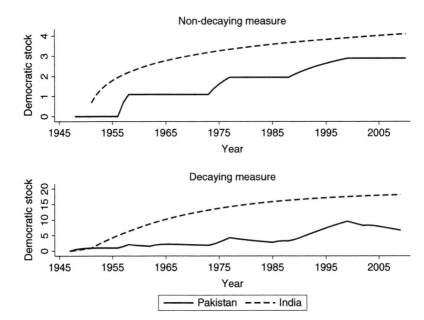

Figure 5.1 India has steadily accumulated democratic experience, while Pakistan has not

unsurprisingly, our results are robust to the more complex, decaying measure.[12]

Elections in Experienced Countries Are More Successful

We are ready to test the impact of democratic experience on the democratic dividend from elections. Chapter 4 introduced our workhorse statistical model of the democratic dividend (i.e., the five-year change in democracy score) in all elections held in the developing world since 1946.[13] We pay special attention to our controls for the country's democracy score in the year of the election and the competitiveness of the election itself. Including these covariates creates a difficult test for our hypothesis, since countries with more democratic experience in their past are more likely to be more democratic and hold more competitive elections.[14] Our model therefore ensures that our estimate of the effect of democratic experience does not erroneously capture either of these other factors.

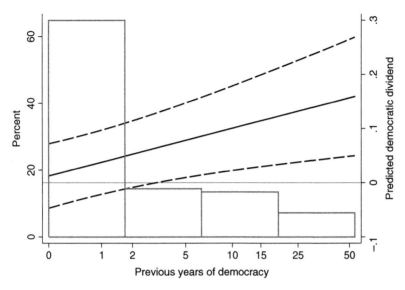

Figure 5.2 Countries in Sub-Saharan Africa with fewer than about three years of democratic experience saw no post-election democratic change

The estimated effect of democratic experience on the five-year democratic dividend from elections is positive and statistically significant. Simply put, post-election democratization is more dramatic the longer a country's past experience of democracy. So two countries with identical current levels of democracy holding equally competitive elections will witness different degrees of democratic change if one has more democratic experience.

How large is this difference? We can answer this question by exploiting a special property of our model. Remember that the democratic dividend tends to be rather small for most elections. So to understand our results, we calculate the democratic dividend predicted by our model holding most variables at their average values and allowing just the key variable to vary. Doing so allows us to see if, all else equal, for example, moving from a country with low democratic experience to one with greater experience generates a larger democratic dividend.[15] This allows us to state in substantive terms how circumstances condition the size of the democratic dividend.

Figure 5.2 plots the predicted democratic dividend for different levels of past democratic experience.[16] The plot is for a highly competitive election held in a typical Sub-Saharan African country during the electoral boom. The plot also draws a confidence interval around the model's prediction, which allows us to see when the democratic dividend is statistically different from zero, and the sample distribution of democratic experience. It is evident that some democratic experience is necessary to capture a democratic dividend after elections and that a lack of such experience has been an important barrier to democratic change in Sub-Saharan Africa. First, the predicted democratic dividend, represented by the solid line, rises as democratic experience increases. Elections more effectively promote further improvements in democracy when they are preceded by more democratic experience. The democratic dividend from an election in a country with ten years of democratic experience is predicted to be ten times larger than the democratic dividend from an election held in a country with no such experience. Second, our model suggests that a minimum of three years of past democratic experience was necessary for elections in Sub-Saharan Africa to yield real democratic change. Below this point, elections yield no systematic democratic change. Third, and perhaps most discouragingly, our data make apparent that few Sub-Saharan African countries holding elections during the electoral boom possessed the experience necessary to harvest a positive democratic dividend after elections. In fact, almost two-thirds of elections held during the electoral boom in the region were held in countries with no previous democratic experience at all and only one-third featured countries reaching the threshold of three years. This is an underappreciated and stunning fact about the electoral boom. Most elections were being held in countries that could not count on even three years of prior democratic experience. In a real sense, this was political experimentation on a grand scale and the fact that many of those elections bore no democratic benefits should hardly be shocking to anyone familiar with the history of democratization in the West. Taken together, these facts are quite conclusive: a lack of democratic experience has been an unavoidable hindrance to promoting post-election democratic change in Sub-Saharan Africa.

What of other regions of the world? We replicate our analysis for each region. Table 5.1 records the number of elections each region witnessed during the electoral boom, the region-specific minimum threshold of democratic experience necessary to generate a positive democratic dividend, the proportion of elections in our sample that

Table 5.1 Previous democratic experience has been critical to successful elections during the electoral boom

Region	Number of elections	Years until positive dividend	Percent above experience threshold	Predicted dividend at 10 years of experience
Middle East/North Africa	91	0	100	0.19
Asia-Pacific	107	2	72	0.11
Eastern Europe	159	4	52	0.10
Sub-Saharan Africa	208	3	33	0.10
Latin America	145	29	22	0.02

fell above that threshold, and the predicted democratic dividend at ten years of past democratic experience. Our findings indicate that regions outside of Sub-Saharan Africa are better positioned to capture the democratic dividend from elections. In Eastern Europe, for example, four years of past democratic experience are necessary to generate a democratic dividend, one year more than in Africa, but a threshold met by over half of elections. The story in Asia-Pacific is even more optimistic; only two years of previous experience is necessary to produce a successful election, a threshold reached in 72 percent of elections. In these three regions, our model predicts that an election held after ten years of democratic rule will yield a substantial democratic dividend. The Middle East and Latin America, however, both stand out. The former's high level of wealth and low level of current democracy predicts that elections, regardless of democratic experience, will succeed in promoting democracy. The opposite is true of Latin America, which has largely been highly democratic since 1988 and where hence the bar is higher for further moves towards democracy. Remembering this protects against mis-interpreting the results – even an initially large democratic dividend in the Middle East from a set of founding elections would fail to close its democratic gap with Latin America, which continues to add incrementally to its democratic stock. And, more pointedly, this counterfactual universe in which

Middle Eastern countries have ten full years of prior democratic experience is far out of reach, as the failures of the Arab Spring become more apparent with each passing day.

Are our results good or bad news for democracy promotion efforts? The answer to this question depends greatly on whether countries are accumulating democratic experience, even haltingly. We explore this question by plotting the average years of democratic experience across time by region in Figure 5.3. Latin America clearly has most rapidly accumulated democratic experience, with the typical country boasting thirty years of democratic rule by the 2000s. The picture is less optimistic in Sub-Saharan Africa and the Middle East, which have lagged behind other regions. Yet the average country in nearly every region reached the thresholds necessary for a successful election by about 2010, indicating that future elections more likely will rest on a cushion of democratic familiarity.[17] One potential threat to that progress would be the breakup of developing countries into still smaller units. The secession of South Sudan is one example of how a new country inheriting little administrative or democratic infrastructure from the rump state is especially at risk of democratic decline or even collapse. South Sudan's government was elected in free and fair elections held as part of the 2010 Sudanese elections. At that point, it was to be the government of the semi-autonomous region of South Sudan and, following the January 2011 independence referendum, Salva Kir became president of the Republic of South Sudan. Yet conflict soon followed and elections that had been scheduled for 2015 have been delayed until at least 2018. The challenges this young nation faces are staggering; indeed it has the dubious distinction of having the highest score on the Fragile States Index. Whether the 2018 elections – if they happen – can move democracy forward is anyone's guess, but our analysis would suggest that any optimism is likely to be disappointed.

The results for our control variables are largely as expected. Elections in more democratic countries tend to witness less democratic change. Uncompetitive elections are as likely to yield a democratic dividend as highly competitive elections. Elections in richer countries also yield a larger democratic dividend. Neither ethnic fractionalization, country size, nor state age condition the democratic dividend. Elections held in more democratic neighborhoods yield a smaller democratic dividend: a surprising finding. Elections between 1950 and 1980 all suffered in comparison with elections held between 1981

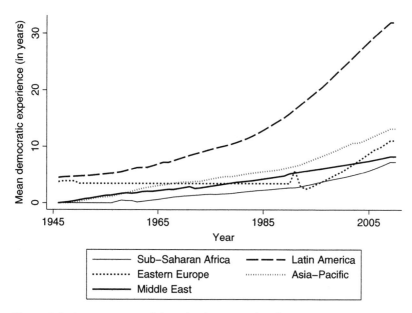

Figure 5.3 Democratic stock has slowly accumulated over time

and 1987. Yet our coefficient on our indicator variable for the electoral boom (1988–2010) is statistically insignificant, suggesting that electoral boom elections did a poorer job of promoting democracy because they were held in worse structural circumstances than during the 1981–1987 period.

Our results thus far strongly support the idea that elections held in countries with longer democratic experience yield a larger democratic dividend, all else equal. Does this finding hold if we alter the measurement of key variables, the estimation sample, or our modeling technique? Happily, it does.[18] We get the same results if we use the decaying measure of democratic stock, if we use the Polity score instead of the UDS measure for democracy, if we shorten the window over which we calculate the democratic dividend from five years to two and if we include a broader panel of control variables.[19] Finally, we distinguish between types of elections and find that our results hold when we restrict our sample to only competitive-executive and only competitive-legislative elections. As expected, when we examine only uncompetitive elections, democratic experience does not matter, confirming the widespread intuition that elections in which competition is severely restricted do little to advance democracy, regardless of prior democratic experience.

Why Does Democratic Experience Matter?

A history of democratic governance improves the conduct of elections, which in turn bolsters future democracy. Even a few years of democratic rule can set the stage for more successful elections in the future. The importance of such experience begs the question of why democratic experience matters. What does democratic experience do that supports the holding of elections? It may well be, for example, that democratic experience's most important contribution to future elections is its incubation of programmatic political parties. Or we may find that citizens' experience with expanded civil and political rights under democratic rule prepare them to hold politicians more accountable.

Our theory of elections and democratization points towards an especially important aspect of democracy: constraints on the executive. Heads of government are uniquely placed to revise the workings of democracy and those who fear losing power in a future elections will weaken democratic rules to their advantage. They are restrained from doing so by other democratic actors, such as opposition political parties and judiciaries, but only inasmuch as they offer a credible constraint on executive power. This is our key mechanism: where chief executives are constrained by other institutionalized actors, the risk of post-election democratic collapse is far lower. We rely on two measures of executive constraints. First, the Polity IV project annually measures the functioning of executive constraints on a seven-point scale, with scores over five indicating strong constraints. We calculate the natural log of the number of years for which a country reached this threshold before the current election.[20] Second, we rely on Witold Henisz's Political Constraints Index, which measures the degree to which policy change is formally constrained by other branches of government, political parties, and sub-federal bodies of government.[21] Higher values on this index indicate a higher degree of political constraint. We take the mean value of the political constraints measure over a country's life since 1960.

What other aspects of democratic experience matter? Strong political parties are a natural candidate.[22] Political parties, particularly
those in the opposition, represent a particularly important check on
executive power. Viable opposition parties also give voters real choice
at the polls on election day. It seems likely, then, that elections held in
countries with a longer history of freely functioning political parties
will better promote democracy. We identify whether political parties are legally banned; legally allowed yet de facto forbidden; or
freely functioning outside the regime.[23] As in our simpler measure of
democratic-institutional stock, we measure the natural log of the number of years with both de jure and de facto freely operating political
parties.

A final consideration is specific events and processes that bolster or
deplete democratic-institutional stock. Our logic of leaks and flows
emphasizes that stocks are replenished by the continued function of
democracy and depleted by events that interrupt it. First, we measure whether an incumbent has ever lost an election or has ever
stepped down from power after one. Democratic governance demands
that incumbents occasionally lose elections and peacefully relinquish
power when they do. This tradition is the stuff of democratic-
institutional stock.[24] Such events might seem commonplace for those
residing in established democracies, but just a quarter of all election-
holding countries in our dataset have ever experienced either of these
events more than once. Second, we capture the occurrence of an
important leak from democratic-institutional stock: the frequency of
military coups. Coups transfer political power violently and extra-
legally, setting a precedent that future political actors can follow in
what John Londregan and Keith Poole label a "coup trap." We calculate the number of coups – both failed and successful – a country has
experienced between 1950 and the election in question.[25]

We re-estimate our core model seven times: each regression substitutes one of the seven component measures just described for our
systemic measure of democratic experience. Figure 5.4 records the
results of these regressions graphically.[26] The striking pattern here
is the centrality of executive constraints to successful elections, consistent with our theory that unconstrained incumbents have a freer
hand to erode democratic governance after elections. Elections do
more to promote democracy when preceded by a longer history of
constraints on executive power, a result that does not vary according

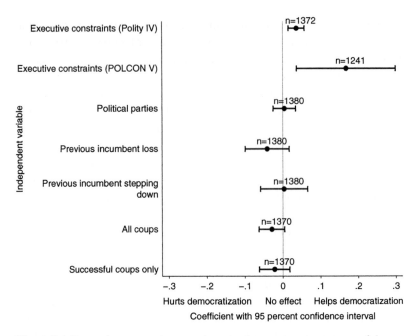

Figure 5.4 Executive constraints are the most important component of democratic institutional stock

to the measure used.[27] Our model predicts that elections in Sub-Saharan Africa during the electoral boom preceded by fewer than seven years of experience with executive constraints produce no democratic momentum at all. These results echo what we have seen earlier: even a modest history of executive constraints suffices to support electoral success, and yet only roughly one-third of elections in Sub-Saharan African countries during the electoral boom met this low threshold.[28]

Our analysis provides weaker results for other components of democratic experience, confirming the preeminence of executive constraints. Countries with a longer history of free political parties do not experience larger democratic dividends. Neither are elections more successful when preceded by a history of incumbent losses or peaceful relinquishment of power. The coup effect, however, is worth considering. While the effect is not as precisely estimated as one might like, it is substantively powerful; our model predicts that even one

attempted coup in a Sub-Saharan African country's past can eliminate the democratic dividend from a highly competitive election.[29]
This is concerning, since the typical election-holding Sub-Saharan
African country during the electoral boom had experienced three coup
attempts.[30]

How Does Democratic Experience Improve Elections?

We now turn to the question of how a democratic past supports
elections today. Democratization undoubtedly is a multifaceted process, consisting of the evolution of a wide constellation of norms,
institutions, and actors. Our modeling strategy thus far has captured
incremental changes to an index that reflects that breadth. Yet we do
not yet understand how democratic experience improves democracy
promotion after elections. Does previous democratic experience galvanize rapid improvements in civil liberties? Or does it matter because of
its impact on electoral competitiveness? Or is there some other aspect
of democratic experience we have missed?

We let theory guide us. Our theory emphasizes that election winners in countries with little democratic-institutional stock will take
steps that deteriorate the integrity of future elections. They will more
likely harass the opposition, use violence to retain power, or stuff
ballot boxes. Fortunately, we can test this intuition using data from
NELDA by first identifying the next election held in the country in
question and then measuring several aspects of the integrity of that
next election. First, we measure *electoral instability*, focusing on the
presence of protests and riots, violence, and opposition boycotts of the
next election. Second, we measure whether the next election includes
harassment of the opposition by the government. Third, we measure
whether the next election *replaces the incumbent*. Finally, we measure
whether the military attempts a *coup* in the five years after the election. We hypothesize that countries with longer democratic experience
should hold elections with less political turbulence, less harassment of
the opposition, a higher probability of incumbent replacement, and
lower probability of a coup attempt.

We re-estimate our model substituting each of these indicators of
the quality of subsequent elections for our broad measure of the democratic dividend. Each regression tests whether democratic experience

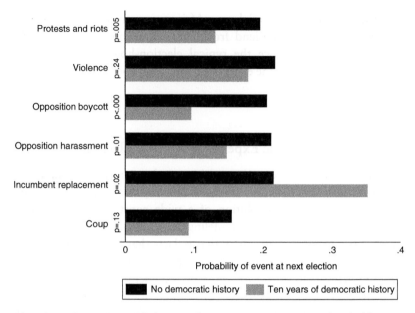

Figure 5.5 Countries with longer democratic experience today hold more competitive elections in the future

yields better elections in the future.[31] We graph our results in Figure 5.5, which records the probability of each event in a hypothetical country with no democratic history versus one with ten years of democratic history.[32]

Figure 5.5 presents strong evidence that elections held in countries with less democratic experience are more likely to bring to power chief executives who then cheat at the democratic game, provoking protesters and opposition politicians. Take post-election protests and riots as an example. The probability of this form of electoral instability declines from 20 percent in countries with no democratic experience to 13 percent in countries with ten years of experience – a difference both substantively and statistically significant.[33] The probabilities of an opposition boycott and harassment of the opposition after the next election also decline. In fact, the probability of an opposition boycott drops by over half, from 21 percent to 10 percent. The probability that the next election replaces the incumbent is also significantly higher in countries with more democratic experience, increasing from 21 percent to 36 percent. The only aspects of tomorrow's elections not affected by today's democratic experience are post-election violence and coups, both of which are relatively rare in the first place.

The democratizing impact of elections is not confined to the conduct of elections. Electoral scholars claim that the electoral process underpins a deeper process of democratization, from the establishment of new political parties to the initiation of new democratic norms and traditions. We therefore define seven new sub-measures of the democratic dividend, with each tracking a different component of democratic change. All but one of these is inspired by the Polity IV project: *executive constraints*, which we have already defined; the *competitiveness of executive recruitment*, or the degree to which real competition exists for the office of chief executive; the *openness of executive recruitment*, or the degree to which all members of the population can run for office; *regulation of executive recruitment*, or the orderliness with which executives are selected; *regulation of participation*, or the legal constraint on political participation; and *competitiveness of participation*, or the ability of diverse groups to voice their preferences. Our last measure is the Freedom House combined measure of *political rights and civil liberties*.[34] We measure the five-year change in each of these dependent variables.

Our theory predicts that elections will more successfully promote these seven attributes of democracy when preceded by some experience of democratic rule. We therefore once again re-estimate our main statistical model, with our new sub-measures of the democratic dividend as the dependent variable.[35] Our results again support the notion that chief executives play a special role in democratic change (see Figure 5.6). Democratic experience is a statistically significant predictor of five of our seven dependent variables. Yet our results also indicate that its importance is uneven. Elections in countries with more democratic experience yield more dramatic improvements in constraints on executives, as well as shifts in how they are recruited and compete for office. The impact of democratic experience is positive and statistically significant for each of these four variables. Our model predicts that an election in a country with no democratic experience does not tighten constraints on the executive, while the same election in a country with ten years of experience will result in a significant improvement.[36] Figure 5.6 also shows that elections in more democratically experienced countries are more likely to improve political rights and civil liberties. Our model predicts that an election in a

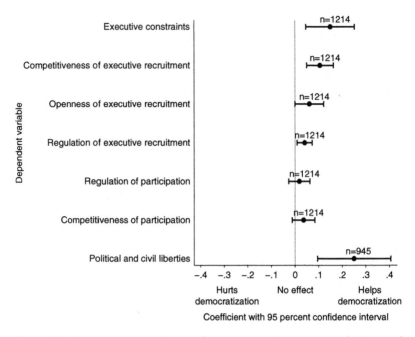

Figure 5.6 Democratic experience galvanizes gains in executive selection and political rights

country with no democratic experience fails to enhance these rights, while an election in a country with ten years of experience is followed by real gains.[37] In fact, the only model where the effect of democratic experience is muted is the one predicting the openness of political participation. This, we suspect, is because universal suffrage was a well-understood norm in the post–World War II era. Indeed, even would-be autocrats saw benefits to expanding the franchise as widely as possible.[38]

Does Democratic Experience Improve Voter Satisfaction?

We know now that elections held in countries with little democratic experience result in less democratic momentum, more entrenched incumbents, and worse elections in the future. It is not a great leap to imagine that voters in these countries will retreat from politics, disillusioned with the prospects for democracy. A deeper fear is that a

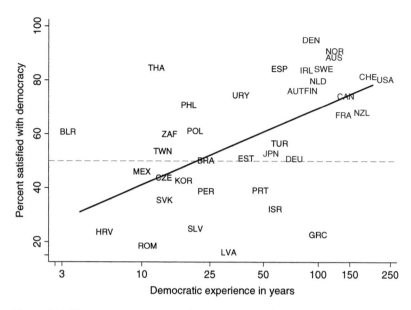

Figure 5.7 Voters report greater democratic satisfaction when democratic institutions are older

vicious cycle of elections and political stagnation will fuel a more permanent cynicism regarding democracy itself, as voters conclude that their problem lies not only with a particular politician or party, but in the weakness of democracy as a system of government. The Comparative Study of Electoral Systems (CSES) represents an ideal means to study this question, since it conducts representative surveys of voters in the years of national elections in a wide sample of democratic countries.[39] Of great interest for our purposes here is a question asking voters whether or not they are satisfied with "the way democracy works" in their country. The wording and timing of this question thus can give us a sense of voters' satisfaction as they head to the polling booths.

Figure 5.7 makes clear that voters do report more democratic satisfaction in countries with a longer experience of democratic governance. It tracks democratic experience in years against the proportion of voters reporting satisfaction with democracy after thirty-eight elections held between 2005 and 2010.[40] The scatterplot depicts developed countries in grey and developing countries in black. We also insert a grey, dotted reference line to indicate countries where a majority or more than a majority of citizens report satisfaction with democracy. Overall, countries with a longer democratic history have more satisfied citizens at election-time. Our analysis predicts that only 40 percent of voters in a country with ten years of democratic experience will be confident in democratic governance, as opposed to roughly 60 percent in a country with fifty years of democratic experience.[41]

Figure 5.7 also suggests that voter confidence in democratic rule remains rather low in the developing world. A majority of voters report democratic satisfaction in only twelve of the twenty-eight elections in our sample, as evidenced by the high proportion of elections falling behind the dotted 50 percent line. In many of these countries, voter satisfaction is dangerously low, as in Greece's 2009 election or Latvia's 2010 election. These figures are in stark contrast to those for developed countries, where a majority of voters report satisfaction with democracy in every election included, with only exception: Iceland's 2009 election in the midst of financial crisis and protests and riots in Reykjavik. Only 47 percent of respondents on average reported satisfaction with democratic rule in the developing world, versus 74 percent in the developed world.

A third and final major trend is cause for deep concern regarding the prospects for democracy in the developing world. Figure 5.7 strongly suggests that the benefits of democratic experience materialize only after a century of democratic governance. The typical developed country in our CSES sample can rely on about a hundred years of democratic experience. Voters in countries with middling levels of democratic experience, in contrast, report drastically different levels of democratic satisfaction. We can see this by examining countries with between twenty-five and fifty years of democratic history, certainly better than most developing countries. The proportion of voters reporting satisfaction with democracy ranges from below 20 percent in Latvia to 60 percent in Poland and 70 percent in Uruguay.[42] These findings stand in rather stark contrast to our cross-national findings earlier in this chapter. There, we reported that even a few years of democratic experience could yield a more successful election. Our analysis of CSES data suggests that a century of democratic rule is necessary before voters become more reliably satisfied with democracy.

Discussion

The epigraph to this book is a snippet from an old song sung by the great Ray Charles. In it, Charles bemoans the dire straits into which he has fallen and asks how, if "them that got are them that gets," he can ever get ahead when he is starting with nothing. The song is an apt metaphor for the lessons of this chapter, which shows that countries with longer histories of democratic governance capture larger democratic dividends after elections, while countries with no such record more likely make little democratic headway, if any at all.

Our theory of elections established a clear expectation that elections are more likely to end in democratic decay when held in countries with less democratic experience. Elections, we argued, are embedded in a set of rules and organizations that define democratic practice, what we call democratic-institutional stock. A deeper stock more tightly binds voters and politicians – especially heads of government – in system whose workings are familiar. The longer and more regularly democracy has functioned, the deeper a society's stock. Winners of elections in countries with little such stock are more likely to weaken democracy by harassing the opposition and cheating during the next election. We hypothesize that elections in countries with little democratic experience do less to encourage democracy.

The statistical evidence reported in this chapter lends robust empirical support to our core hypothesis. Countries harvest a larger democratic dividend from elections when they have a longer history of democratic rule first. This effect holds even when we control for the competitiveness of the election and the country's current democracy score. Our finding is also robust to different measures of key variables, the inclusion of different control variables, and the sample of elections studied. Our statistical analysis also indicates that some previous democratic experience is essential to a successful election. The typical Sub-Saharan African country holding a highly competitive election since the electoral boom, for instance, would require three or more years of democratic experience to yield even a small democratic dividend. Elections held in countries with no such history fail to yield any democratic momentum. Sadly, most Sub-Saharan elections are held in countries lacking even this minimal background in democratic politics. Elsewhere, the news is brighter: in the Middle East, Asia, and Eastern

Europe, our analysis predicts that a majority of countries could hold successful democratizing elections.

Our core theoretical expectation is robustly supported by our findings. Yet our theory of democratization and elections also has clear implications for why and how a history of representative governments supports democratic change after elections. Our theory places election winners under a microscope: their policy choices go a long way to determining the direction of political change. Our results in this chapter support that view. We find that democratic experience matters mainly because it incubates institutional constraints on chief executives. We also find that elections in more democratically experienced countries succeed mainly because they advance improvements to how executives are recruited, compete for power, and are constrained by other actors. Presidents and prime ministers find it far more difficult to subvert the democratic process after elections held in more experienced countries. We find that the probabilities of harassment of the opposition, boycotts by the opposition, and protests and riots during the next election cycle all decline when an election is held in a country with a longer democratic history. Crucially, the probability of incumbent replacement also rises. Finally, we find that democratic experience conditions the impact of elections on voters. Voters witness larger expansions of their political rights and civil liberties after elections in countries with more democratic experience. They also report higher levels of confidence in democracy.

This brings us back once more to the words of Ray Charles and Ricca Z. Harper. If elections fail to advance the cause of democracy without a background in representative government, yet elections themselves are a vital aspect of democratic practice, how can countries gain democratic experience in the first place? Our findings suggest that even highly competitive elections often fail to propel democratic change where we most passionately wish for it – in places with long histories of repression. It seems highly possible that such elections are bound to fail, ensnaring countries in a vicious cycle of elections, democratic stagnation, and citizen disengagement. We offer three rejoinders to this pessimistic conclusion. First, our findings, as in all statistical research, are probabilistic. Our model predicts that a country with little or no democratic-institutional stock will fail to gain democratic momentum, all else equal. Yet these predictions come with confidence intervals. And all else is only rarely equal in the hurly-burly of the political world. Some countries can overcome a history of dictatorial rule through successive elections, whether through luck or leadership, or because other systematic factors (e.g., wealth) weigh in the country's favor. Second, the passage of time has witnessed the slow accumulation of democratic experience in every region of the globe, as we saw in Figure 5.3. Elections may often fail to support lasting political change, yet we can hope that even short-lived democratic experiments will set the stage for successful elections in the future. Third, a renewed commitment to democratic assistance to countries with non-existent or limited democratic history might improve the conduct of elections. Policies such as election observation, democratic assistance, and foreign aid are premised on the intuition that they can substitute for a depleted democratic-institutional stock. We will explore their efficacy empirically in Chapter 8.

Next, however, we turn to another condition that plagues elections in poor countries: an insolvent national government. Citizens might lose their confidence in democratic practice during an economic collapse, even in the most democratically experienced countries. Data from the CSES suggest that only one-quarter of Greeks reported satisfaction with democracy as they headed to the polls in 2009 at the dawn of a financial crisis that continues today. In the same year, Iceland went to the polls, also in the midst of economic crisis. Between 2007 and 2009, the percentage of Icelanders satisfied with democracy collapsed, from 71 percent to 42 percent. In two countries with long experience with democracy, economic crisis dramatically reduced confidence in democracy. In Chapter 6, we argue that these cases reflect a broader pattern in which elections in countries with shrunken fiscal space result in democratic stasis or even backsliding.

6 Starved States: Fiscal Space and Elections

Governments spend money – lots of it. Governments would spend even more if they could, as the needs and wants of their citizens know few limits. Governments differ less in their desire for resources than in their ability to generate them, what they choose to do with them, and how well they do it. While the spending power of any government would be the envy of ordinary citizens, it is true that governments are not equally endowed, and that, while all governments might face fiscal constraints, these bind tighter and more harshly for some than others.

The ability to deliver public services to citizens is a primary function of modern states everywhere. However, doing so is increasingly expensive, as the scope of demands made by citizens continues to grow. When governments fail to provide services of sufficient quality and quantity, citizens must obtain private substitutes from the marketplace or religious and social organizations. Governments face steep costs when they fail to meet voters' needs, however, as President Dilma Rousseff of Brazil discovered when major protests broke out in Brazil over the price of public transportation. Samuel Huntington foresaw such troubles, warning that citizens' demands would overwhelm states lacking robust institutions to channel such demands. His concern was that weak institutions – principally the absence of strong political parties – would fail to provide avenues for peaceful opposition.

Huntington's prediction in *Political Order in Changing Societies* might appear unduly pessimistic in hindsight. Only six years following its publication, in 1974, the Third Wave of democracy commenced in Iberia. An optimist might conclude that these events rendered anachronistic Huntington's original prediction that the inability to generate basic public goods would doom states to chronic instability. Not so fast. Huntington worried that popular protests would undermine weak institutions and that vulnerable governments would respond by resorting to praetorianism. They did, but only for as

120

long as that option remained available. The advent of the electoral boom soon after the Berlin Wall crumbled galvanized a sea change in international politics. Elections became the sole route to international political legitimacy and governments everywhere and of all stripes rushed to secure electoral mandates. The electoral boom might suggest that Huntington got it wrong – rather than undermine democracy, popular participation provoked by poorly performing states appeared to have bolstered it. Indeed, Huntington himself, in a series of lectures that became *The Third Wave*, appears to admit this.[1]

To our thinking, it is the later Huntington that got it wrong, while his earlier work – though requiring repairs – has weathered nearly five decades of scrutiny admirably well. The key is to decouple in our minds the holding of elections from the establishment and consolidation of democracy. One cannot have a modern representative national democracy without elections, nor can such a democracy be built without elections to approve constitutions and elect interim governments. Yet one can certainly have elections without democracy. In fact, as we have already shown, the typical election in the developing world does little to further democracy's cause. All too often, things worsen after elections.

The solution to popular protests in the 1960s and 1970s was simple: forcibly clear protesters from the street and clamp down on dissent with authoritarianism. The 1990s rendered such tactics more politically costly – leaders had to adapt. The ideal option clearly was that they would have recognized the passing of an era and permitted genuinely free and fair elections. If you were an incumbent leader facing pressure to hold real elections for the first time, you might be forgiven for thinking that the deck was stacked against you. With little to no democratic-institutional stock accumulated, and an impoverished treasury, your public policy record was thin. Leaders of impecunious states could not hope to implement broad public policy initiatives that could focus their re-election campaigns, nor could they promise to do so in the future to dubious electorates. So, again, they adapted, but not in ways conducive to deepening democracy.

Across the developing world, leaders faced with limited fiscal space seek other ways to win elections. A common strategy is to engage in populist appeals that often worsen the problem by encouraging inflationary spending that weakens the economy. Another is to eschew broad public goods entirely – since the state cannot afford them even if

it were capable of implementing the required policies – and to emphasize instead narrowly targeted appeals via clientelistic and patronage
networks. Too often this shift is driven by a cynical exploitation
of ascriptive cleavages such as ethnicity, language, or tribal kinship.
There are sensible strategic reasons for this, since co-ethnic clientelistic exchanges are more credible and enforceable.[2] But the damage to
the body politic and national democracy can be quite grievous due to
a loss of legitimacy with excluded groups. Of course, if neither pop-
ulism nor ethnic clientelism is enough, leaders can always resort to
more heavy-handed tactics such as repression of the opposition, and a
variety of fraudulent tactics leading up to and on election day.

The point is simple: limited fiscal space harms democracy via its
effect on the electoral strategies adapted by incumbent leaders. This
effect is distinct from, though related to, the deleterious effects of
poverty and economic crisis on democratic consolidation. In the next
section, we survey the literature linking economic conditions to democratic transition and survival. We do so because these are important
arguments to consider in their own rights, but also to force ourselves
to clarify the distinguishing features of our fiscal space argument vis-
à-vis existing economic explanations. Then, we describe our empirical
strategy for measuring the concept of fiscal space and for testing our
main hypotheses. We conclude this chapter by discussing the implications of our findings for democracy promotion efforts, but reserve
for later a fuller consideration of strategies to ameliorate the negative
democratic consequences of limited fiscal space.

Economic Theories of Democracy

For at least sixty years, political scientists have investigated the
relationship between economic conditions and the likelihood of democratic transition and consolidation. Two main sets of findings are
worth recalling here, both because they highlight important facets of
the democratization process and because they relate to the fiscal space
argument presented here. Clearly this is a stylized reading of a voluminous literature. Our purpose is selfish: we seek the key insights relevant
to our inquiry and leave aside plenty of valuable findings that are more
tangential.[3]

The modernization theory school provides the clearest early articulation of why better economic conditions should be congenial to

democratic development. At its core, the argument operates at the micro level, where it posits that individuals more likely adopt pro-democratic views as well as the ancillary attitudes towards tolerance of diversity and dissent and support for principles of equality that undergird democratic practice. While one might – and should – debate the operationalization of some of these concepts in applied survey research, the fact remains that the body of evidence in favor of this proposition is quite impressive. Globally, people with improved economic situations (i.e., richer people) are more likely to express support for democratic principles and institutions.[4]

A parallel construction of the modernization argument occurs at the national level, with some scholars arguing that economic development would make democracy more probable for the nation-state. Seymour Martin Lipset argued almost sixty years ago that richer countries were more likely to enjoy the stable and legitimate national institutions conducive to democracy.[5] Phillips Cutright confirmed this insight in a series of studies in the early 1960s, using more sophisticated regression analyses than Lipset had employed.[6] But Huntington arrested the momentum of the modernization juggernaut with his devastating critique in 1968, and O'Donnell and Schmitter followed up with their analysis of the bureaucratic authoritarian regimes of Latin America.[7]

More recently, a pair of important books appears to have put the nail in the coffin of modernization theory. Adam Przeworski and colleagues show quite comprehensively that since at least 1950, economic growth and the level of development do not predict transitions to democracy.[8] If anything, the path to democratization appears quite idiosyncratic. However, Przeworski et al. do find that, beyond a fairly high level of economic growth, democracies survive at much higher rates. The Lipset hypothesis appears spurious – rich countries are more likely to be democratic not because national wealth spurs democratization, but because rich democracies persist while poor democracies revert to authoritarianism. India is an important exception, though its success also poses a problem for conventional modernization arguments. Daron Acemoglu and James Robinson offer a different reason for suspecting that any relationship between wealth and democracy is spurious. They argue that colonial-era institutions drive the establishment, or lack thereof, of post-colonial democracy, and that democracy, by promoting the rule of law, might in fact promote economic development.[9] That is, the causal arrow is probably the opposite of what the modernization theorists had posited!

Fifty years of scholarly scrutiny might have landed some severe body blows on the corpus extolling modernization theory, yet several recent articles have breathed new life into it. Carles Boix and Susan Stokes tackle the Przeworski et al. argument vigorously.[10] Przeworski et al., they admit, might be correct in the period they study, viz. 1950–1990, but a longer perspective validates Lipset. Prior to 1950, the relationship between economic development and democratic transition was considerably stronger than it has been in the post–World War II era. Besides, as Acemoglu and Robinson argue, institutions themselves influence development, which opens the possibility that any relationship between democracy and development uncovered in the time period studied by Przeworski et al. is the result of endogeneity. Ryan Kennedy concurs with the broad thrust of the Boix and Stokes rejoinder, though his analysis suggests that modernization theory is better conceptualized as conditional on regime type.[11] Higher economic growth makes autocratic transition to democracy less likely, as autocratic leaders are bolstered by strong economic performance. Poor growth records, on the other hand, make transitions to democracy more likely but they also increase the risk of democratic backsliding. Michael Miller illuminates one potential causal mechanism at work here: strong economic growth reduces the risk of violent removal for autocratic leaders significantly.[12]

The insight that poor economic conditions might doom fledgling democracies animates Ethan Kapstein and Nathan Converse's *The Fate of Young Democracies*.[13] Kapstein and Converse suggest, however, that focusing on economics might be misleading. Echoing Huntington, on whose broad shoulders much of this body of work stands, they argue that the real culprits are the weak political institutions that are too often found in young democracies. The weakness of these institutions harms democracy by allowing would-be autocrats to usurp power and undermine checks and balances. This perspective is consonant with ours. As we have shown in the previous chapter as well as in prior work on post-conflict democratization and elections, one of the biggest deficiencies for developing countries is that they lack the benefit of adequate time to accumulate sufficient democratic-institutional stock. But time matters and the US Supreme Court's landmark *Marbury* v. *Madison* decision establishing the principle of judicial review again presents an instructive case: the decision was handed down in 1803, a full fourteen years after George Washington assumed power and not until the United States was on its fourth elected president. Yet as our analysis in Chapter 5 makes clear, most developing countries today do not have the luxury of fourteen years of accumulated democratic stock or multiple peaceful alternations of power. Even more pointedly, the principle of universal suffrage, the sine qua non of modern democracy, took the better part of two hundred years to be guaranteed by law in the United States.

Kapstein and Converse also contribute to the debate about the economic pre-conditions for democracy by shifting our analytical focus away from levels of economic growth to the volatility of that growth. Given their limited institutional stock, young democracies tend to find economic crises particularly devastating, as the resulting dislocations to citizens generate demands and protests that quickly overwhelm the state and allow populist dictators to seize power. The Latin American record highlights the danger of inflationary crises in which citizens' purchasing power is eviscerated overnight. Suddenly impoverished and unable to meet even their most basic needs, citizens demand immediate action by the state and, in their desperation, are susceptible to the siren calls of personalistic leaders who promise better futures and find easy scapegoats in the ruling classes, international capital, religious and ethnic minorities, or immigrants. The fate of Weimar Germany illustrates the worst that can result.

Economic development, growth, and crises clearly matter for our understanding of democratic transition, consolidation, and survival, but these arguments require tweaking to help answer the puzzle motivating our book: why do some elections contribute to the deepening of democracy (alternatively, add to a country's democratic-institutional stock), while others appear to erode it? Put differently, what is it about elections under poor economic conditions that reduces their democratic dividend?

Answering such questions requires changing our vantage point. Rather than identify the broad economic correlates of individuals' democratic value orientations or of national democratization efforts, we want to delve more deeply into the nature of elections in the developing world. This move is justified in no small part by the near-universality of elections globally. While earlier studies could have marked the onset of a "democratization episode" by the holding of an election, that would not be very helpful today. Instead, we must move away from studying democracy per se and toward analyzing elections.

So why is the democratic dividend of elections higher in some places and at some times? A partial answer is found in the incentives and opportunities available to the incumbent leaders who are now forced to seek return to office by subjecting themselves to the will of the people. In countries where elections are well established, we expect politicians to run for re-election on the basis of the public policy records they have amassed during their terms in office. These records ideally emphasize public goods built and enhanced because of the candidate's leadership. However, while all leaders might be tempted on the campaign trail to claim complete credit for their initiatives, the fact is that successful public policy is expensive, and reliant on considerable bureaucratic capacity which is expensive to establish in its own right. Barack Obama's presidential re-election campaign in the United States in 2012, not to mention the opposition campaign of Mitt Romney, focused largely on the passage of the Affordable Care Act, which sought to establish a national healthcare mandate. However, one can only have an election fought on the merits of a national healthcare system in a country with sufficient resources to contemplate building one in the first place. Elsewhere, elections are fought on far less grandiose terms.

What strategies are available if one is a leader of a young state, lacking the prior institutional history required to build bureaucratic expertise and capacity or the fiscal resources required to fund national public good provision? Obviously, one can still promise to build such programs and claim credit for initial efforts to do so, but attentive voters will recognize those promises as lacking credibility. It pays therefore to build a more immediate campaign strategy. The central tactic is to shift the focus away from national public goods and towards more targeted provision of patronage to ethnic groups that support the leader. Such patronage is distributed via existing clientelistic networks and is cheaper on the whole, even if such targeted goods are more expensive per person than corresponding public goods. One can also enforce the reciprocity of votes more easily; conversely, the tangible nature of patronage rewards makes incumbent promises more credible to voters. Patronage and clientelism are not favorable to the long-term establishment of democratic institutions, but at least they involve some sort of credible relationship between voters and candidates.[14] Furthermore, the delivery of patronage requires formal and informal networks, which may not even exist in some developing countries lacking strong parties or clearly delineated ascriptive or regional identities. In those countries, the choices for incumbents are even starker and result in the use of repression and coercion of opposition candidates and supporters, as well as blatant fraud, to secure victory when necessary.

The argument outlined earlier yields a clear testable hypothesis that elections held in countries where leaders have more limited fiscal space to enact large public policy programs will have a lower democratic dividend than those held in situations where leaders enjoy the fiscal flexibility required to provide public goods to citizens. This hypothesis complements the democratic-institutional stock hypothesis developed and tested in the previous chapter by highlighting another factor limiting the democratic utility of elections in the developing world. In the remainder of this chapter, we provide an empirical test of this hypothesis, followed by a discussion of the implication of our results.

Fiscal Space and the Democratic Dividend

Fiscal space refers most generically to the ability of governments to spend on projects and initiatives. One can conceive of it, in effect, as the country's spending ability, which in turn is a function of the country's income stream and fiscal obligations. Where fiscal space is limited, politicians are unable to make credible promises to voters; this erodes party loyalty and increases electoral volatility as voters try other candidates who promise greater goods in exchange for votes.[15] To operationalize fiscal space, we would ideally estimate the revenues available to each government through taxation and transfers from sub-national units from the central government and subtract from that number monies committed to a standard set of non-discretionary budget categories such as civil administration, debt servicing, and law and order. The resulting measure would indicate the fiscal space available to governments to pursue other, more discretionary, projects.

Constructing such a measure cross-nationally is unfortunately difficult for both conceptual and operational reasons, since it requires agreement on which budget categories should be considered "non-discretionary" across states and also on commensurable and fine-grained budgetary category data. Instead, we choose a simpler focus on the tax revenues of the national government. To ensure the comparability of these figures, we measure them in per capita terms and in constant US dollars. The advantage of this approach is that it maximizes data coverage, since tax data are reasonably easily available for most countries over the time span we wish to cover.[16] The disadvantage is that it ignores the fixed costs of governance, or what we might consider non-discretionary spending. Disaggregated budgetary data for enough categories of spending simply do not exist for the cross-national time series we have built here. However, if anything, this limitation of our measure understates the disadvantages facing developing countries, since the fixed costs of running the state should comprise a larger constraint on their spending than in higher-revenue countries. Likewise, by ignoring debt-servicing burdens and the differential access to international credit markets cross-nationally, focusing solely on tax revenues understates the fiscal disadvantage faced by developing countries.

The extent of this fiscal disadvantage is considerable and widening, which should concern us in its own right even if our intuitions regarding the importance of fiscal space for democratization turn out to be wrong. Fiscal space matters for a host of desirable attributes. For instance, it correlates positively and statistically significantly with a battery of World Bank Governance Indicators. It also correlates positively with the level of democracy as measured by Polity and Freedom House. And it correlates positively with GDP per capita. All these correlations are in the theoretically anticipated positive direction, but they are not so strong as to suggest that we are simply measuring regime type or government efficacy in a different guise. Our point, rather, is to establish a prima facie case that our concept of fiscal space is worth investigating for its possible effects on the democratic dividend of elections. Further suggestive evidence for this hypothesis comes from the observation that, in the developing world, the correlation between fiscal space and the governance indicators and GDP per capita, respectively, is strongest in the 2000s. This suggests a separation of fates for the countries in the developing world. While some are making slow, steady gains along several key dimensions and are narrowing the gap with developed countries, for too many others there is no such "unity of goodness." Instead, this latter set is mired in the kinds of development traps highlighted by Paul Collier in *The Bottom Billion*, unable to escape cycles of violent conflict, poor governance, and poverty.[17]

We can also compare fiscal space directly across political indicators. For instance, in the developing world, democracies on average enjoy more fiscal space than non-democracies, but the average gap is not very large in absolute terms ($160 per capita), bolstering our contention that fiscal space is not simply democracy in different clothing. However, the gaps are much more striking when we compare fiscal space across different levels of governance. Within the developing world, the difference in fiscal space endowments between high-governance and low-governance states is twenty-fold ($925 vs. $21). This supports our causal mechanism that fiscal space enables better governance, but also raises the concern that any relationship we uncover between fiscal space and the democratic dividend of elections is simply picking up the effect of better governance rather than of fiscal space. Ideally, we would simply control directly for governance in our regression models. Unfortunately, the World Bank Governance Indicators are only available since 1996 and so controlling for them is not an option. Therefore, we control for GDP per capita and economic growth, which serve as effective proxies for governance. This also helps account for the fact that wealthier countries should have larger tax bases, and hence larger tax revenues. Obviously, a key feature of our theoretical framework is this correlation of fiscal space with governance and prosperity, but our goal in the statistical analysis is to isolate, to the extent possible, the contribution of fiscal space to the democratic dividend of elections. Controlling for possible confounds therefore is sensible. We also utilize temporal lags of fiscal space throughout to ensure its value is measured prior to the measure of our dependent variable.

To get a better feel for this notion of fiscal space, establishing a benchmark is useful. Over the entire period for which we have data, the United States has a per capita tax revenue of $3,197 (in constant figures). By 2005, the most recent year for which we have cross-national data, the US figure rises to $6,000. As a group, the OECD average in 2005 is $7,331, higher than the US value since the US's European counterparts tax more and have smaller populations than the United States. How does the developing world compare? Since 1960, the developing world average is just $580 – only one-fifth the

US average. However, that is not the worst news: by 2005 the average per capita tax revenue for the developing world plummets to a mere $98. Compare that to the $7,331 average for the developed world *in the same year*. For the governments of the developing world, and the citizens they must serve, this is a chasm in possibility.

The gulf between the tax resources available to developed and developing countries grows with each passing year (see Figure 6.1). While a full explanation for this widening gap is beyond the scope of this book, three simple considerations help make sense of it. First, as we have argued throughout, a key dynamic at play globally is the changing set of countries in the global sample. The newly independent countries of the 1960s and 1970s entered the world as sovereign states at much lower levels of economic development than did their developed counterparts. In this very real sense, the average developing country instantly became poorer. Second, inflation and population growth are much higher in the developing world, and currencies are weaker. Considering tax revenue in per capita constant US dollars highlights the developing world's disadvantages, while measuring it as a proportion of GDP (as is often done in cross-national research) masks it. Third, the electoral boom came on the heels of the global debt crisis of the early 1980s, which rendered micro- and macroeconomic interventionism unpopular in influential development circles. Governments in the developing world slashed tax burdens in an attempt to comply with advice from development banks, submitted themselves to be rated by credit ratings agencies, and granted new power to Western-trained technocrats.

Another comparison paints an even bleaker picture. Figure 6.2 plots the fiscal space enjoyed by Sierra Leone's governments since the country's independence from the United Kingdom in 1961. We also mark the beginning and conclusion of that country's civil war, which is estimated to have killed between 50,000 and 300,000 people, not to mention the countless more that suffered non-fatal injuries, long-term health damage, and displacement. Over the non-conflict years (i.e., before 1991 and after 2002), Sierra Leone's per capita tax revenue was $492. During the conflict period of 1991–2002, the average per capita tax revenue dropped to $2!. Yet that does not capture the full scale of the devastation to Sierra Leone's public institutions wrought by the conflict. In the pre-conflict period, the average fiscal space was $1,286, even when we include the last few years before conflict broke out but

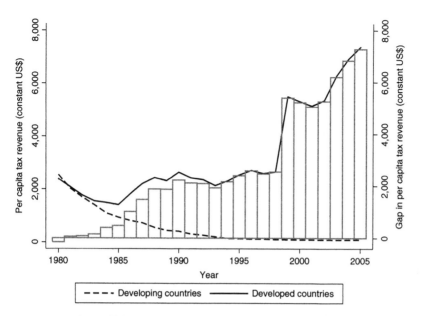

Figure 6.1 The gulf between the tax resources available to developed and developing countries grows with each passing year, 1981–2005

after the attempted coup in 1987. This was well above the developing country average as the country's leaders exploited its vast natural resources. But the civil war changed that permanently. For the fifteen years for which we have reliable data since the conclusion of the civil war in 1991, the average per capita tax revenue is a mere $1.75. What can a government do with less than two dollars per head to spend? What chance does it have of building high quality public services and basic national infrastructure, especially after a decade of war? And how does an elected leader build a record worthy of re-election with such meagre resources to deploy?

One answer to these depressing questions – indeed our answer – is that governments can do precious little with such limited fiscal space and that, consequently, elections must be contested through clientelistic and ethnic appeals, and won by repression and rigging.[18] We turn next to a statistical analysis of a global sample of developing countries since 1960 to establish the generalizability of our claim that fiscal space explains why some elections yield a richer democratic dividend than others.

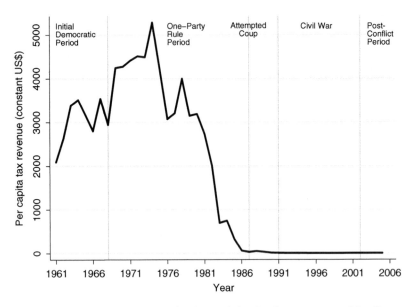

Figure 6.2 Civil war permanently changed the fiscal space enjoyed by Sierra Leone's governments, 1961–2005

The Benefits of Fiscal Space for Elections

Our statistical model follows the template used in the two previous chapters. Once again, what we wish to know is if elections conducted under specific theoretically indicated conditions yield better democratic outcomes. Our unit of analysis is an election for national executive office, and our dependent variable is the change in the country's level of democracy five years after the election. We control for the country's present level of democracy throughout, which provides some insurance against concerns that our measure of fiscal space is capturing quality of governance. Recall also that we control for GDP per capita, which helps ensure that our measure of fiscal space does not simply capture the impact of wealth. We also revert to including a full set of country fixed effects, since there is sufficient over-time variation in our main variables to warrant doing so.

Two modifications to our baseline model are worth noting. First, we include a quadratic term, the square of the fiscal space measure. This allows us to examine whether the impact of fiscal space dissipates past

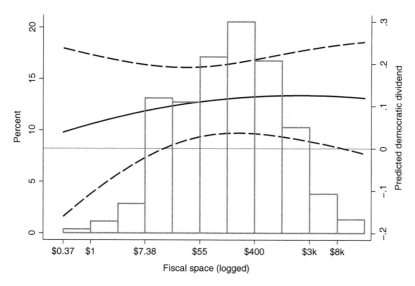

Figure 6.3 As fiscal space increases, elections yield a greater democratic dividend

some threshold. Doing so helps address another concern, namely that the conversion of nominal local currency measures of tax revenues into constant US dollars leads to some distortions in countries experiencing currency crises or hyperinflationary episodes. In those situations, the conversion into constant US dollars leads to misleadingly high values in the right-hand tail of the measure. Second, for similar reasons, we also include a direct measure of the incidence of a high-inflation episode.[19]

The regression results support our argument well. Simply put, greater fiscal space enhances the democratic dividend. Figure 6.3 plots the predicted democratic dividend of increased fiscal space using the estimates of our regression model and holding the values of our control variables at the levels observed in the developing world sample during the electoral boom period. The positive-sloping line indicates that as fiscal space increases, elections yield a greater democratic dividend, which confirms the main hypothesis in this chapter. The plot also includes 95 percent confidence intervals, which allow us to identify the point at which this estimated effect becomes statistically significant. Thankfully, from the point of view of democracy promotion, this is an achievable goal: a country with about fourteen dollars in fiscal space will yield a democratic dividend of roughly 0.10. Thankfully, the average fiscal space in the 1990s for Sub-Saharan African countries is roughly forty-eight dollars. As the histogram shows, however, about 10 percent of countries in our sample lack even this low level of fiscal space. Figure 6.3 also allows us to examine where the effect becomes insignificant. In this case, that point is not until a country has at least $8,000 in per capita tax revenues (measured in constant figures). Recall that the OECD average is over $7,000; therefore, for the range of data relevant to the observed world, the effect of additional fiscal space is positive and statistically significant.[20]

The fiscal space result discussed earlier is robust to different modeling decisions. Here we provide an overview of the various tests we conducted to explore the boundaries of our empirical work.[21] A primary consideration might be whether we have gotten the lag structure correct. We used the five-year change in democracy to be consistent with the models used in the other empirical chapters in the book, but it is obviously possible that alternative time periods are more appropriate. Happily, our results do not vanish if we use the two-year change in a country's democracy score following an election. Rather, they grow stronger, since we are using the government's fiscal space in a given election year to predict the change in the democracy score five years hence. That is a very conservative estimate of the effect of fiscal space, since the effect will naturally dissipate over time. It is no surprise, then, that narrowing the window to just two years post-election yields a stronger effect. Another way of checking if our results are robust to altering our treatment of time is to use the five-year moving average of fiscal space to ensure we are not simply picking up the effect of an election-year expansion.[22] Using the moving average smoothes the fiscal space trend and yields consistent results. Lastly, the results hold if we use random instead of fixed effects.

A second set of robustness checks involves using the Polity index of democracy instead of the Unified Democracy Scores (UDS). We realize of course that Polity is one of the indicators that feed into the UDS but, since prior studies often use only the Polity scale, we do so here for sake of comparability. Our results do not change. Elections held where governments have greater fiscal space yield positive democratic dividends, while those held where governments have little fiscal ability to implement public policy do not. Recall that the model controls for economic development levels so this effect is not simply an artifact of rich countries, or countries with higher state capacity, having more fiscal space. Further, the results hold if we use a battery of alternative dependent variables, including disaggregating the Polity score into its various key components.

Nor is the positive result a function of our relatively parsimonious model specification. Adding more variables to the model reduces the effective sample size due to missing data, but we do so to assess the robustness of our results to the inclusion of additional control variables. Our most expansive model specification includes seven additional variables. Since the most plausible challenge to our results is that our measure of fiscal space is simply capturing the effect of other economic conditions, we augment the model by including a measure of economic growth (in GDP per capita) as well as an indicator for whether the country experienced a crisis (negative growth) in a given year. These are in addition to the level of GDP per capita and the high inflation indicators already included in the baseline model. Next, we control for domestic instability, such as the number of protests and anti-government demonstrations. Membership in democratic inter-governmental organizations, which scholars have shown influences democratization and the quality of elections, is also included.[23] We control for the country's level of trade openness and dependence on oil rents as a source of revenue to account for alternative explanations from the globalization and oil curse literatures.[24] Our models hold in this augmented model, which is unsurprising given that our original model included country-level fixed effects, which effectively capture any unobserved country-level factors that might affect how elections work to forward democracy. Finally, we also test whether our results hold when we restrict our control variables to inflation, real GDP per capita, current democracy, and our regional and time period indicator variables. Such a model increases our number of cases, allowing us to check whether our results are sensitive to missing data – they are not.

Another potential concern in our results is that the power of fiscal space holds only for certain types of elections. We test this intuition by re-estimating our results for different sub-samples of elections. Our results are robust to this testing: fiscal space increases the democratic dividend from elections when we restrict our sample to only competitive, executive, legislative, and competitive legislative elections. They do not hold, however, for sub-samples of uncompetitive executive elections. This makes sense: if an election does not meet even a minimal threshold of competitiveness, more fiscal space will not make the outcome any more democratic.

The result that fiscal space increases the democratic dividend of elections, even after controlling for economic growth and level of development, provides strong evidence in favor of our theoretical framework. But the statistical analysis presented earlier, while yielding an admirably robust association between fiscal space and post-election democratic dividend, does not tell us if the causal mechanisms posited by our theory are the right ones. In the next section, we dig deeper into the causal mechanisms behind our main result.

The Effect of Fiscal Space on Governance Outcomes

Does fiscal space provide elected leaders the opportunity to enact large-scale public policies that benefit broad swathes of their citizenry? Does it allow them the possibility of building a policy record on which they might stand for re-election? We are not naïve – some leaders might squander the opening provided by such resources by enacting inefficient, even wasteful, programs that hemorrhage funds to corruption. Others – kleptocrats – might just loot their country's treasuries for purely personal profit. Such inefficiencies and corruption are the backbone of criticisms of higher tax burdens. We would be silly to deny such likelihoods, but our argument is not deterministic. It simply asserts that with more resources, the probability a leader builds a better functioning state and, in so doing, augments the country's institutional legitimacy that is vital to democratic deepening, increases. The statistical results mentioned earlier support the claim that greater fiscal space increases the democratic dividend of elections; however, to substantiate our favored causal mechanism, we need different data.

The contemporary gold standard for assessing causal claims is an experiment. However, this is a poor fit for our circumstances. Even if we had a few billion dollars in grants to assign as revenues across treatment and control groups, we are not sure that the complaints of the governments assigned to the low-revenue group would be worth our while.[25] We adopt, therefore, a time-trusted strategy and consider other observable implications of our argument.

The first of these is that greater fiscal space facilitates better governance, which in turn adds to the stock of institutional legitimacy in a given state.[26] We use the World Bank Governance Indicators as our measure of the quality of governance in a given country. Based on expert surveys, the World Bank provides measures of a country's governance in several different domains.[27] We use the indicator for government effectiveness, since it most closely approximates the theoretical construct of interest. We measure each country's average score for the 2000s and use it as our dependent variable. We then measure each country's average fiscal space for the prior decades to provide some cover against the concern that fiscal space is caused by governance.

Figure 6.4 shows these two measures plotted against each other.[28] The strong positive relationship is striking and the plot reveals some noteworthy patterns.[29] For instance, Singapore's success as a governance exemplar is evident – its effectiveness score exceeds what we would predict given its fiscal space. More generally, the countries above the line are disproportionately established democracies, while those below the line are countries in the developing world. Clearly, the relationship between fiscal space and government effectiveness is not deterministic and other factors matter, but the positive relationship is apparent. Indeed, it remains even if we use the average fiscal space from the 1980s to predict government effectiveness in the 2000s. The lower graph in Figure 6.4 provides that correlation. The relationship is weaker as the effect dissipates over time but the conclusion persists: more fiscal space is correlated with better-performing governments.

Another way of observing this relationship is to examine more discrete indicators of government performance. Do governments use these higher revenue streams to provide the sorts of public goods we have argued increase institutional legitimacy? It appears they do. We use the median value of fiscal space as a convenient threshold and separate our sample of developing countries into two halves to see if having more fiscal space is associated with higher values of these indicators – it is. For instance, "low" fiscal space countries on average report a 43 percent literacy rate, compared to a 59 percent rate for "high" fiscal space states. This is important since literacy – and education more generally – is often held up as a canonical public good.[30] A similar distinction emerges if we consider the public good of infrastructure production. Low-fiscal-space states report just 37 percent paved roads, while their better-resourced counterparts report 43 percent. Similarly, road density in low-fiscal-space states is 27 kilometers

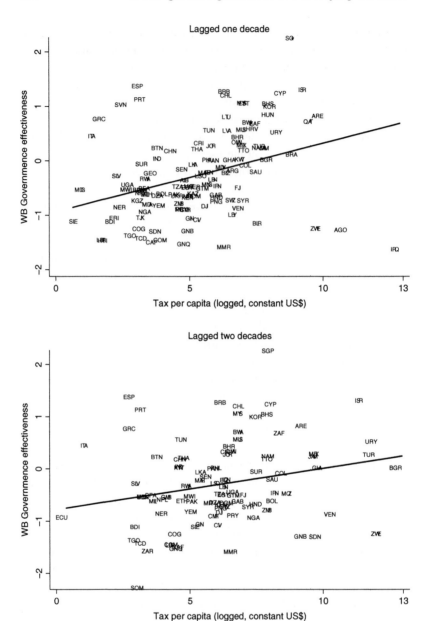

Figure 6.4 More fiscal space is correlated with better-performing governments

of road per square kilometer, compared to 40 kilometers per square kilometer in the other group. These differences are not simply statistical chance either, but are statistically significant at the 95 percent confidence level.

A final piece of corroborating evidence comes from thinking about an electoral implication of our argument. When governments have tax revenues, they are more likely to build public policy programs, and can compete for office on the basis of the record they assemble while in power. However, if they cannot make public policy because of a lack of resources, they are more likely to resort to extra-legal means of securing political survival. We use the NELDA project's coding of whether there exists compelling evidence that the opposition was subject to government harassment leading up to the election. As fiscal space decreases, the probability of such opposition harassment having occurred increases, which is consistent with our argument that low fiscal space reduces both leaders' policy options and their options for retaining office. We can also observe this effect in the probability of election boycotts, which are lower after elections in which incumbents had greater access to fiscal space. Our analysis also reveals that improvements in executive constraints and political participation are more likely to follow elections in countries with wider fiscal space.[31]

Fiscal Space and Voter Satisfaction with Democracy

The final piece of our evidence is at the individual level. An implication of our story is that where states are able to spend more because of higher fiscal space, they should emphasize public-good provision. The evidence presented earlier supports this claim. Leaders are therefore able to run on their policy records and so electoral malfeasance is less necessary. Citizens therefore should express greater satisfaction with democracy. If this last step in our logic is correct, it would bolster our key theoretical contention that fiscal space adds democratic consolidation by increasing the stock of institutional legitimacy.

We again use the third module of the Comparative Study of Electoral Systems (CSES) data. This module maximizes the number of developing countries in the sample, while remaining temporally proximate to our tax revenue data. Given the return to legitimacy, we expect that more recent data would yield even sharper results, but

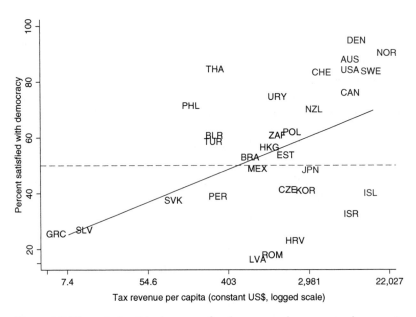

Figure 6.5 The relationship between fiscal space and aggregate democratic satisfaction is strong and positive

leave such an analysis to a future time when updated tax data are available.

We focus on a single question from the CSES, which asks respondents how satisfied they are with the way democracy works in their country. Note that this is not the same as a more abstract notion of whether they support democracy.[32] Respondents do not have to have read Robert Dahl's *Polyarchy* – though we imagine they would have loved it as much as we did had they done so – to know what democracy is or is not. They simply have to state if they are happy with how democracy is working in their country, which allows them to focus on issues of process and service delivery. We calculate the share of respondents in each country who say they are at least somewhat satisfied with democracy and plot this proportion against the country's fiscal space in Figure 6.5.

The positive relationship between fiscal space and aggregate democratic satisfaction could not be clearer.[33] Just as evident is the toll taken by the financial crisis on both the fiscal resources and the public morale of citizens in Greece. Further inspection of the scatterplot also reveals that the countries with greater experience with democracy tend to fall above the line and those that have made more recent transitions to democracy fall below it. Democratic stock works in conjunction with fiscal space to boost satisfaction with democracy, but, as we have argued and shown throughout this book, these two essential commodities are in rare supply in many of the world's fledgling democracies.

Discussion

Economic explanations of democratic transition, performance, and consolidation have a long and storied tradition in political science. Theories have been constructed linking the level of economic development, the rate of economic growth, the depth and frequency of crisis, and the structure of the economy to various dimensions of the democratization process. In this chapter, we have sought to add to this voluminous and influential body of scholarship by making contributions in two distinct areas. First, we focus on the fiscal space enjoyed by states in deciding their spending priorities. The ability of states to levy taxes on their citizens has been an important focus of study in political economy.[34] Here, we use it as an explanatory variable and, by controlling for economic development and growth, are able to identify the effect of having more fiscal resources at one's disposal over and above the effect of having a prosperous economy. This move allows us to shift our theoretical focus away from the effects of economic prosperity on individual-level attitudes towards modern democratic values and towards the ability of elected leaders to provide the public goods their citizens desire.

Our second contribution builds directly on this insight. Rather than study broad historical shifts in regime type, where the presence of elections is a definitional criterion for democracy, we focus on elections as the unit of analysis itself. The ubiquity of elections worldwide means that regimes of dubious democratic quality are just as likely to hold elections as bona fide democracies. By taking elections as given, we are able to identify the conditions under which elections help create better democracies, or, alternatively, set countries further along an illiberal path. This focus on elections also makes our research relevant (we hope) to scholars working on questions concerning the quality of elections.

Our analysis provides strong evidence for the argument. Using data from all developing country elections since 1960, we find that elections held in countries with higher fiscal space yield larger democratic dividends. Many elections in the developing world yield no democratic dividend at all because their tax revenues are too low to sustain good governance. Further analysis yields evidence consistent with our posited causal mechanisms: high fiscal space predicts government effectiveness even two decades later; is correlated with better outcomes in public-good provision; and is less likely to be associated with allegations of government harassment of opposition groups and boycotts by those groups. These are better-run states, and the result, survey evidence shows, is citizenries that are more satisfied with how democracy is working in their country. This satisfaction facilitates a virtuous pro-democracy cycle.

The flip side of that happy picture is bleak. Our analysis suggests a vicious cycle in which election-holding countries can become ensnared. Elections are held as a marker of democratic transition in countries with minimal fiscal space. Those elections result in the election of governments with little means of improving the lives of their citizens and precious little time until the next election. These governments turn to patrimonialism and democratic shenanigans to win the next election. Elections become increasingly fraudulent until protests, a coup, or international pressure force a derided incumbent from power. Then the cycle restarts, trapping countries in a vicious circle of bad elections and poor governance. The policy question we must tackle is how fiscal space and bureaucratic capacity can be built in the cauldron of election competition in new, fragile democracies.

Three implications of our argument might help us answer this question. First, when elections are being held in states with low fiscal space, pro-democracy organizations and observers should be on alert for electoral misconduct, since leaders will need to rely on such tactics to a greater degree than their counterparts with more public policy options. Second, to paraphrase Monsieur Clemenceau, public finance reform is too important to be left to the tax economists at the International Monetary Fund and World Bank. The importance of higher taxes for democracy-building should be recognized and leaders must be provide incentives to make the difficult choices required to raise adequate revenues to meet their citizens' needs. These challenges are even greater in a global economy, where capital mobility makes taxation more complicated. Third, as the Sierra Leone example demonstrates, conflict can have a devastating impact on tax receipts. This is but one of the many negative effects of conflict, of course, but it provides a distinct mechanism for understanding the challenges of post-conflict democratization. The next chapter delves deeper into the question of how conflict and its legacy affect elections, and to that analysis we now turn.

7 | *Violent Votes: Conflict and Elections*

Journalists and political observers like to describe elections in combative terms. Elections pit candidates and political parties in "campaigns" in which they "fight" for votes, particularly in tightly contested "battleground" states or provinces. Candidates hopefully can access a large "war chest" to finance their campaigns. An uneven election might be described as a "rout," in which one side deals another a "crushing defeat." The use of militaristic metaphors to describe elections should not surprise us; elections by their very nature involve a contest for political power. The promise of democracy is in part the replacement of irregular war with regular elections, bullets with ballots, and armies with political parties. Democracy does not eradicate humans' relish for political combat, but the hope is that it channels that competition into a commitment to peaceful political campaigns.

It is therefore ironic that elections have increasingly been held in the shadow of organized political violence. The electoral boom spread elections to countries scarred by successive waves of civil conflict. The incidence of civil conflict exploded after the mid-1950s, from a low of only 6 percent of sovereign states in 1955 to a high of nearly a quarter in the early 1990s, just as the electoral boom took shape. The electoral boom often found itself spreading to conflictual societies. Nearly two of every five elections during the electoral boom took place in countries either mired in civil conflict, as in Colombia, or within ten years of one, as in post-war Liberia and Cambodia. The electoral milieu also more frequently featured ethnic strife. Only 5.5 percent of elections were held while an ethnic war occurred in the 1960s; by the 1990s, that proportion had nearly tripled.

Quite clearly, the specter of organized political violence has become an unwelcome yet common feature of the electoral environment over the last thirty years. Scholars have suggested that this trend is no mere coincidence. They argue that elections surged precisely because the international community more frequently acted on two preferences. First, the United Nations and other organizations, particularly after the publication of *An Agenda for Peace* in 1992, committed themselves to a more robust portfolio of preventive diplomacy, conflict mediation, and post-war peacebuilding. Conflicts that ended in the 1990s consequently were far more likely to be ended through peace talks held under the aegis of the United Nations and other international organizations.[1] Second, these same organizations began to place elections and democratization at the center of their post-war program of peacebuilding. Societies dominated by civil violence only waited several months before setting themselves to the tasks of drafting constitutions and holding democratic elections. Marina Ottaway labeled this process "democratic reconstructionism."[2]

We investigate the impact of civil conflict on elections in this chapter, concluding that elections in conflict and immediately post-conflict situations should worry democracy promoters. Holding elections might be in the short-term interests of Western interveners in civil conflict situations, but we will show that such elections hurt long-term democratic development. Given that our previous research has already demonstrated that elections held rapidly after civil conflict in new democracies hasten conflict recidivism and hamper economic recovery, the case against such elections is pretty damning.[3] Violent conflicts require political solutions, but our research makes clear that "quickie" elections are not a panacea but can actually worsen the situation. We need to generate new ideas for helping these troubled societies recover.

We are not the first to examine the interrelationships between elections and violent political conflict, but previous scholarship has not explicitly examined whether conflict hinders democratic change after elections. We consider this issue carefully. Elections in peacetime should allow fair competition for power among different coalitions, confer legitimacy on a new government, and replenish or at least begin to fill the well of democracy. This is already a high bar for many young democracies, as we have already seen. Yet elections in conflictual societies confront yet another daunting burden – solidifying an often tenuous peace. We suggest that politicians taking power after elections in conflictual societies find it far more difficult to generate performance legitimacy and far easier to abrogate democratic rules. A recent history of political violence is also likely to alter indelibly a country's political economy in ways that make democratic rule more unstable, even for the most sincerely committed democrats.

This chapter provides evidence for this argument: elections held during conflict and in its aftermath yield a smaller democratic dividend than those held during peacetime. Elections held while conflict is ongoing yield a negative democratic dividend – that is, conflict is "democratization in reverse." Such "conflictual" elections are more likely to be followed by violence and opposition boycotts and less likely to be followed by progress in civil liberties and political rights. Ethnic secessionist conflicts are particularly harmful to the democratic dividend from elections. Finally, elections held after the cessation of violence – what we term the "recovery" period – can yield positive democratic gains but only if we are patient. Those held within a year of the conflict do nothing for future democracy, but waiting even one more year turns that around in the positive direction. This is consistent with our earlier research showing that early post-conflict elections are especially worrisome for conflict recidivism and economic recovery. Here, as is so often true in politics, timing is everything.

Guatemala provides an excellent illustration of many of the dynamics afflicting post-conflict democratization efforts. Guatemala successfully concluded a long, brutal civil war two decades ago, holding elections during conflict partially as a means to bring peace. At a macro-level, Guatemala presents a successful case of post-war peacebuilding, with no large-scale political violence since 1996 and a robust democracy by cross-national measures. Yet Guatemalans themselves are not very convinced. We document a form of democratic stasis in Guatemala; voters report little more satisfaction with democracy today than they did in 1996. One reason for this democratic ennui is their physical insecurity; Guatemalans report frighteningly high levels of crime. Our results suggest an extension to our original theory: even where elections during and after conflict are followed by the building of formal institutions of democracy, continued post-conflict human insecurity yields citizens with little faith in democratic governance.

War by Other Means? Elections and Conflict

Scholarly efforts to understand the dynamics linking democracy and war have generated a rich literature spanning several decades. This search began as an empirical evaluation of the "democratic peace thesis," which states that democratic countries almost never go to war against each other, though they do fight wars with non-democracies.[4] Two explanations for the democratic peace dominate. First, democratic practice develops a different culture of conflict resolution, encouraging alternatives to armed violence. Second, democratic institutions constrain leaders from initiating war, since voters and political opponents will punish leaders for ill-advised military actions that lead to significant losses.

The mature democratic practice and consolidated democratic institutions that undergird democratic peace theory are in limited supply across the developing world. So it is hardly a surprise that, while mature democracies tend towards more pacific relations, immature democracies are especially war-prone. In young democracies, with their inchoate democratic and administrative institutions, democratization encourages nationalist out-bidding among politicians, presaging violent conflicts, not only between countries, but also within newly democratizing societies.[5]

The impact of political regimes on civil war's incidence has received significant attention in recent years. For the most part, there is little evidence that civil wars are more likely in autocratic than in democratic regimes, though Paul Collier argues that democracy raises the probability of violence in poor countries.[6] Other authors have attended specifically to the question of whether elections make civil war more likely. Cederman, Hug, and Krebs find that they do, contending that episodes of democratization raise the probability of civil war, and Cederman, Gleditsch, and Hug find that first and second elections during democratization raise the probability of ethnic civil wars.[7]

Global trends inspired another group of actors and scholars to examine the interrelationship between violent conflict and democracy. The United Nations' *Agenda for Peace* dedicated it to an ambitious mission of mediating violent conflicts and building the peace after their conclusion. The end of the Cold War, meanwhile, had created a newfound zeal for democracy promotion. The conclusion of long civil wars during the 1990s in Central America (e.g., Guatemala in 1996) and Sub-Saharan Africa (e.g., Mozambique in 1992) provided ideal cases for applying these principles, and a new model of internationally sponsored peacebuilding – one that placed elections at the center of a liberal agenda including economic reform, transitional justice, and peacekeeping missions – was born. Peacebuilding paired elections with United Nations Peacekeeping Operations (UNPKOs) as part of an effort to transition societies from war to peace, economic recovery, and liberal democracy. Yet scholars voiced doubts that this model could be successful in post-war countries. Nicole Ball argued that post-war elections present dangers in countries lacking previous experience with democratic competition. Barbara Walter agreed, arguing that former belligerents' inability to commit credibly to peace would require heavy international intervention in the short run to relieve distrust; democracy might act as a conflict resolver only in the long run. Roland Paris, foreshadowing Mansfield and Snyder, argued that post-war countries suffer from a series of socio-political pathologies that make political liberalization and economic reform a dangerous enterprise.[8]

Our own research on post-war liberalization was among the first to subject these suspicions to serious statistical scrutiny. We argued that new post-war democracies complicate the creation of durable commitments to peace, since constraints on executives would be observed mostly in the breach. We found that post-conflict democratization tended to retard economic reconstruction, all else equal.[9] We next examined the impact of elections on post-conflict countries, finding that elections held within the first post-conflict year in more established democracies and the first two post-conflict years in new democracies hastened the return of political violence.[10] Others examined the same question with a different dataset and statistical models and came to similar conclusions.[11] Yet not all post-conflict elections are deemed dangerous. Aila Matanock, for example, finds that elections following negotiated settlements in which former armed groups compete as political parties against their erstwhile enemies tend to prolong the peace.[12]

These contributions enrich our understanding of conflict and democratization and, in the process, challenge the premise that democratization and elections necessarily engender more peaceful politics. Yet there is also agreement that consolidated democracies are desirable. An important question is whether the birthing pains of early elections are a necessary price to pay on the path to someday having an established democracy. Put differently, while the research surveyed earlier is convincing that elections can raise the probability of civil conflict and hamper economic recovery following conflict, an open question is the one asked here – are elections held during civil conflict and in its wake less successful at promoting democracy than those held during peacetime?

We expect that elections during and after violent political conflict should generate a smaller democratic dividend than those held during peacetime. Elections held during or after conflict may very well raise the expectations of voters to impossible-to-reach levels, as the moment of transition creates a moment of unguarded optimism.[13] A newly elected leader, particularly as conflict ends, takes office facing the daunting challenge of high expectations and a constrained ability to meet them. We argue that conflict hinders the development of stocks of performance and democratic-institutional legitimacy. Politicians elected during and soon after conflict will find it difficult to generate performance legitimacy, since leaders lack access to the whole of the national territory and face violent political opponents. The most immediate means to performance legitimacy remains on the battlefield, by physically punishing one's enemies. Election winners therefore will divert scarce funds formerly earmarked for public goods to military spending.[14] Political violence also avails incumbents and their political opponents of the ability to remain in power by eroding democratic practice. Incumbents can more easily suspend elections and restrict political participation, particularly of identity groups deemed supportive of an insurgency. Conflict likely magnifies the importance of the military in political life, making coups far more likely. Nor does the conclusion of conflict necessarily support the holding of better elections. The economic destruction and political dysfunction during conflict likely long outlasts the conflict itself, complicating elections long after the international community has turned its attention to other hotspots.

Recent scholarship undergirds this argument, documenting clearly that elections held during and after conflict take place in unpromising economic, political, and social environments. Conflict slows economic growth, spurring Collier to declare civil war "development in reverse." Continued post-war economic stagnation exacerbates the risk of recurrence, leading to a "conflict trap" in which conflict slows economies, which only raises the risk of further conflict.[15] Civil war also undermines public health, an effect that lasts long after conflicts end.[16] Politically, post-war countries likely suffer from severe political mistrust and weak institutions and typically exhibit little improvement in the rule of law.[17] Sarah Daly argues that the organizational capacity created by insurgent groups lasts long after conflict ends, making a return to conflict more likely.[18] The result is a persistent high probability of further conflict; Collier et al. estimate the probability of conflict recurrence within five years at 44 percent. Conflicts also create psychological traumas that scar refugees, ex-combatants, and civilians, which ultimately reduces social capital. Conflicts also may harden ethnic identities, as people caught in the middle form a "conflictive ethos" in which they form negative beliefs regarding adversaries, which can complicate political reconciliation.[19]

Sri Lanka's 2010 presidential elections illustrate these dynamics well. The Liberation Tigers of Tamil Eelam (LTTE) had fought since 1983 to establish an independent state for the Tamil minority in the north and east of the country. The war killed tens of thousands of Sri Lankans over twenty-six years of intermittent fighting. The Sri Lankan state, however, finally inflicted a crushing defeat on the LTTE, reestablishing complete control of the north of the country. Incumbent President Mahinda Rajapaksa, basking in political popularity among the Sinhalese majority, exercised his constitutional right to call for new elections four years into his term. Presidential elections were then held in January 2010, only eight months after the end of the civil war, with hundreds of thousands of citizens in displacement camps. General Sarath Fonseka, the head of the armed forces and often recognized as the architect of the defeat of the Tigers, resigned his position to run against Rajapaksa. The resulting election featured many of the abrogations of checks on the executive that our theory would predict. State television nearly totally ignored Fonseka's candidacy while lavishing non-stop coverage of the Rajapaksa campaign. Fonseka's hotel in Colombo was surrounded by a hundred government troops on election night, purportedly for his own protection, and he was arrested only two weeks after the election on charges of plotting a coup. He eventually was convicted on charges of corruption and served two years in jail. Freedom House's 2011 report on Sri Lanka also notes that political reforms subsequently pushed by Rajapaksa's government reduced the powers of the electoral commission, invoking an opposition boycott and criticism from human rights groups.[20] As of August 2015, thankfully, Sri Lanka's authoritarian slide appears to have been arrested. Rajapaksa has suffered two ignominious defeats, first to his effort to win another term as president and then to his attempt to return to power as prime minister. This is a positive step but rebuilding the trust destroyed by the conflict will take many years and concerted efforts by Sri Lanka's leaders.

Elections during Conflict are Democratization in Reverse

Testing the hypothesis that elections during and soon after civil conflict yield a smaller democratic dividend than those held during periods of peace requires a measure of civil conflict. Existing measures can be divided into two groups, one that defines and measures civil war and another that defines a broader array of civil conflict. Melvin Small and J. David Singer initiated a focus on what they termed "intrastate" war as part of the larger Correlates of War (COW) project at the University of Michigan that had until that time focused on war between countries. The authors defined civil war as sustained fighting between organized groups resulting in at least a thousand battle deaths per year, with the weaker side (usually an insurgent group) effectively resisting the stronger so that it inflicted at least 5 percent of the battle deaths. The global intensification of civil violence in the 1990s and attendant interest from policymakers and academics spurred modifications to COW's criteria, including a requirement that the incumbent government be a party to the conflict.[21] A second group of scholars, associated with the Uppsala University Data Program (UCDP) and Peace Research Institute Oslo (PRIO), has eschewed an exclusive focus on war in favor of a broader notion of armed civil conflict. They define civil conflict as "a contested incompatibility that concerns government and/or territory where the use of armed force between two parties, of which at least one is the government of a state, results in at least twenty-five battle-related deaths."[22]

Our hypothesis that conflictual societies will tend to have more problematic elections does not provide precise guidance as to whether we should prefer the higher or lower threshold for organized political violence.[23] We choose the lower threshold recommended by the UCDP and in our robustness analyses verify that the impact of conflict on the democratic dividend from elections does not depend on conflict's intensity. Our theory focuses on the importance of armed challenges to the state and how they condition the democratizing impact of elections. Opting for a stricter focus on only war would rule out the possibility that lower levels of violence affect elections. Colombia illustrates why that would be a poor choice. The country has experienced political violence since the early 1960s, as the state has battled leftist insurgent groups, drug cartels, and occasionally para-military groups. Yet the COW project codes Colombia as beginning a civil war only in 1989, while the UCDP codes a continuous conflict since 1964.[24] The war-focused definition likely misses key aspects of how conflict has affected Colombia's elections. The National Front, a period between 1958 and 1974 in which Colombia's two traditional political parties agreed to alternate in office, represented a response to civil conflict in the 1940s and early 1950s and likely limited Colombia's political development even though the conflict would not have qualified as a "war" under definitions imposing higher thresholds for battle-related deaths.

We distinguish between three types of elections: those held during peacetime, those held while a civil conflict is ongoing, and those held during a recovery phase following the cessation of violence. Our earlier work found that early post-conflict elections are the most fragile from the perspective of preventing conflict recurrence and generating economic recovery.[25] Therefore, we distinguish between each of the first two years of recovery and those that follow. We add this set of indicators for conflict and recovery period to our model of the democratic dividend from elections.

The regression results are clear. The conflict variable has a statistically significant negative effect on the five-year democratic dividend.[26] To ease interpretation we calculate the predicted size of the democratic dividend under conflict. We conceive of conflict as a state into which countries might fall, but not all countries are equally likely to experience the conflict state. For an accurate picture, we need to hold other factors at reasonable values too. What we want to know is how elections held in conflict situations differ from those held in peacetime and so we estimate the substantive effects holding the other factors in our model at values relevant to those states. Figure 7.1 reports the predicted democratic change five years after an election held under peacetime, conflict, and post-conflict states. Peacetime elections, thankfully the vast majority of elections in our sample, do yield a positive democratic dividend, but these gains are wiped out and reversed when elections are held during conflict. In that unfortunate circumstance, the estimated democratic dividend is negative. Switching from a country holding a peacetime election to one holding an election while an active conflict rages results in a quarter-point negative swing over a five year period. Recall that the average country in our dataset experiences essentially no change in its democracy score in the five-year period following an election. Given that perspective, it is not hyperbole to say that conflict is devastating for future democracy and arguably an understatement to say that holding elections while in conflict does not help. The proportion of elections held in conflictual societies also helps us contemplate the substantive import of these results. Nearly one-fifth of elections since 1946 have taken place in countries in the midst of violent civil conflict, a set of elections predicted to engender a negative democratic dividend. The better news is that elections held after conflict has ended can yield more positive effects on future democracy, but only if the international community and local authorities do not rush the election. Elections held in the first year after the conflict do nothing for democracy moving forward. But elections held in the second year or after do generate positive democratic dividends. As mentioned earlier, this is consistent with findings that early post-conflict elections are bad for maintaining peace and generating economic recovery.

One other result from our model is striking. As we have seen consistently throughout this book, compared to elections held in the 1980s, elections held in earlier decades resulted in smaller democratic dividends. But in contrast to earlier analyses, we find that elections held in the electoral boom yielded a greater democratic dividend than those held during the 1980s. This is because we are now explicitly controlling for one of the biggest changes in the profile of election-holding countries over the past seven decades: those that began holding elections in the 1990s were far more likely to do so in the shadow of conflict as the international community adopted a peacebuilding paradigm predicated on the principle of democratic reconstructionism. This positive effect of the 1990s is apparent in Figure 7.1. All the predicted democratic dividends move rightwards towards positive territory. During the electoral boom, conflictual elections no longer harm democracy, but they do nothing to advance it either. Rather, even as the positive effect of peacetime elections grows, the effect of conflict is to nullify these gains. In a sense, this is good news and reflects just

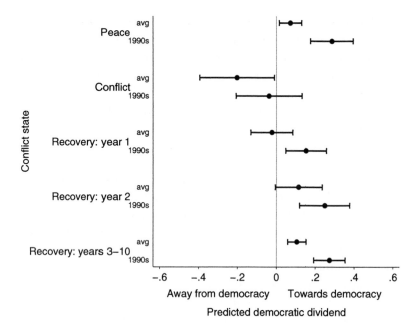

Figure 7.1 Conflict hurts the democratic dividend of elections

how much the international community has done to support fragile countries holding elections but, in another sense, the democratic
opportunity costs of conflict are also stark. While the rest of the
developing world inches towards deeper democracy, countries holding
conflict elections are lucky to hold still.

The negative effect of conflict on the democratic dividend following elections is robust to altering the details of the statistical model
used.[27] One telling finding is that if we shorten the window for democratic change to two years, the effect of conflict is still negative but the
size of the effect is smaller than in the five-year model. This suggests
that things worsen as the negative dynamics inherent in post-conflict
politics ossify. Another interesting finding is that using the Polity measure of democracy, the effects of conflict are much weaker. We suspect
that this is because the Polity score focuses exclusively on the formal
rules governing democracy, which tend to change less, while the UDS
measure captures the smaller creeping changes that undermine democracy. We will provide evidence for this interpretation in the following text.

A final observation about conflictual elections is that they are not very legitimate affairs. In fact, 80 percent of elections held during conflict or during a recovery period do not meet our threshold for being even minimally competitive. When we limit the analysis only to these non-competitive elections, the results grow much more depressing for democracy's prospects. Here, as before, peacetime elections are the best and conflictual elections are bad for future democracy, but, in addition, elections held in the first year following conflict have a huge negative democratic dividend. Holding all else equal, these early post-conflict elections yield a negative effect three times as large as the conflict effect estimated earlier! This adds to the body of evidence militating against holding early elections in post-conflict states with few of the institutions required to ensure genuinely free and fair elections.

What Types of Conflict Harm Democracy the Most?

Conflict hurts democratic change following elections. Our argument is that this negative effect is due to the poor quality of politics and process surrounding elections held in conflictual and immediately post-conflict settings. Understanding why conflict has this negative effect on future democracy is important given the international community's commitment to holding elections in these settings.

Conflict comes in various forms, from military coups pitting a renegade military wing against the state, as in Pinochet's seizure of power in Chile in 1973; to full-scale war, as in Liberia's two civil wars, each of which ended with United Nations Peacekeeping Operations (UNPKOs); to low-intensity insurgency that never metastasizes into a full-fledged war, as in India's Naxalite rebellion. Understanding what types of conflict are especially harmful to democracy's prospects is important to inform policymaking for democracy promotion and peacebuilding in fragile societies.

We first turn to the question of conflict intensity. Civil conflicts vary widely in their brutality. Especially violent civil conflicts that kill thousands, result in widespread abuse of civilians, and envelop the entire country tend to dominate our collective consciousness. Yet only roughly one-third of conflict years reach conventional thresholds for war. Globally there are 1,300 country-years of conflict (i.e., a year in which a particular country experienced a conflict). Half of these saw fewer than 200 combatant deaths; the other half experienced more, with some witnessing deaths by the thousands.[28] The impact on civilians also varies; roughly 42 percent of years with ongoing conflict do not feature one-sided violence against civilians, a figure suggesting that conflict does not necessarily place civilians in widespread, extraordinary danger.[29] The point is that there exists potentially relevant variation in conflict intensity that might inform our understanding of its effects on elections and democracy.

We do not have strong priors about the relationship between conflict intensity and the resulting democratic dividend of elections. On the one hand, it is intuitive that higher-intensity conflicts might especially hurt the conduct of elections. They may more dramatically erode social trust and shorten the time horizons of politicians seeking elective office, driving election winners to cement their hold on power by oppressing election losers. More violent conflicts might convince politicians that violence is the only means to power, weakening elections' ability to sustain democratic change. More violent conflicts are more likely to displace massive numbers of civilians, complicating the process of registering voters. Finally, especially damaging conflicts might create the excuse for politicians to clamp down on civil liberties, retarding democratic progress. Yet, on the other hand, one could argue plausibly that persistent low-level violence is more damaging for long-term trust in governmental institutions and has a withering effect on the social fabric. Such armed violence against the state, even if it does not kill as many people as in other places and times, should also undermine faith in law and order and allow politicians to use armed groups (e.g., party militias) to intimidate opponents.

Three different measures of conflict intensity are available to evaluate these claims. First, the Uppsala Conflict Data Project records the number of *battle deaths*, capturing the intensity of fighting for political power.[30] A related indicator is whether a conflict reached the "war threshold," indicating that it killed 1,000 combatants or more in that year. Lastly, we see if *one-sided violence* makes a difference.[31] The data are available only from 1989 until 2010, which limits our sample to only 711 elections.[32]

Figure 7.2 presents the results. Interestingly enough, lower-intensity conflicts have a worse effect on democracy after elections than do large-scale conflicts. We suspect that this is because low-level conflicts last longer and are less likely to have formal ends such as negotiated settlements or peace agreements, or even outright victories by one side

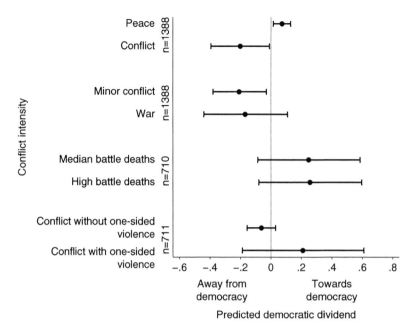

Figure 7.2 Low-level violence harms the democratic dividend of elections

or the other. The underlying issues therefore remain unresolved and societal polarization is higher. The other possible indicators of conflict intensity are less instructive. Using battle deaths as a measure of intensity yields nothing, and neither does the indicator for one-sided violence in conflict.

The answer to our question of what types of conflict are worst for democracy does not appear to lie in their intensity. Conflicts vary not only in intensity, however, but also in kind. Scholars have long categorized conflicts into types along two axes. First, scholars have studied the divergent aims of armed opposition groups. Many seek to violently capture control of the state itself, fighting to reform the nature of the state or at least to seize the material benefits from control of the capital. The Cuban Revolution, in which Fidel Castro's forces fought a successful insurgency against the government of Fulgencio Batista, is a classic example of a war fought to change the nature of the state. Other groups battle to force the central government to accept the secession of a part of the national territory. The Tamil Tigers, for instance, fought a long-running war to allow Tamil-dominant areas to secede from Sri Lanka, ending only in the Tigers' defeat in May 2009. Second, scholars have concentrated on the politics of ethnic violence, differentiating ethnic conflicts from those fought over other incompatibilities. We once again might compare the Cuban Revolution with civil war in Sri Lanka. The latter centered in part on ethnic differences between a Tamil minority and the Sinhalese majority, while the former focused on class differences. Wars fought for control of the central government may also have an ethnic basis, as in the Great Lakes region of East Africa, where overlapping conflicts in Burundi, Rwanda, Uganda, and the Central African Republic have pitted Hutus against Tutsis in efforts to control the state.

We therefore test whether the type of conflict matters for its impact on the democratic dividend from holding elections. Our first test classifies the aims of insurgent groups as either control of the state or secession. We disaggregate conflict using indicators for whether an ongoing conflict was fought over control or territory.[33] The model therefore allows us to compare the impact of each type of conflict directly. Our results indicate that secessionist conflicts are a much more serious danger to elections than those in which a government faces a challenge to its rule at the center.

The findings presented in Figure 7.3 point clearly to the corrosive effects of separatist conflict on elections. Elections held during conflicts over control of the state generate no democratic dividend. Given that peacetime elections yield a positive democratic dividend, this null effect should be interpreted as the opportunity cost of conflict. Yet the 7 percent of elections held during a territorial conflict pay a high price, with a negative democratic dividend almost twice the size of the effect of conflict in general. The same is true of elections occurring in the small minority of cases where both types of conflict exist.

We will return to the question of secessionist conflicts in the text that follows, but first turn to the question of ethnic conflict, using data from the Ethnic Armed Conflict Dataset. This project identifies ethnic civil conflicts by identifying whether the armed opposition stated its aims in ethnic terms, recruited mainly among co-ethnics, and allied with other armed organizations based in the same ethnic group.[34] We once more estimate our workhorse model, only this time using indicators for *Non-ethnic conflict* and *Ethnic conflict*. Here again we have a winner in a dubious competition: ethnic conflicts are worse for democracy, with a large statistically significant negative effect on the

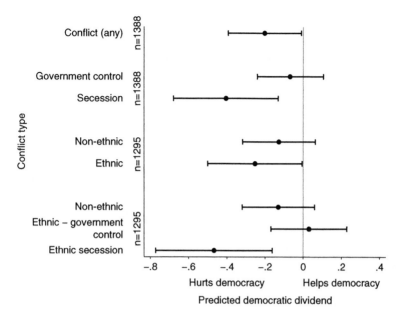

Figure 7.3 Ethnic secession is particularly harmful for the conduct of elections

democratic dividend. Non-ethnic conflicts pay the opportunity cost of conflict, but do not retard the cause of democracy as dramatically as ethnic conflicts.

One issue deserves further thought. Non-ethnic conflicts are almost exclusively fought over control of the center, while ethnic conflicts are mostly secessionist. Do these negative effects compound each other? To find out, we estimate one last model with three mutually exclusive indicators for *non-ethnic conflict, ethnic control of center,* and *ethnic secession.* The answer, unsurprisingly, is that secessionist conflicts that have an ethnic basis are the most devastating for democracy following elections. When elections are held in this situation, democracy deteriorates dramatically. We cannot emphasize this finding enough. Elections can be wonderful things but in an environment of ethnic secessionist movements, campaigns will be rife with ethnic outbidding appeals, low trust, high violence, and little respect for law and order. Little wonder that the data are so unequivocal that such elections will harm rather than aid democracy. Our main conclusion in this section is straightforward: ethnic conflicts, which are nearly completely fought for secessionist reasons, are the primary conflict type that reduces the democratic dividend. Such conflicts are more likely to be characterized by the sort of low-level persistent violence that we also found harms democracy.

Having identified the types of conflict that hurt the democratizing power of elections the most, we turn now to an investigation of why they do so. We begin by considering the kind of elections a country holds in the future. An election today should yield elections tomorrow, preferably ones that show real democratic progress, rather than a slide towards electoral authoritarianism. We focus on three important qualities of a country's next election: electoral instability, including post-election protests and riots, election-related violence, and opposition boycotts; whether the next election featured harassment of the opposition by the incumbent; and whether the next election replaces the incumbent.[35]

We find statistically significant effects for two important factors: elections held during conflict today more likely yield a next election that features post-election violence and boycotts by the political opposition. These are substantively large effects. The probability of an opposition boycott in the next election more than doubles when the current election is held during conflict while the probability of future post-election violence rises from 18 to 26 percent. In other words, the probability of future electoral instability rises when current elections are held in conflict. This electoral instability hurts democracy directly by undermining its legitimacy and by constraining the ability of elected leaders to rule in ways that build democratic institutions.

Democratic Stasis and Insecurity in Post-war Guatemala

The politics of post-war Guatemala illustrate our argument about the nature of elections in conflictual societies. Guatemalans endured a long and brutal civil war, which began in the early 1960s and ended with a peace agreement in 1996. Two hundred thousand people died or vanished in over thirty years of violence, according to a 1999 report of the Comisión para el Esclarecimiento Histórico (Commission for Historical Clarification, or CEH). The origins of the prolonged conflict can be found in the 1954 CIA-backed military coup deposing President Jacobo Árbenz Guzmán who, since his election in 1950, had enacted massive land reforms that threatened the interests of large landowners and foreign corporations. A series of coups and sham elections followed, cementing the military's hold on political power. The first phase of the war consisted of a leftist insurgency similar to those in other Central American societies, as the Partido Guatemalteca del Trabajado (Guatemalan Labor Party, or PGT), formerly the Communist Party, and a group of disaffected army officers known as the Movimiento Revolucionario 13 de Noviembre (Revolutionary Movement November 13, or MR-13) clashed with a series of military governments. These insurgent groups were nearly defeated by the late 1960s, yet were eventually replaced by a series of groups dominated by indigenous Mayans left landless by government repression. The military again relied on indiscriminate violence to battle insurgents, yet the conflict remained a stalemate until a peace process began in the late 1980s. The peace agreement signed in December 1996 in Mexico called for democratization and civilian control over the military.

Political repression and conflict remained intertwined throughout Guatemala's civil war. Successive military regimes banned political parties, executed political opponents, and forcibly displaced civilians from their land. Yet elections still took place, even while Guatemala remained far less than democratic; over a dozen presidential and legislative elections took place between the 1954 coup and the conclusion of the civil war. Arguably these elections and the process of democratization represented a way forward for Guatemala as peace negotiations slowly brought the war to an end in the early 1990s. The inauguration of Jorge Antonio Serrano Elías in 1991 represented the first transition of one civilian government to another, yet Serrano continued human rights abuses and in 1993 attempted a failed self-coup. The self-coup inaugurated a series of positive democratic steps, as a package of constitutional changes and another presidential election in 1995 took place before the conclusion of the peace agreement in December 1996. The peace agreement contained clauses on democracy, indigenous rights, political decentralization, civil-military relations, and land reforms. The United Nations participated in its negotiation and contributed to its enforcement through a peacekeeping operation beginning in 1997.

Guatemala represents a particularly interesting case for our theory, since the conclusion of the civil war in 1996 was inextricably bound up in a process of elections, which served as markers of a transition to fuller democracy. Our cross-national analysis may well qualify Guatemala as a success. It regularly holds competitive elections for national office. Candidates of several different parties have held the presidency and the 2007 elections saw the inauguration of Guatemala's first leftist president since 1954, a symbolic victory given that a military coup against a left-leaning leader incited Guatemala's civil war. Guatemala qualifies as a de jure democracy by any cross-national measure, with nearly twenty years of continued formal democratic experience since the conclusion of its civil war.

Yet beyond formal cross-national markers, just how well does democracy function in post-war Guatemala? Surveys of voters help answer this question. The conclusion of the civil war also fortunately coincided with the initiation of surveys by the Latinobarómetro in Guatemala. The Latinobarómetro conducts roughly twenty thousand interviews in eighteen countries of Latin America each year, asking series, of questions regarding respondents' political, economic, and social views. The project first conducted surveys in Guatemala in 1996, the year of the peace agreement, and has continued until 2010.[36] We fortunately can assess how Guatemalans themselves have regarded democratic progress in their country since the conclusion of war, allowing a more granular view of the success of elections since 1996. Guatemala presents a unique opportunity; we know of no other country that has so continually been surveyed since the conclusion of its civil war for such a long period of time.

We begin our analysis in Figure 7.4, which displays the percentage of Guatemalans who reported either full or partial satisfaction with democracy and a preference for democracy over all other forms of government over time.[37]

Figure 7.4 hints that Guatemalans do not regard their post-war political development quite as rosily as the experts who rate Guatemala's formal democratic institutions. The series on democratic satisfaction supports our idea of contingent legitimacy bestowed by elections. Democratic satisfaction has tended to rise ahead of elections and collapse soon afterwards. We observe a surge in democratic satisfaction after the 1996 peace agreement; democratic satisfaction more than tripled from 18 percent in 1996 to 57 percent by 1998, one year before elections in 1999. That satisfaction quickly fell back to earth, however, dipping to just above 20 percent after the 1999 elections. This pattern repeats itself before the 2003 elections, though less dramatically; democratic satisfaction rose to nearly 40 percent

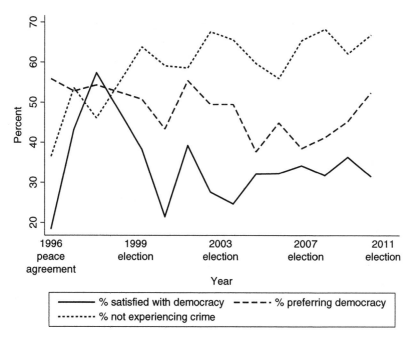

Figure 7.4 Guatemalans' confidence in democracy has not grown since 1996

in 2002, but fell again to the mid-20s by 2004. By 2010, one year before elections in 2011, only about one-third of Guatemalans expressed satisfaction with the state of their democracy. The proportion of Guatemalans who voiced an unqualified preference for democratic governance, meanwhile, fell steadily during the post-war period until the 2007 elections, from a high in the mid-50s to just below 40 percent, though it has since recovered.

This piece of evidence regarding Guatemala's post-war history does little to convince us that elections have successfully convinced citizens that democracy functions well and is the best means by which to govern. Rather than a slowly rising proportion of Guatemalans voicing faith in democracy, we instead observe democratic stasis and the declining ability of elections to raise Guatemalans' faith.[38] What explains this gap between the cross-national ratings of democracy and Guatemalans' own understanding of how democracy works in their society? Figure 7.4 indicates one possibility – physical security. For each survey year, we record the proportion of citizens reporting that they were *not* the victim of a crime, which we consider a proxy for citizens' physical security. This proportion predictably increased dramatically between 1996 and 2000, as the military retreated to the barracks and insurgents disarmed; while less than 40% of Guatemalans met this minimal standard of physical security in 1996, over 60% did by 2000. Yet this is shockingly low for a putatively well-functioning democracy. In any year in the last twenty since the peace agreement was signed, fully 40 percent of Guatemalans report having been a victim of crime. Put differently, a slightly larger proportion of Guatemalans report being the victim of a crime than report satisfaction with democracy!

Surveys of Guatemala's post-war voters suggest strongly that they feel physically vulnerable, even many years after the war ended. This finding would not surprise observers of Guatemalan post-war history. Legislation passed in 1996 declared a general amnesty for nearly all political crimes committed during the war, allowing many involved in human rights abuses to escape scrutiny.[39] According to one report in *The New Yorker,* the conclusion of a formal peace agreement allowed elements of the state's security apparatus to evolve into criminal organizations that engage in kidnapping and drug trafficking.[40] Guatemala also suffers from contagion from violence in Mexico and Honduras. The grim consequence has been Guatemala's perennial ranking as one of the world's most crime-ridden societies. Nor has the Guatemalan state proved capable of reducing this insecurity. Nearly 98 percent of violent crimes in Guatemala escape prosecution, despite the election in 2011 of President Otto Pérez Molina, who committed the Guatemalan military to restoring security.[41]

Guatemala is hardly unique in the perpetuation of cycles of violence after the conclusion of civil war. In nearby El Salvador, gang violence reached proportions that required a truce sponsored by the government and the Catholic Church in 2012, a truce that has still seen eleven people killed per day since 2013. Roughly sixty thousand El Salvadorans belong to one of several powerful gangs involved in the truce.[42] Indeed, every society in Central America has experienced an uptick in homicides since 1999, even in countries that have ended long-standing civil conflicts.[43] The diffusion of small arms after civil wars exacerbates the problem; the failure of post-war demobilization programs after Mozambique's civil war allowed small arms to spread, worsening crime not only in Mozambique, but also in its neighbors.[44]

This brief discussion suggests that the shadow of civil conflict might constrain democratic progress through physical insecurity. This accords with the World Bank's assessment that a "legacy of mistrust" in societies affected by violence reduces the impact of public programs.[45] This continuing threat to public peace erodes citizens' trust in democracy, an erosion that elections, no matter how formally honest, cannot overcome. Peace agreements or the victory of one side or another bring wars to a formal end. And the largely rapid holding of elections and formal functioning of democracy also may take hold in post-conflict countries. Yet these formal achievements may not improve the actual lives of citizens, who continue to suffer insecurity born of crime years after civil wars end. A first postwar election might bring a surge of optimism for the future among citizens weary of years of violence, of course. Yet the reality of continuing crime and insecurity and economic stagnation may weaken their faith in these possibilities. Our argument about the ephemeral nature of contingent legitimacy applies especially well; elections alone cannot sustain citizens' hope for democracy without delivering material gains.

A preliminary test of this intuition is supportive. Across all Latin American countries, we calculate the proportion of citizens reporting satisfaction with democracy by whether or not they have experienced a crime for each of year of the survey beginning in 2001 and ending in 2010. Figure 7.5 reveals that, in every year, secure citizens are more likely to report democratic satisfaction than are insecure citizens, a difference that is statistically significant in five of the ten years for which we have survey data.[46] These results strongly suggest a means by which civil war impedes the ability of elections to foment democracy; continued physical insecurity impedes democratic faith amongst citizens, even as the formal practice of democracy continues unabated.

Discussion

Democracy and violence have a surprisingly intimate relationship. Each of Samuel Huntington's waves of democracy involved organized political violence. The First Wave featured the French Revolution, American Revolution, and wars of independence in Spanish America.

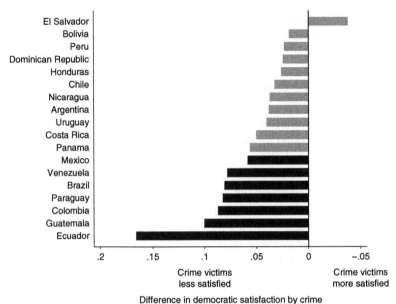

Figure 7.5 Latin Americans report far more confidence in democracy when they are not victims of crime

The Second Wave arose from the ashes of World War II and liberation struggles against colonial powers, bringing democracy to West Germany, India, Israel, and a host of other countries. Democracy's Third Wave has been no different. Many of the late arrivals to the Third Wave held their first elections in the shadow of violent civil conflict, particularly after the early 1990s. The societies of El Salvador, Liberia, Serbia, Sri Lanka, and Timor-Leste (to name a handful) differ on many dimensions, but share the basic challenge of building democracy either during or in the aftermath of violence since the dawn of the electoral boom.

Do violent civil conflicts limit the democratizing power of elections? Our answer is an unqualified yes. Violent civil conflict undermines election winners' ability to build legitimacy through respecting democratic norms and providing public goods. Officeholders during civil conflict lack unfettered access to broad swaths of their national territory and whatever fiscal space might have been earmarked for building clinics and schools is more likely to be spent on military weaponry. Their best means of retaining office are likely to be violent repression, private goods to key constituents, and democratic chicanery. Perhaps many incumbents seeking re-election in such environments would prefer to govern differently, but they do not have the option of being prime minister of Japan or Switzerland. They must play the hand they are dealt. Elections during conflict therefore bring to power leaders who possess little power to deepen democracy, and instead might reverse it. The same might be said of elections held in fragile societies still reeling from war, since the political, social, and economic consequences of civil conflict far outlast the ostensible end of the conflict. Elections thus held years after the shooting stops may still take place in an environment characterized by ethnic enmity, economic stagnation, large refugee populations, new political rules, and widespread disease. Elections thus may prove unable to promote democracy for years after a conflict ends.

Our cross-national statistical results offer robust empirical support for this argument. Elections held during civil conflict are especially bad for future democracy. Elections held very early in the recovery or post-conflict period are also problematic, but elections held later in the recovery period aid a rebound in democracy. The negative effect of conflict appears to be quite general and a disaggregated analysis does not show strong differences between ethnic and non-ethnic conflicts or secessionist and control-of-center conflicts. The most robust result from our effort to disaggregate conflict is that persistent low-level conflict is the most damaging to democracy. The overall finding of a negative effect of conflict on election's democratic dividend is consistent with previous research on post-conflict elections that finds elections held soon after conflicts in nascent democracies result in faster conflict recurrence and slower economic reconstruction than those held later. Of course, our analysis here differs in the sets of comparisons it makes. Here, we are comparing elections held during peacetime with those held during or soon after conflict, and we compare not the odds of further conflict or economic recovery, but democratic change. These findings taken jointly suggest most clearly the importance of time: post-conflict democratization can work, but attempting to make the transition too rapidly can unravel a fragile peace and undermine economic recovery. Patience is what is most needed in these difficult situations.

Four findings regarding the impact of civil conflict are worth high-lighting in conclusion. First, ethnic conflicts pose a graver threat to elections than non-ethnic conflicts. Second, ethnic conflicts fought over secessionist goals are more likely to disturb electoral success than those fought for other reasons. Third, elections held during conflict are likely to be followed by violent elections in the future. Finally, elections held in the shadow of conflict yield smaller advances in civil liberties and political rights. These findings help us understand the circumstances under which conflictual elections might yield especially weak democratic change and should provide policymakers with clues for how best to structure their interventions in these troubled settings.

Our discussion of Guatemala's post-civil war experience also reveals two patterns worth noting. First, survey data suggest that Guatemalans were barely more confident in the state of their democracy in 2010 than they were in 1996. They have tended to feel a surge of democratic optimism in advance of elections and then lose that optimism in the first couple years after them. This provides evidence in favor of our broader argument that elections provide a short grace period of contingent legitimacy, but the everyday challenges of life in post-war Guatemala have tended to swamp such feelings and return democratic optimism to pre-election levels. There is little evidence of growing democratic confidence in Guatemala. Elections in post-war Guatemala may have produced the practice of formal democracy, but Guatemalans themselves feel little connection to that practice. Second, continuing physical insecurity has contributed to this trend. For the roughly one-third of Guatemalans who report being the victims of crime, their physical security remains at risk. We find a large and significant democratic optimism gap between Guatemalans who have and have not been the victims of crime. This suggests a larger pattern that we could not test directly with our cross-national data but that is consistent with our finding about the dangers of persistent low-level conflict; elections in post-war states may produce formal democratic practice (e.g., elections, parties, etc.), but they are animated by disaffected citizens whose lives can scarcely be called "post-war." Crime and physical insecurity after civil wars represent a major barrier to democratic consolidation in these societies.

As we write these words in March 2016, civil war continues in Colombia, where talks have made slow progress towards a final peace agreement over two decades after Colombians wrote a new constitution while violence raged; in Syria, where an initially peaceful uprising against dictatorship led to a brutal conflict that now involves several of its neighbors, not to mention Russia; and in Somalia, where a fragile elected government continues to rely on its neighbors to fight a Islamist insurgency. Each of these countries bears witness to the connection between civil conflict and democracy. We have suggested here that conflict disrupts the link between elections and the process of democratization. Yet, as we have already seen, the international community has developed a range of tools – disarmament, demobilization, and reintegration (DDR) programs for ex-combatants, specialized packages of foreign aid and technical advice, UNPKOs, etc. – designed to help war-torn countries end their conflicts and transition to a more peaceful state. We next turn to the question of whether these programs, as well as those meant to address weak democratic institutions, make a difference.

PART III

Democracy Promotion for the Twenty-first Century

8 | Democracy Promotion for the Twenty-first Century

National elections are a signal event in all countries and deservedly so. They represent the assertion of popular sovereignty over political elites in a manner unimaginable to our near ancestors. Even in countries with longer experiences with popular elections, it is only in the most recent decades that principles of universal suffrage have been protected and enforced. Today's elections are the sole source of legitimacy for rulers around the world. A mere handful of states are yet to hold elections for national office, but resist only at the cost of international isolation and domestic protest. The rise of elections as a means not only for choosing political leaders, but also for building democracy, has been one of the major political changes of the last fifty years (and, by extension, of recent human history). Yet facts are stubborn things – even as cleaner, more transparent elections have spread to all corners of the globe, their capacity for promoting democracy has diminished. Rather, as we have shown throughout this book, elections in the developing world have all too often either hurt the cause of democracy or, at best, contributed little to its advancement. This is especially true precisely where we most dearly wish elections to succeed: in societies with long histories of authoritarianism and little state capacity.

Commentators from *The Economist* to Larry Diamond increasingly worry about a democratic backlash worldwide. The disappointments of the Arab Spring tempered electoral enthusiasm, if any still existed after watching the unraveling of Iraq and Afghanistan. The events unfolding in Hungary – where Prime Minister Viktor Orbán has publicly denounced liberal norms in favor of an illiberal state while winning his third consecutive election in 2014 – bode ill for the health of liberal democracy in that member of the European Union and NATO, both of which are considered democratic bastions.[1]

Our pessimistic findings notwithstanding, we come not to bury elections but rather to praise them. For all their limitations, there are no politically feasible alternatives to elections as a peaceful means for choosing legitimate leadership. The proverbial genie has escaped the bottle and alternatives to mass suffrage – whether apartheid-like restrictions on suffrage, military dictatorship, or rule by clerical fiat – are normatively beyond the pale. Too often, however, the focus of international democracy promotion actors has been on the election as a solitary event, rather than on the political-economic milieu in which election winners must rule. Where these contexts are deficient, the reality of electoral politics creates perverse incentives that warp the country's democratic trajectory. The consequence has been a pro-liferation of "authoritarian elections" called by "pseudo-democrats" in which election fraud and opposition harassment are the dom-inant campaign strategies. A sincere effort to promote democracy requires grappling with the structural inadequacies that undermine elections and thereby democracy. What is needed is a rethinking of the democracy promotion enterprise that goes beyond the current emphasis on elections as distinct events divorced from democracy; to save elections, we require a holistic analysis of their structural impediments.

Our theory of legitimacy stocks, flows, and leaks accomplishes these goals. It suggests a new interpretation of democracy promotion and novel empirical means for its evaluation. Our logic is simple: democ-racy promotion must augment low stocks of legitimacy if it is to suc-ceed. The electoral boom spread elections to places with low stocks of legitimacy or persistent leaks. Efforts at democracy promotion should help plug those leaks and refill low stores of legitimacy. In places with weak democratic institutions, democracy promotion should enhance their legitimacy in order to forestall post-election democratic col-lapse. In fiscally impoverished countries, democracy promotion should enhance the powers of governance of beleaguered election winners. In conflictual societies, democracy promotion should focus on promot-ing security for all citizens and augmenting trust between erstwhile enemies. Our framework suggests that if international interventions cannot augment low stocks, they will fail to promote democracy. This is normatively attractive too, since it requires that democracy promo-tion efforts bolster the political fortunes of citizens trapped in difficult circumstances.

This chapter offers a new analysis of democracy promotion. We ask two questions. First, does the use of a given strategy reduce the constraining effect of democratic inexperience, limited fiscal space, and conflict? Second, does democracy promotion work best where structural constraints are tightest or does it only benefit elections in already fortuitous circumstances? We do not endeavor to provide a comprehensive assessment of democracy promotion, but instead focus on whether it supports successful elections in challenging circumstances.

Where possible, we build on our workhorse statistical model used throughout the book, but with a new twist. Each of the statistical models we present here interacts one of the three structural variables we have analyzed previously with an indicator for the presence of a particular kind of democracy promotion. The interaction term can be interpreted directly to reveal if the democratic dividend of elections increases where we have the right interventions in place. Further, our model tells us the extent to which international interventions "subsidize" structural deficiencies, all else equal, and whether they have their biggest impact where the structural deficiencies are the deepest. In each case, we match the intervention to the structural problem. We expect that foreign aid, for example, is most crucial to politicians where fiscal space is most constrained. Importantly, we do not always have cross-sectional time-series data for all theoretically interesting democracy promotion strategies. Given that it is beyond the scope of this chapter to collect such data, our discussion will at points necessarily be more speculative. Our hope is that the findings we report in the following text below will motivate further research seeking to improve the design of democracy promotion interventions.

We start this discussion by considering how we might compensate for the lack of democratic-institutional stock, given its importance for the quality and efficacy of elections in the developing world. Many democracy promotion strategies should be re-interpreted as attempting to do just this but without the benefit of the theoretical framework presented here to guide their efforts. Second, we ask if official development assistance (ODA) can compensate for the lack of fiscal space. Considerable attention has been paid to the effects of official development assistance on economic growth and various human development outcomes; however, we seek to refocus the discussion by considering its effects on democratic development. Finally, we ask if UN peacekeeping missions can ameliorate the negative effects of prior civil conflicts on democratic change following elections.

Taken as a whole, our results are encouraging and indicate several strategies that help bolster the democratic dividend of elections. A point worth underscoring at the outset is that, in several cases, our analysis shows that whether interventions succeed is timing-dependent. For instance, sending election monitors and making aid threats conditional on democratic performance do increase pro-democratic change following elections, but only in new democracies. Once a country has been a democracy for a few years, such efforts are less successful. This is relevant for the EU's response to democratic backsliding in Hungary. A second point to keep in mind is that null results need not always mean that the intervention did not work, but could in fact be evidence that not enough was tried in the first place. International aid, for example, does not augment sufficiently the limited fiscal space of states; more aid is not correlated with better post-election democratic performance, but a closer look suggests that inadequate levels of aid, coupled with how aid is delivered, might well be the reason for the poor democratic performance of aid. In post-conflict situations, our results make clear that the shift in focus to peacebuilding following Boutros-Ghali's *An Agenda for Peace* has paid dividends. Elections held where UN peacekeeping missions had an explicit election mandate yield a positive democratic dividend. We conclude with a discussion of the key questions for future research on democracy promotion.

Democratic Inexperience and Democracy Promotion

Chapter 5 documents a pernicious catch-22: countries with little democratic-institutional stock will find it hardest to build that stock through elections. In the West, the solution to this conundrum largely involved incubating institutions and regulating competition over decades and centuries, often as women, minorities, and men lacking property were denied the vote.[2] Even if we disregard the manifest injustice of such a road to liberal democracy, that path is closed to the contemporary world, where international norms and the demands of restive citizens demand mass-suffrage elections early in the process of democratization.

A generation of democracy promoters representing Western governments and non-governmental organizations (NGOs) have crafted a wide range of initiatives designed to support liberal government.

They have trained opposition groups, tutored election commissioners, and donated funds to NGOs. We regard such efforts as an attempt to supplement the meager democratic institutional stocks upon which elections must rest. We discuss four such efforts here: election monitors, and three elements of democracy assistance – US democracy aid, threats to reduce ODA, and aid to political parties.

Election Monitors

Election monitors are a ubiquitous presence in elections in the developing world. Delegations of observers from other countries descend on election-holding societies to examine voter lists, visit polling places, and issue long reports on elections. Susan Hyde argues that inviting monitors to assess elections has become an international norm that constrains even less-than-democratic incumbents.[3] Three of every five elections in the developing world during the electoral boom were monitored, versus only one in ten before it. Recent scholarship has recognized this rising importance. Judith Kelley goes so far as to state that "international election monitoring has become the primary tool of democracy promotion."[4] Both Hyde and Kelley have analyzed the impact of monitors on the quality of elections. These analyses have advanced our understanding of whether monitors encourage the participation of otherwise skeptical opposition groups, reduce incumbents' vote share, shift how incumbents cheat, and generally improve election quality.[5] Our question here, however, is a different one: do election monitors expand the democratic dividend in the years after elections, especially those held in countries with little democratic-institutional stock?

To find out, we test to see if the effect of democratic experience on the democratic dividend of elections differs depending on whether or not election monitors were present. Put differently, our model allows us to test whether election observers boost the democratic dividend and whether their ability to do so depends on democratic stock. Figure 8.1 highlights three patterns in this analysis.[6] First, election observers have a positive impact on the democratic dividend in countries with no democratic experience. Substantively speaking, it is a very large effect; our model predicts that a typical country in sub-Saharan Africa with no previous democratic experience holding an election would actually see its democracy score decline.

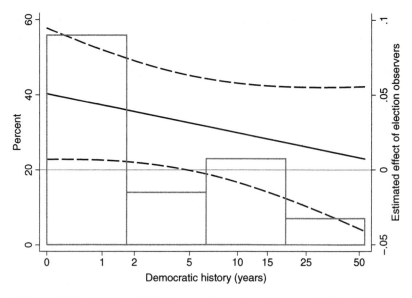

Figure 8.1 The democratizing impact of election observers declines in countries with more democratic experience

But the presence of election monitors turns the democratic dividend positive.

Second, the presence of election monitors softens the constraints of democratic inexperience. The impact of democratic experience falls by half and becomes statistically insignificant when monitors are present.

Third, the liberalizing impact of election monitors declines with the democratic experience of the country in question. Election observers have a large and positive impact on the democratic dividend from elections in societies with little democratic experience, as we have already seen. Yet this impact declines as democratic experience deepens such that election monitors no longer promote post-election democratic change once a country has surpassed five years of past democratic experience, all else equal. This finding is consistent with our theory of stocks of legitimacy. Election monitors have their largest impact in low-legitimacy contexts, where their expertise in election administration can supplement inexperienced institutions and assuage distrustful politicians' concerns. They have less of an impact where politicians more readily understand and accept the rules of the political game and election administration has improved.

This positive effect of election observers in new democracies holds only when we estimate a model of short-term democratic change in which our dependent variable records the two-year change in a country's democracy score. The results do not hold when we seek to explain longer-term democratic change (i.e., over five years from the election). This suggests that election monitors exert a temporary change in the politics of democratizing countries. Their presence shifts the dynamics of democratization for two years, but after that point, other forces largely dictate democratic change. Just as we found in our analysis of the effect of electoral quality in Chapter 4, electoral monitors may open a short-term window of liberalization by enhancing electoral integrity, but after that point, other interventions are necessary to sustain democratic progress.

Our finding that the impact of election monitors on the democratic dividend from elections dissipates as countries accumulate democratic experience suggests that monitoring organizations such as the Carter Center might be well-served by reducing their presence in more democratically experienced countries. Election monitors observe 70 percent of elections in countries with fewer than five years of democratic experience, but continue to observe 59 percent of elections in countries over that threshold and roughly half of elections held in countries with twenty or more years of experience. Election observers actually monitored fourteen elections since 1988 in societies with more than fifty years of democratic experience, including Costa Rica's 2006 and 2010 elections and Italy's 2008 elections. A typical election observer mission can cost around $3.7 million; organizations engaged in election observation therefore spent approximately $52 million on these missions. Our theory and findings imply that election observers might do more to promote democracy by concentrating more resources on countries early in their processes of democratization, while modifying their programming in more experienced countries. We do not advocate an abandonment of election observation in the latter set, but rather a shift towards a lower-cost set of programs tailored to the divergent needs of more consolidated democracies.

Democracy Assistance

Election observation may represent the most high-profile form of democracy promotion in countries with little democratic legitimacy, but it is hardly the only intervention attempted by the international community, particularly in the West. The United States Agency for International Development (USAID), for instance, touts democracy as one of its major goals, alongside economic growth, poverty eradication, and education. Within its sector focused on democracy, governance, and human rights, USAID describes programs dedicated to building civil society, ensuring free and fair elections, promoting transparency, and protecting human rights.[7] That USAID initiated and dramatically expanded this aid program just as the electoral boom began should not surprise us. Between 1990 and 2004, democracy aid rose from around $100 million to nearly $900 million; the proportion of total USAID assistance taken up by democracy and governance programs rose from 2 to 12 percent. The official aid agency of the United States quickly added democracy promotion to its core mission.

Does such democracy aid work? Steven Finkel, Aníbal Pérez-Linan, and Mitchell Seligson conclude that it does, finding that democracy and governance aid supports democratic change in its recipients.[8] Simone Dietrich and Joseph Wright find that democracy aid encourages transitions to multiparty democracy, but does not increase support for opposition parties in elections.[9] We ask a slightly different question: does democracy assistance amplify the democratic dividend from elections? Our conceptual emphasis on democratic experience suggests it should. Democracy aid should help to improve election administration, strengthen the rule of law, and encourage respect for civil rights. In other words, it seeks to deepen democratic-institutional stock in the short-term, substituting for the decades- or even centuries-long process of building stock through trial and error and the development of democratic norms. We test this expectation by inserting a measure of outlays from USAID's democracy and governance program into our model.[10] We also create an interaction term of this measure with our measure of democratic experience. Our expectations echo those for our analysis of election monitors: democracy aid should have its largest impact in countries with little democratic experience.

As anticipated, democracy aid bolsters the democratic dividend from elections in low-experience countries, but has little impact in more experienced countries (see Figure 8.2). The impact in low-democratic-experience countries is statistically significant at the 90 percent confidence level until a country reaches two years of democratic experience. Past this point, the effect is indistinguishable from

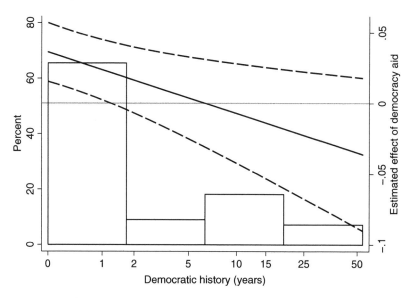

Figure 8.2 The impact of democracy and governance aid is positive for low-democratic-experience countries

zero. But perhaps this decline in the impact of democracy aid should not worry us: as we observed in Chapter 5 and can see again in Figure 8.2, the distribution of democratic experience in Sub-Saharan Africa is highly right-skewed – most countries lack any experience whatsoever.

Our analysis suggests that as countries accumulate democratic experience, further democracy and governance aid does not have a substantial effect on electoral success. This finding implies that USAID should change the emphasis of its programming in countries with more democratic experience. We do find a strong statistically significant relationship in our data between democratic experience and democracy aid: countries with more democratic experience receive less democracy aid. USAID sends its democracy and governance aid to where the democratic-institutional stock is at its shallowest; this is a sensible policy. But the policy also means that USAID's political principals need to be patient when assessing results. Investing in the hardest cases is the right thing to do but also means that we need to be realistic and patient in waiting for results.

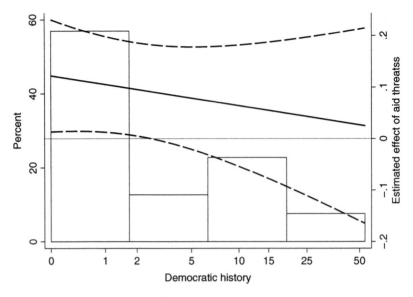

Figure 8.3 Aid threats more likely accomplish their goal of promoting post-election democratic change in countries with less democratic experience

Democracy aid helps elections in countries with little past experience succeed in promoting democracy. But can threats to withdraw aid galvanize democratic change after elections? By threatening to withdraw valuable aid flows, Western governments have tried to encourage incumbents to make good on their promises to hold free and fair elections and simultaneously to embolden democracy activists and opposition forces.

Do such threats actually work? They might if they discourage incumbents from engaging in fraud and post-election shenanigans, particularly when weak public institutions might fail to stop them. We test this possibility with data from NELDA, capturing whether a threat to cut off foreign aid occurred during the electoral process. We interact this measure with our measure of democratic experience to examine whether aid threats do less to encourage successful elections in more democratically experienced countries. We graph our results in Figure 8.3, which plots the impact of aid threats across levels of democratic experience and also graphs the distribution of democratic experience in Sub-Saharan Africa in the 2000s. We find evidence that aid threats do expand the post-election democratic dividend for countries with no democratic experience; the effect is positive, large, and statistically significant. However, the impact of aid threats is no longer statistically reliable once democratic experience exceeds roughly three years. Thus, here again the policy implication is clear: aid threats work best when countries are in their earliest stages of developing their democratic institutions. Rather than coddle such countries, democracy promoters must be willing to use threats to cut off aid at the earliest signs of possible malfeasance. Once countries get past those early days when they are most dependent on international assistance, democracy promoters lose their leverage rapidly.

Democratic experience matters for the success of elections but getting the necessary experience is no mean task. To help aspiring democracies get over the initial hump, democracy promoters have developed a range of possible interventions. Our results suggest that these interventions can and do work but with two important caveats. First, all the strategies surveyed – monitors, aid, and threats to cut off aid – work best in the very first few years of a country's democratic trajectory. Second, these interventions are most effective over the short run. When we extend the window over which to assess their effect to five years post-election, we find no results in any of these cases. This is consistent with our contingent legitimacy argument. The interventions discussed here are principally aimed at enhancing the integrity of the electoral process. Better elections are good for democracy but only to an extent. They get the country on the right path, but whether the progress towards better democracy is sustainable depends on whether deeper structural issues can also be resolved.

A good example of such a structural issue is the weak state of political parties in most young democracies. Scholars of comparative politics have long recognized the importance of political parties to stable democratic politics. Samuel Huntington argued that political parties represented the key organization for creating "political order in changing societies."[11] The analysis of political parties continues to unite scholars today. Scholars of African politics have studied the emergence of party systems in Africa in great detail. The emergence of opposition parties has especially preoccupied scholars who see such organizations as essential to democratic transitions. Adrienne LeBas, for example, explains their emergence as a function of past patterns of authoritarian rule. Shaheen Mozaffar and J. R. Scarritt agree, arguing that a pattern of short-lived political parties owes much to Sub-Saharan Africa's authoritarian past.[12]

The process of democratization by elections thus occurs in part because elections should encourage an opposition to coalesce, especially in the form of strong political parties. Thomas Carothers states the problem plainly: "The troubled state of political parties in new or struggling democracies is a central challenge to democratization."[13] Do international interventions to foster the development of opposition parties help this process? Carothers studies this question carefully, concluding that aid from Western countries likely has had only a limited impact on the development of robust opposition parties.[14] He also recommends changes to aid to political parties, including more rigorous program evaluations. Such evaluations have thus far eluded the grasp of experts in comparative democratization. We still lack data on aid to political parties in foreign countries, which often is given by a wide constellation of Western governments, political parties, and NGOs, making systematic data collection difficult. This is a worthy effort for future data collection.

Can International Aid Bolster Fiscal Space?

Chapter 6 argued that the lack of fiscal resources inhibits incumbents from pursuing policy initiatives that improve citizens' economic lives. Where public resources remain meager, leaders focus instead on cheaper projects that can be targeted at ethnic kin or favored localities, not to mention strategies of electoral manipulation, to secure re-election. Our evidence in Chapter 6 supports that contention. We find that elections held in countries and years where fiscal space is more ample yielded larger democratic dividends. This result holds even though we control for the country's economic growth, level of development, the occurrence of economic crisis, as well as the economy's dependence on oil rents as a source of income. *Ceteris paribus*, having higher tax revenues makes elections more democratically fruitful. The problem facing new democracies is less an overly burdensome state, than one that lacks tax revenues. This tax "deficit" is likely to be exacerbated in coming years by the pressures of globalization that make traditional sources of revenues such as tariffs less feasible.[15] This continues a pattern of declining tax revenues per capita around the world.

For many governments, official development assistance (ODA) – foreign aid, in other words – remains a vital supplement to inadequate fiscal resources. Yet such aid does not lack for detractors, precisely for this reason. For political economists, foreign aid represents a type of "found" money that corrodes democratic accountability and public policymaking.[16] When rulers have little need for citizens' money, they tend to have little need for their voice, either. We do not deny these criticisms of foreign aid, though we emphasize that the preponderance of evidence is actually much more positive about aid's long-term macroeconomic effects than its critics admit.[17] Nonetheless our brief here is narrower. When fiscal space through taxation is limited, does aid serve to augment governments' spending ability? If so, if aid allows governments to provide public goods that bolster the state's legitimacy, might it not bolster the democratic dividend from elections?

To answer these questions, we gather data on ODA inflows to developing countries. We measure these in per capita terms to capture the size of these flows and to make them directly comparable to the fiscal space measure introduced and utilized in Chapter 6. We prefer the per capita metric to the share of GDP or share of budget alternatives that are better suited to capture relative dependence on aid. We interact the per capita aid measure with the fiscal space measure and add this interaction term to our statistical model. If aid plays a fiscal-space-expanding role, the interaction term's coefficient should be negatively signed and statistically significant. This would tell us that increases in aid boost the democratic dividend at low levels of fiscal space, but that the marginal effect of increasing aid diminishes as fiscal space increases. Put simply, aid matters most when governments are broke, and least when they are flush.

Our analysis does not support this positive conjecture of aid's possible effects on elections. The interaction term is not statistically significant. Calculating the marginal effect does not alter this conclusion: as Figure 8.4 shows, at no level of fiscal space observed in our sample does aid have a statistically significant effect on post-election democratic change. Given that aid is a major policy mechanism for providing fiscal support to developing countries, this null finding begs explanation.

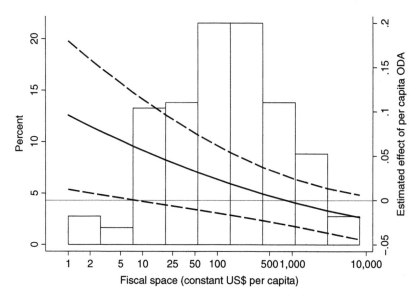

Figure 8.4 ODA does not increase the democratic dividend of elections

The most obvious explanation for the lack of an aid-induced democratic effect is that aid's critics are correct – aid creates perverse
incentives for governments to reform their tax administrations and
therefore undermines the government–citizen accountability relationship. Governments might simply use aid to buy support.[18] Deborah
Bräutigam and Stephen Knack argue that higher aid levels create a
collective-action problem that reduces tax collections and lowers the
quality of governance.[19] Our analysis is insufficient to substantiate
such criticisms, though the null finding certainly is consistent with
it. We will return later to a further consideration of the implications
of this criticism for democracy promotion, but for now consider two
other possible explanations for the null effect.

The first alternative interpretation is that aid levels, rather than
being too high, are in fact inadequate to compensate for the low
levels of fiscal space available to developing countries. Consider Figure 8.5. In all regions other than Sub-Saharan Africa, levels of aid are
considerably lower than tax revenues; in Sub-Saharan Africa, aid def-
initely plays a major supplementary role and, in per capita terms, is
almost equivalent to tax revenues. Yet even when aid is high, the combined fiscal space provided by aid and taxes is still very low. Compare

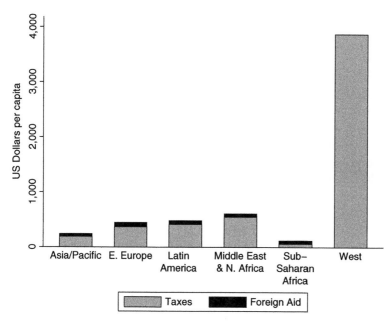

Figure 8.5 Aid and tax revenues around the world

the combined height of the bars in all of the world's regions to that of the West alone and the gulf in resources available to governments is apparent. There are many problems with aid, but one could argue quite persuasively, as Jeffrey Sachs has, that the real problem is that the aid given to poor countries is too little to be helpful rather than too much.[20]

A second alternative explanation concerns the delivery mechanisms of aid. An important concern for Western aid donors is the absorptive capacity of recipient countries. Low capacity means that a lot of the aid given is wasted or stolen due to inefficient procedures, rampant corruption, and shoddy implementation. Increasingly, therefore, donor governments choose to bypass the state agencies in recipient countries and to give the aid directly to civil society and private sector organizations that can demonstrate a credible commitment to utilizing aid effectively.[21] This strategy allows donors to exercise greater scrutiny over the use of their money and to demand higher auditing standards. From the perspective of the donor, this bypass strategy can make a lot of sense, especially if it is used to bypass the worst-governed state governments. From the perspective of citizens in recipient states, bypassing might also be a good strategy if it means that access to medicine, healthcare, and education, for example, are no longer mediated by inefficient and corrupt state institutions. But from the long-term perspective of building state institutions that have some claim to legitimacy, bypassing might be harmful, as citizens come to associate well-functioning public goods with non-state providers and the state with aspects that either perform poorly by comparison (e.g., state hospitals versus an NGO-run health clinic) or that are coercive (e.g., the police). Testing this conjecture is beyond the scope of this book, though experimental work by Simone Dietrich and Matthew Winters suggests the concern is not unfounded. Further, other research by Dietrich suggests that this trade-off is understood by donor agencies themselves. The French officials Dietrich interviews explicitly justify their preference for giving directly to governments rather than bypassing them in terms of wanting to help build stronger state institutions in recipient countries.[22]

There exist plausible and often contradictory explanations for why foreign aid does not yield a positive democratic dividend. It is worth recalling that our analysis mentioned earlier does indicate that democratic aid and aid conditionality can at times induce positive change; the null result in this section concerns development aid generally rather than aid targeted at elections. Nonetheless, regardless of one's preferred explanation, the crisis of low fiscal resources remains.[23] Aid is, at best, a short-run fix for low fiscal space. The real solutions to the fiscal crisis facing developing countries must come from tax reform and capacity-building that allow governments to raise revenues sufficient to meet their governance challenges. Forging such a path requires difficult political choices, and democracy promoters must embrace the challenge by partnering with international financial institutions to help countries identify both the technical solutions and the political will necessary for tax reform. This, in turn, will necessitate a different organizational model in Washington, DC (or London or Paris or Brussels for that matter). Not far from our offices, it is commonplace for discussions about economic reform and assistance to occur at the World Bank and the IMF entirely separately from conversations at USAID and the US State Department about elections in the very same countries. Democratic consolidation following elections requires those who wish to help to embrace a better coordinated and holistic approach that does not ignore the messiness of real-world politics.

Conflict and the Power of UN Peacekeeping Operations

Our prior research on elections and democratization in post-conflict societies found that hastily held post-conflict elections in new democracies raise the risk of conflict recurrence. These findings echo a wider literature on peacebuilding that generally has emphasized the dangers of elections and democratization in post-war countries. Aila Matanock, in contrast, argues that peace agreements that enshrine the participation of combatant groups in post-war politics may lead to a more durable peace. Her research more broadly raises the question of whether international interventions aimed at building peace may also boost the democratic dividend from elections.[24]

One such intervention has received consistent attention from scholars of war and peace: United Nations Peacekeeping Operations (UNPKOs). The end of the Cold War opened new possibilities for the UN to engage in international diplomacy and peacebuilding, as the end of Cold War competition removed roadblocks to action in the Security Council. Secretary-General Boutros Boutros-Ghali clearly grasped these new opportunities in *An Agenda for Peace*, which dedicated the UN to conflict prevention and post-war peacebuilding. The growing number of UNPKOs represented a practical outgrowth of these momentous changes. Only eleven UNPKOs were mandated between the end of World War II and 1987. That number grew fivefold to fifty-five during the period between 1988 and 2011. UNPKOs could be found in Sierra Leone, El Salvador, the former Yugoslavia, and beyond. UNPKOs not only expanded their international presence, but also the scope of their missions.[25] They continued to monitor ceasefires, as they had before the late 1980s, but now supervised the demobilization of soldiers, trained police forces, and in extreme cases, as in East Timor and Bosnia-Herzegovina, fully assumed the powers of the state.

UNPKOs also administered elections in conflictual societies for the first time in the United Nations' history. Before the dawn of the electoral boom in 1988, not a single UNPKO had had this mandate; after the electoral boom two of every five did. Given this expansion in the UN's mandate to support elections, we ask whether they successfully improved the democratic dividend from elections held in war zones. Scholars have already found that they bolster the peace.[26] In so doing, they have highlighted the UN's ability to fortify trust between erstwhile enemies and prevent misunderstandings from becoming outright crises. UNPKOs, however, should also improve elections. Page Fortna, for example, argues that politicians who might otherwise fear political exclusion if they lose elections will trust the process more with UN peacekeepers and monitors on the ground.[27]

We therefore test whether UNPKOs expand the democratic dividend from elections. We begin by collecting data from the United Nations Peacekeeping website on the dates and mandates of UN missions.[28] We then interact an indicator for whether or not a UNPKO was present with an indicator for whether the country is currently experiencing civil conflict or within ten years of one. Our model indicates that UNPKOs have little effect on the success of elections. They have little direct impact on the democratic dividend, nor is their impact heightened in conflictual societies.

Yet such a model may well fail to capture how UN missions affect elections in conflictual places. Fortna's argument regarding the impact of UNPKOs on the risk of political exclusion should hold whenever peacekeepers are present to contain potential outbreaks of violence, but perhaps the mechanism only holds when UNPKOs explicitly are mandated to administer elections. We therefore re-estimate our model, substituting an indicator variable that only takes on a positive value if a UNPKO with an elections mandate is present for our more general UNPKOs measure. Our results are summarized in Table 8.1, which reports the predicted democratic dividend for elections held in peacetime, conflictual societies without a UN mission with an election mandate, and conflictual societies with such a mission. Elections held in peacetime are predicted to yield a positive democratic dividend. Conflictual history in the absence of UN missions erases the positive effect of elections. But when UNPKOs with a mandate to monitor elections are present, elections yield a positive democratic dividend once more. This provides evidence that UNPKOs with an electoral mandate are successful in buoying elections in conflictual societies.

This analysis suggests two lessons. First, we provide a more direct test of Fortna's argument that UNPKOs should help preserve peace by reducing the danger of elections. Our results are broadly consonant with her argument and with the findings of Steinert and Grimm:[29]

Table 8.1 UNPKOs with a mandate to monitor elections bolster the democratic dividend in conflictual societies

Conflict status	Predicted democratic dividend
No conflict	+ 0.02*
Conflictual without UN	−0.01
Conflictual with UN	+ 0.05*

Note: * $p < 0.05$. Based on fixed-effects regression of 1,472 elections in 136 developing countries.

elections in conflictual societies more likely yield democratic momentum if a UN mission with an electoral mandate is present, though not if a UNPKO more generally is present. This contributes to a generally sanguine assessment of the power of UNPKOs to preserve the peace in post-conflict countries.[30] Second, our findings suggest that the United Nations has at times succeeded in promoting post-conflict democratic change, if only at the margins and when they empower their missions to monitor elections. Marina Ottaway argues that post-conflict peacebuilding efforts have grown in scope and complexity, and with only limited success. She contends that, "the international community must rethink its approach to postconflict reconstruction and scale it down to something that can realistically be achieved."[31] Our research and that of Steinert and Grimm suggests the opposite. When the United Nations expands the mandate of its peacekeeping operations to include elections, it helps support democratic change. More generally, a pragmatic dedication to democratic reconstructionism can be valuable in supporting elections in the developing world.

Discussion

The first seven chapters of this book explored the structural impediments to democratization by elections. Our theory of stocks of legitimacy emphasized how elections are embedded in a set of structures that either inhibits or supports democratic change after elections. We identified three major structural barriers: democratic inexperience, constrained fiscal space, and a history of violent political conflict. Our subsequent empirical chapters provided evidence that broadly supported this argument. The impact of elections on democratic change, we found, suffers when politicians and voters have little practical experience with democratic rule and when politicians have little access to the fiscal space necessary to provide public goods when they win office.

In this chapter, we analyze how democracy promotion affects the success of elections in building democracy. We conclude that international interventions in support of democracy should focus on addressing the structural constraints that inhibit political change after elections. Efforts to improve the proceedings on election day itself are always welcome, of course. Yet without addressing the core gaps in institutional legitimacy in democratizing countries, the seed of clean elections is planted in rather rocky ground. To stretch this metaphor, improving the quality of the seed may help, but fertilizing the ground in which the seed is planted deserves our attention too. We therefore seek not to evaluate democracy promotion as a whole, but instead to examine whether international interventions soften the constraints of democratic inexperience, tight fiscal space, and violent conflict.

Our findings should encourage democracy promoters in the West, for we find many of their favored interventions do bolster the democratic dividend of elections in low-legitimacy contexts. Election monitors, democracy and governance aid, and threats to cut off foreign aid, for example, help supplement the impact of elections in countries with little prior experience of democracy. These effects tend to fade after democratizing countries accumulate several years of democratic experience, but their success early in the democratization project is encouraging. International development aid, however, does little to soften the negative impact of constrained fiscal space. We also find, however, that aid levels remain rather inadequate to the task. Finally, we examine the impact of United Nations Peacekeeping missions on elections in conflictual societies. We find that such missions do not generally accelerate democratic change in conflictual societies, but missions with a mandate to observe elections do. The United Nations can reinforce elections when they are held amidst political violence. Indeed it is one of the few actors that has a chance.

Our aims in this chapter were limited. We sought to establish a prima facie case for whether certain democracy promotion strategies help compensate for the structural weaknesses of states that limit the democratic utility of their elections. Rather than an exhaustive evaluation of democracy promotion, we searched for the most basic evidence that international interventions promote democratic change in difficult structural circumstances. By this standard, our evidence is encouraging. Yet much work remains. We highlight two avenues for future research. First, we have not analyzed how foreign interventions support the development of opposition parties in democratizing countries.[32] Scholars and practitioners agree on the importance of political parties, but we lack the kinds of data we need to evaluate the success of Western programs designed to support them. Second, we have not accounted for the non-random assignment of international interventions. Our evidence here might be unduly pessimistic if we think that democracy promoters devote more attention to "harder" cases, or elections whose underlying odds of success are rather low. Conversely, our analysis might erroneously encourage us if democracy promoters sensibly dedicate themselves to "easier" cases. Given the policy stakes and the difficult conditions under which democracy promotion efforts must operate, we invite others to engage such methodological issues more rigorously and hope that the findings reported in this chapter illuminate multiple paths for future research.

9 | *Conclusions*

The political shockwaves of the late 1980s – the collapse of Communism, breakup of the Soviet Union, and end of the Cold War among them – yielded an electoral boom that swept the world in a matter of only ten years. The raw numbers by themselves are striking: the proportion of countries in the developing world holding competitive elections for executive office more than doubled between 1988 and 1998. The countries of the developing world held more elections in the twenty-two years between 1988 and 2010 than in the forty-one years between 1946 and 1987. Not only did elections become more numerous, they also grew in integrity. The elections of the electoral boom have featured increased competition among more numerous political parties freer from harassment by incumbents. By our reckoning, the proportion of elections dubbed at least minimally competitive increased from about 60 percent before 1988 to 87 percent afterwards.

Yet the raw numbers of the electoral boom, however impressive they may be, cannot do justice to the electoral boom's impact on politics around the world. The manner in which political leaders are chosen transformed rapidly and fundamentally in Latin America, Eatern Europe, Sub-Saharan Africa, South Asia, and East Asia. No longer did military juntas, ruling parties, dueling armed factions, or ruling families dominate the choice of chief executives. Politicians instead faced electorates in mass-suffrage elections, sometimes for the first time in a generation. South Africans voted in the first post-apartheid election, sweeping Nelson Mandela to power with over 85 percent turnout. Ninety-eight percent of Chileans turned out to vote to end General Augusto Pinochet's rule. The same dictator who had continually used repressive means to remain in power simply accepted the verdict of the Chilean people and left power, leaving behind an amended democratic constitution. These and other elections around the world symbolized the promise of democracy, peaceful political change, and a new dawn of politics.

This optimism ironically was often felt most strongly in the West, where politicians and intellectuals interpreted the electoral boom as the triumph not of local elites over repression, but of a Western ideal of liberal democracy. Francis Fukuyama offered the most optimistic and forceful formulation of this premise. Writing only one year into the electoral boom, Fukuyama wrote that, "What we may be witnessing is not just the end of the Cold War, or the passing of a particular period of post-war history, but the end of history as such: that is, the end point of mankind's ideological evolution and the universalization of Western liberal democracy as the final form of human government."[1] Detractors immediately seized on Fukuyama's triumphalism, but he undoubtedly captured some part of the Western zeitgeist. Western political leaders echoed Fukuyama's basic premise that the spread of free elections and democracy marked the commencement of a "new world order" in world politics, "where diverse nations are drawn together in common cause to achieve the universal aspirations of mankind – peace and security, freedom, and the rule of law."[2]

The subsequent twenty years would frustrate the hopes of voters around the world and of Western elites seeking credit for a new dawn of democracy. For many observers, elections themselves were the culprit, especially when they brought to power political leaders who themselves muzzled dissent, dissolved legislatures, and hounded opposition parties. Voters have elected Charles Taylor in Liberia, Vladimir Putin in Russia, Hun Sen in Cambodia, and Hugo Chavez in Venezuela, each in free and fair elections. Democratic progress in countries holding elections has stalled. Our cross-national evidence supports this claim: elections have yielded little in the way of a democratic dividend since the dawn of the electoral boom in 1988. Elections have more often yielded coups and instability than stable democratic politics in Pakistan, Thailand, and Haiti. They have sparked violent street battles in Côte d'Ivoire and Kenya. The African National Congress (ANC) still lacks a viable political opposition in South Africa, more than two decades after Mandela's historic victory in 1994. In Turkey, Recep Tayyip Erdoğan, first as prime minister and more recently as president, sought legislation allowing his government to block Internet sites, violently put down peaceful protests in Istanbul, and built an immense presidential palace for himself.

These recent frustrations have produced in Western observers a form of democratic depression, just as the outset of the electoral boom produced democratic euphoria. The editors of *The Economist* wrote a long essay in March 2014 entitled, "What's Gone Wrong with Democracy?" In it, they plainly pinned the democratic malaise around the world on an obsession with elections *qua* elections:

Many nominal democracies have slid towards autocracy, maintaining the outward appearance of democracy through elections, but without the rights and institutions that are equally important aspects of a functioning democratic system. . . One reason why so many democratic experiments have failed recently is that they put too much emphasis on elections and too little on the other essential features of democracy.[3]

The sense that Huntington's Third Wave of democracy has gone astray has been acknowledged by no less an authority than Larry Diamond, who admits that, "it's a difficult and messy time for democracy and freedom around the world. We have been in a global democratic recession for something like a decade."[4] He sees a "gray zone somewhere in between electoral democracy and electoral authoritarianism" developing in Pakistan, Kenya, Turkey, and beyond. These concerns are developed more fully in a recent volume edited by Larry Diamond and Marc Plattner called *Democracy in Decline?* under the auspices of none other than the National Endowment for Democracy. These voices, each possessing unchallenged liberal credentials, articulate the realization that the electoral boom has yielded weak democratic practice. Indeed, the Diamond and Plattner volume comes almost exactly twenty years after they published another volume, much more optimistically titled *The Global Resurgence of Democracy.*[5]

Western intellectuals, case evidence, statistical evidence, and book titles all suggest that the elections of the electoral boom, while more numerous and transparent than those at any previous point in world history, have generally not succeeded in building democracy in the developing world. This basic empirical puzzle has inspired this book's two questions. First, why have so many elections been followed by democratic collapse or inertia, while others have been followed by democratic change? Second, do steps taken by the international community support democratic change after elections?

We conclude our investigation by reviewing our findings, discussing their implications for international interventions, and considering future research into elections.

Electing Democracy?

This book makes a rather simple conjecture: the success of elections depends mightily on the political-economic context in which they are embedded. We present a theory of stocks of legitimacy that generates testable hypotheses regarding when elections will promote democracy and when they will end in democratic stasis or authoritarian reversals. All election winners enjoy a brief electoral honeymoon in which the halo of their victory shines brightly. This contingent legitimacy does not last forever, even for the first democratically elected presidents and prime ministers who replace despots. Voters soon abandon even the most inspiring incumbent who fails to enhance their incomes.

Not all incumbents can easily take steps to expand the economy, however. Their ability to do so depends on their performance legitimacy, or the capability inherited from past governments to provide public goods that underpin economic growth. Election winners who take charge of a state with robust stocks of performance legitimacy more easily can initiate programs to support the poor and industrial policies to attract international investment. Election winners who take charge of a state with only shallow stocks of performance legitimacy, in contrast, possess little ability to expand human development. These incumbents at best command sufficient capacity to provide private or club goods to favored cliques – a home region, co-ethnics, or elements of the military and/or police, for example. Yet doing so likely fails to reach enough voters to secure re-election. Self-interested politicians can still win re-election, sadly, by altering electoral rules, limiting media freedom, and harassing the political opposition. Their ability to do so depends on the depth of democratic-institutional legitimacy, the total strength of formal and informal democratic rules and practices. A deep stock of democratic-institutional legitimacy prevents the kinds of shenanigans favored by desperate and unsuccessful incumbents, while a shallower stock enables them.

Our theoretical framework explains why some elections expand democracy while others disappoint expectations: elections in contexts characterized by shallow performance and democratic-institutional legitimacy generate a smaller democratic dividend. Low-legitimacy political environments avail election winners of little authentic means of winning re-election, while leaving open fraudulent roads to power. We identify three particular political-economic contexts that we argue are low-legitimacy. First, countries with little democratic experience have little in the way of democratic-institutional legitimacy. Second, incumbents with little access to fiscal space likely lack the performance legitimacy needed to win office on their competence alone. Finally, incumbents embroiled in civil conflict likely have little means of enhancing performance legitimacy other than through continued violence.

We bring to bear a wealth of evidence to test this theoretical framework. The core of this effort of research has been the statistical analysis of a cross-national data set of all elections held globally since 1945 using data primarily from the National Elections in Democracy and Autocracy (NELDA) project and supplemented as needed by a variety of other sources. This analysis allowed us to estimate what we call the "democratic dividend" from elections, or improvements in the formal exercise of democracy. We also carefully studied surveys of voters in elections around the world from the Comparative Study of Electoral Systems (CSES) and the Latinobarómetro. These analyses allow us to analyze not only formal measures of democracy, but voters' stated faith in the democratic process as they head to the polls. Finally, we relied on short vignettes of elections and post-election change in countries ranging from India to Guatemala to elucidate the logic of the argument and clarify our results.

Our evidence largely supports our theory of stocks of legitimacy. We emphasize three major findings. First, elections in countries lacking democratic experience generate little democratic change. The electoral boom spread elections to many countries with either little prior experience of democracy or a tortured history of democratic elections followed by authoritarian interruptions, often through military coups. A history of political repression in these societies is precisely why elections prompted such hope. Consider the history of Sub-Saharan African elections, frequently the focus of scholars of democratization by elections. We find that elections since 1988 held in Sub-Saharan African countries with fewer than six years of democratic experience yield no democratic dividend at all. Sadly, the vast majority of Sub-Saharan African countries do not meet this minimal threshold of democratic experience. Our survey data further support this proposition; voters in countries with longer democratic experience report far more satisfaction with democracy.

Second, elections in countries with meager fiscal space also produce far smaller democratic dividends. The elections of the electoral boom have often taken place in constrained fiscal straits, a product of two historical forces. On one hand, countries with well-developed fiscal space were often already holding elections before the commencement of the electoral boom in 1988. On the other hand, the electoral boom coincided with the neoliberal turn in political economy, as developing country leaders were compelled to slash the size of the state in the wake of the global debt crisis of the early 1980s and the end of the Cold War. The gap in fiscal resources available to sovereign nations is staggering, with the OECD states on average having seventy times the fiscal space of the average developing countries. As our analysis shows, this gap influences not just the quality of life citizens enjoy but also the democratic dividend from elections. Our analysis makes clear that the fiscal space threshold required for countries to reap a positive democratic dividend is not that high in absolute terms but too many developing countries still come up short. Again, our survey data translate these results in terms of voter satisfaction with democracy: voters in countries with more expansive fiscal space are far more likely to report satisfaction with democratic governance.

Third, conflict has a major negative impact on the democratic dividend from elections. We documented that elections since 1988 have frequently occurred in societies where political competition previously occurred at the point of a gun. Such elections occurring during or soon after civil conflict result in democratic regression compared to those held during peacetime. Further, elections held in the first year after recovery do nothing to further democracy, which is consistent with our previous research that concluded that elections held within one or two years of the end of conflict in new democracies tend to slow economic reconstruction and endanger the post-conflict peace.[6] Given that so many of the world's youngest democracies are holding their elections in the shadow of conflict, we encourage future research on elections during and after civil war, especially concentrating on the particular array of circumstances that promote successful elections. Aila Matanock, for example, finds that post-conflict elections in which former rebel groups participate more likely encourage peace.[7] We focus on a different aspect of the post-conflict environment – continuing physical insecurity. We examine Guatemala's post-conflict history, finding that citizens today evince no more confidence in democracy than they did twenty years ago. We argue that the high rate of crime, a direct result of the civil war, threatens democratic legitimacy among Guatemalans.

Supporting Elections in Low-Legitimacy Societies

The cumulative body of evidence presented in this book makes clear that the success of elections depends crucially on the political-economic context in which they occur. Elections held in poor countries with little democratic experience or fiscal space and in the wake of conflict do far less to promote democracy than those held in more propitious circumstances. The research in this book thus calls into question the notion, promoted by the literature on democratization by elections, that competitive elections can galvanize democratic change if they are sufficiently free and fair and properly designed. We instead suggest that democratic progress depends little on the nature of elections as discrete political events and more on the structural environment in which they are embedded.

This perspective naturally leads to more pessimism regarding interventions to ensure successful electoral competition in the developing world. Elections experts focus on how modifications to the electoral process itself – sharper election monitoring, for example, or more advanced voter registration – might forestall post-election democratic reversals. Our emphasis on structural conditions suggests that such optimism is misplaced. There are no technical fixes for a tortured political history featuring little in the way of a free media, competitive opposition political parties, or constraints on the executive. Nor can democracy promoters easily help domestic leaders expand fiscal space; aid flows represent a drop in the bucket compared to tax revenues, even though too many developing countries have opaque and ineffective tax systems. What is needed is tax reform so that states can raise the revenues they need to govern, but this is often politically unpalatable.

At the core of the electoral paradox is an immutable reality: most countries with structural advantages already have democratized.

Tomorrow's democracy promoters must necessarily work in far more challenging structural environments. What policy advice does our book suggest for democracy promoters, aside from a somber recognition of the structural challenges to elections in low-legitimacy societies? Our theory and evidence suggest strongly that democracy promoters should focus less on the technical administration of elections and more on addressing the structural barriers to post-election liberalization. We focus on three sets of such policies. First, we find that election monitors, democracy and governance aid, and aid threats all help countries with little past democratic experience. In turn, these interventions soften the constraint of depleted stocks of democratic institutions.

Second, we examine the impact of international aid on the success of elections for governments with narrow fiscal space. In theory, aid might temporarily enlarge the fiscal resources available to new governments, allowing them to compete for re-election on their merits. We find little evidence to support this assertion, however. We instead show how aid typically is given in such small amounts that it pales in comparison to the fiscal resources available to most states. Our findings therefore suggest that aid is not being given in the amounts necessary to supplement fiscal space in a meaningful way. We also point to the possible danger of "aid bypass," in which donor governments eschew recipient governments out of a fear of corruption but by doing so miss opportunities to bolster state capacity and legitimacy.[8]

Finally, we study the impact of United Nations Peacekeeping Operations (UNPKOs) on the democratic dividend from elections held in post-conflict countries.[9] Scholars of civil conflict mostly agree that rapid post-conflict democratization, especially through elections, raises the risk of a return to conflict, though some scholars are hopeful that third-party enforcers can ameliorate such problems.[10] UNPKOs might fulfill an important function in our theoretical framework by solving problems related to post-conflict distrust. We find that UN missions do not generally bolster the democratic dividend from elections, but that missions with a clear mandate to prepare for and monitor elections do make a difference in post-conflict elections. This is consistent with emerging literature on the utility of UN peacekeeping. Lisa Hultman and her colleagues show that UN missions play a crucial role in protecting civilians caught in the crossfire of warring groups during civil war and also lengthen the duration of post-conflict peace.[11] Gabriella Lloyd focuses on the role UN missions have played in facilitating police reform. Protecting civilians from warring parties and promoting greater legitimacy of police institutions are vital policy issues given our findings on the concerns about physical security in post-conflict societies and the negative effect such concerns have on democratic satisfaction.[12]

A cynic might point out that our attempt to identify how foreign interveners might bolster elections in the developing world is ironic given that the rest of the book could be read as a criticism of foreign interventions to promote elections in the first place. This is a fair criticism that forces an important clarification. Our concern throughout the book has not been with the idea or practice of holding elections. To us, elections are unequivocally the most important and radical institutional reform governing state–society relations in the last several centuries. But the historical record and our analysis in this book is equally unequivocal: countries that attempt elections without the right conditions do more damage to long-term democratic development than not. Today's developing countries are the first to hold elections offering universal suffrage rights from their very start. The developed democracies today went about it differently, holding elections that featured contestation between elites but with limited participation by the masses. While none of the elections held by Britain and the United States in the 1800s would pass muster as democratic today, the fact remains that they permitted the establishment of sustainable democracy.[13]

Obviously, no one is advocating limiting the franchise in today's developing country elections. We certainly are not. But delivering on democracy's promise requires understanding why "free and fair" elections do not always build democracy. Our answer, stated bluntly and a little unfairly, is that democracy promoters are idealists and have not engaged in a hard-nosed analysis of the realities of electoral politics. Politicians want to win elections and will do so using whatever means they have at their disposal. Where they can make big public policy splashes that affect large swathes of their nation, they seize that opportunity. But that does not mean they will eschew other strategies of intimidating opponents or buying votes or voters or just stealing an election outright. The democracy promotion community has focused its efforts on raising the costs of malpractice by requiring election monitors and generating more sophisticated techniques of election audits. But we have ignored the ugly truth that politicians who see no viable alternative will find a way around any hurdle to cheating that we create. The lesson from the history of successful democracies is only partially about better law and order and cleaner elections. The other part is about growing state capacity that led to the ability to make public policy that matters for citizens. Of course, corruption continued (and indeed continues) but electoral integrity grew too. The problem now is that our collective obsession with "good governance" blinds us to the need for governments to govern. When aid agencies bypass the state because it is corrupt, or when multilateral lenders eschew infrastructure investment because it is rife with graft and cannot be subjected to randomized controlled trials, the state shrinks to the detriment of democracy. Here, once again, Samuel Huntington's brilliant *Political Order in Changing Societies* got it right: the "degree" of government matters too, not just its "form."[14] He had it right in one other regard too, in his criticism of our innate desire for a "unity of goodness."[15] Low corruption and high democracy are both desirable goods but examples of countries that achieved both simultaneously are vanishingly rare for a reason.

Democracy Promotion in the twenty-first Century

Our research contributes to important debates regarding elections, democratization, and public policy. Most importantly, we fuse two theoretical perspectives on political liberalization. A long-standing structuralist tradition has tended to concentrate on slow-moving social and economic changes and their impact on the viability of political democracy. This tradition harkens back to modernization theory, which identified socioeconomic pre-conditions for democratic change. A more recent electoral literature has focused instead on the power of elections as agents of political change. The democratization-by-elections school has hypothesized that if elections are sufficiently free, frequently held, and properly designed, democratic change will follow.

Our theoretical framework has synthesized these two strands of research – as well as insights from international relations and political economy – that unfortunately have tended to work in isolation. Our approach recognizes that autocrats and opposition movements, scholars, and Western democracy promoters all regard elections as prime instruments of political change in the world today. Yet it also argues that elections are embedded in a political-institutional environment that conditions their democratizing impact. This theoretical fusion changes the questions we ask of elections and democratization. Research on elections has overwhelmingly concentrated on whether elections generally contribute to democratic change or support authoritarian stability. More rare have been studies that conceptualize the democratic dividend from elections as varying and contextual.[16] Our theoretical synthesis and statistical analysis fill this gap by examining how the democratic dividend varies across political-economic contexts. A rigorous analysis of variation in the contexts in which elections occur might assist policymakers in identifying potentially troublesome elections and considering their policy responses more seriously. At any rate it will save us from feigning shock when elections do not go well in South Sudan, should they end up happening in 2018.

Like any single book, this one leaves unanswered several questions, all of which deserve significantly more scholarly attention. First, experimental work on elections should try to link the structural conditions under which electoral competition occurs and the democratic outputs that result. Laboratory experiments have already shed light on classic political-economic theories of voting and provided evidence of retrospective voting.[17] Such experiments might also help us understand the conditions under which elections more likely support democratic cooperation, especially if conducted in a developing democracy context. One might, for example, ask participants in an experiment to elect a leader who then controls distribution of a valuable resource, the amount of which could be randomly manipulated. Participants could then play a public goods game as a measure of their success in cooperation. If cooperation obtains more readily when the elected leader has greater access to resources, this might provide evidence corroborating our results about the importance of fiscal space to democratic politics. Such work remains relatively new to political economy, but offers a new road forward, one that allows corroboration of findings from the observational data used here.

Second, the relationship between conflict and democratic change after elections demands further examination. Elections in conflict situations are democratization in reverse, especially in cases of ethnic secessionist conflict. Early post-conflict elections can also be harmful and at best produce no democratic change. Our analysis of post-war politics in Guatemala suggested one potential explanation for this pattern: continuing violence after the war, now the result of crime, deepened Guatemalans' sense of insecurity and diminished democracy's post-war luster. Yet there are other potential means by which conflict conditions democratic change, including the probability of electoral violence, effects on social trust, and adaptation of formerly violent actors into political parties.[18] Further analysis of these questions is needed to shed light on the political path societies travel after the shooting ends.

Finally, further survey analysis might help us understand how voters perceive elections as a means to political change, and the success of interventions intended to promote democracy. Cross-national measures of democracy, which focus primarily on formal assessments of civil rights and political institutions, often do not correlate with citizens' own assessments of their country's democratic strengths and weaknesses. Exploring how citizens' perception of democracy shifts after successive elections might help us understand further whether and when elections improve their perceptions of opposition parties, sense of their own political freedoms, and rating of international interventions designed to support democracy.

Universal suffrage national elections represent the most radical transformation of the balance of power between citizens and their rulers in a millennium. Unsurprisingly, scholars and practitioners have poured considerable thought into improving the conduct of elections. But elections are fundamentally a means rather than an end in themselves. If the goal is to make steady irreversible progress towards a state of universal democracy, where leaders are constrained by laws and citizens are empowered to act as political agents, then elections are no longer the "silver bullet" they were once thought to be. Yet there is no normatively acceptable alternative to elections, nor do we wish to suggest there need be one. Elections can work to further the cause of human freedom through political democracy, but only if we make it possible for them to do so. Otherwise the them that's got will remain the them that gets.

Appendix A
Data Appendix: Sample, Variables, Sources

The preponderance of evidence described in this book is based in the statistical analysis of a time-series cross-section (TSCS) dataset consisting of nearly 9,000 annual observations of 165 countries between 1946 and 2010. The analysis does not include so-called "microstates", usually defined as those countries with populations below 500,000. Such countries include Kiribati, Belize, and Iceland, even when they hold elections that otherwise match our empirical criteria. Missing data also constrain the sample; economic data are largely missing for East Germany, Poland, and other Communist countries during the Cold War, for example. We attempt to minimize the statistical threat from missing data by avoiding data sources with poor coverage whenever possible.

The remainder of this appendix describes the definitions, sources, and coverage for the elections that comprise the sample for most of our graphs and models. We also provide summary statistics for the dependent variables, particularly democracy and economic development; independent variables, especially those centered on fiscal space, conflict, and democratic stock; and control variables that are used in the analysis.

Creating a Global Sample of Elections

Data on elections are drawn from Version 3 of the National Elections across Democracy and Autocracy (NELDA) dataset, collected by Susan D. Hyde and Nikolay Marinov and available for download at http://hyde.research.yale.edu/nelda/ (Hyde and Marinov 2012). NELDA includes information on all elections for national legislatures, constituent assemblies, and/or executives in which some proportion of the general population votes. The data thus exclude local elections and those in which only a central committee or institution votes. NELDA otherwise includes elections in which the franchise is highly restricted, as in apartheid-era South Africa, or highly uncompetitive, as in Syria during the al-Assad regime. NELDA represents an excellent match for our conceptual focus for several reasons. First, the dataset covers wide spatial and temporal domains, which generates a large sample of elections for us to analyze. Second, Hyde and Marinov collect data on several important aspects of the electoral process in which we have theoretical interest, including competitiveness, outcomes, economic conditions, and international pressures.

The NELDA dataset is recorded at the election-round level. It therefore records as separate observations multiple rounds of the same election. It also includes separate observations for general elections in which legislative and executive elections are held on the same day. So, for example, the dataset includes three observations for Peru's elections in 2000, which kept incumbent Alberto Fujimori in power. Peru held a general election on April 9, 2000, which is recorded as two separate events, one for the legislative election and one for the presidential election. A run-off for the presidential election was held on May 28, 2000, as Fujimori barely failed to obtain 50 percent of the vote in the first round. This run-off also receives a separate observation, for a total of three.

Our dataset is comprised of annual observations by country of whether and what type of election was held in a particular year. We take a few steps to condense NELDA into an annual format. First, we collapse multiple observations for general elections into single observations, using commands provided by Hyde and Marinov and available on NELDA's webpage. This process gives precedence to executive elections, so that the combined coding of general elections is merely the coding for the presidential election. Second, we combine multiple-round elections into single observations. Where NELDA's coding of electoral attributes varies across rounds of the election, we vary our approach. In some cases, as in the status of relations with the outside world, we take the observation from the first round. In other cases, as in whether the incumbent left office, we take the observation from the last round. Finally, in cases of electoral quality, we often take a worst-case approach, coding the fullest extent of electoral malfeasance. If only one round exhibited evidence of allegations of media bias, for example, we code the entire election as exhibiting that evidence. There remain a few countries that had multiple general elections in the same calendar year. For these countries, we privilege

Table A.1 List of elections analyzed

Country	Election year
Afghanistan	*49L, 52L, 55L, 61L, 65L, 69L, 69L,* 88L, 04P, *05L*
Albania	*49L, 58L, 70L, 74L, 78L, 82L, 87L,* 91L, 92L, 96L, 97L, 01L, 05L
Algeria	*62L, 63P, 64L, 76P, 77L, 79P, 82L, 84P, 87L, 88P,* 91L, 95P, 97L, 99P, 02L, 04P, 07L
Angola	92G
Argentina	46G, 48L, 51G, 54G, 57C, 58G, 60L, 62L, 63G, 65L, 73G, 83G, 85L, 87L, 89G, 91L, 93L, 94C, 95G, 97L, 99G, 01L, 03G, 05L, 07G
Armenia	91P, 95L, 96P, 98P, 99L, 03P, 60L
Azerbaijan	*91P, 92P, 93P, 95L, 98P,* 00L, 03P, 05L
Bahrain	72C, *73L,* 02L, 06L
Bangladesh	73L, 78P, 79L, 81P, 86P, 88L, 91L, 96L, 01L
Belarus	94P, 95L, 00L, 01P, 04L, 06P
Benin	60G, *64G, 68P, 70P, 79L, 84L, 89L,* 91P, 95L, 96P, 99L, 01P, 03L, 06P, 07L
Bhutan	*07L*
Bolivia	47P, 51G, 56G, 58L, 60G, 62L, *64G,* 66G, 78G, 79G, 80G, 85G, 89G, 93G, 97G, 02G, 05G, 06C
Bosnia-Herzegovina	96G, 98G, 00L, 02G, 06G
Botswana	69L, 74L, 79L, 84L, 89L, 94L, 99L, 04L
Brazil	47L, 50G, 54L, 55G, 58L, 60P, 62L, 66L, 70L, 74L, 78L, 82L, 86L, 89P, 90L, 94G, 98G, 02L, 06L
Bulgaria	46C, *49L, 53L, 57L, 62L, 66L, 71L, 76L, 81L, 86L,* 90L, 91L, 92P, 94L, 96P, 97L, 01P, 05L, 06P
Burkina Faso	*65P, 70L, 78P, 91P,* 92L, 97L, 98P, 02L, 05P, 07L
Burundi	*65L, 81C, 82L, 84P,* 93P, 05L
Cambodia	*55L, 58L,* 62L, 66L, 72P, *76L, 81L,* 93C, 98L, 03L
Cameroon	60L, 64L, *65P, 70P, 73L, 75P, 78L, 80P, 83L, 84P,* 88G, 92P, 97P, 02L, 04P, 07L
Central African Republic	*64P, 81P, 86P, 87L,* 92G, 93G, 98L, 99P, 05G
Chad	*62L, 63L, 69P, 90L,* 9P, 97L, 01P, 02L, 06P
Chile	46P, 49L, 52P, 53L, 57L, 58P, 61L, 65P, 65L, 69L, 70P, 73L, *88P,* 89G, 93G, 97L, 99P, 01L, 05L
Colombia	46P, 47L, *49P,* 51L, 53L, 58P, 60L, 62P, 64L, 66P, 68L, 70G, 74G, 78P, 82P, 86P, 90G, 91L, 94P, 98P, 02P, 06P

Table A.1 (*cont.*)

Country	Election year
Comoros	*78P, 82L, 84P, 87L,* 90P, 92L, 93L, 96P, 02P, 04L, 06P
Congo	*61P, 63L, 73L, 79L, 84L,* 89L, 92P, 93L, 02P, 07L
Congo, Dem. Republic	65L, *70P, 75L, 77P, 82L, 84P, 87L,* 06L
Costa Rica	46L, 48G, 49G, 53G, 58G, 62G, 66G, 70G, 74G, 78G, 82G, 86G, 90G, 94G, 98G, 02L, 06G
Côte D'Ivoire	*60G, 65G, 70G, 75G, 80P, 85P,* 90P, 95P, 00P
Croatia	92G, 93L, 95L, 97P, 00P, 03L, 05P, 07L
Cuba	46L, 48G, 50L, 54G, 58L, 93L, 98L, 03L
Cyprus	68P, 70L, 76L, 81L, 83P, 85L, 88P, 91L, 93P, 96L, 98P, 01L, 03P, 06L
Czechoslovakia	46L, *48L, 54L, 60L, 71L, 76L, 81L, 86L,* 90L, 92L
Czech Republic	96L, 98L, 00L, 02L, 04L, 06L
Djibouti	*81P, 82L, 87G,* 92L, 93P, 97L, 99P, 03L, 05P
Dominican Republic	46C, 47G, *52G, 55C, 57G,* 62G, 66G, 70G, 74G, 78G, 82G, 86G, 90G, 94G, 96P, 98L, 00P, 02L, 04P, 06L, 07P
Ecuador	48P, 50L, 52G, 54L, 56G, 58L, 60G, 62L, 68G, 78P, 79L, 84L, 86L, 88L, 90L, 92L, 94L, 96L, 97C, 98L, 02L, 06L, 07C
Egypt	50L, *56P, 57L, 57P,* 64L, 65P, 69L, 70P, 71L, 76P, 79L, *81P,* 84L, 87P, 90L, *93P,* 95L, 99P, 00L, 05P, 07L
El Salvador	50G, *52L, 54L,* 46P, *58L,* 60L, 61C, 62P, 64L, 66L, 67P, 68L, 70L, 72L, 74L, 76L, 77P, 78L, 82C, 84P, 85L, 88L, 89P, 91L, 94L, 97L, 99P, 00L, 03L, 04P, 06L
Equatorial Guinea	*83L, 88L, 89P,* 93L, 96P, 99L, 02P, 04L
Estonia	92L, 95L, 99L, 03L, 07L
Ethiopia	*57L, 61L, 65L, 68L, 73L, 87C,* 94C, 95L, 00L, 05L
Fiji	72L, 77L, 82L, 87L, 92L, 94L, 99L, 01L, 06L
Gabon	*61G, 64L, 67G, 69L, 73G, 79P, 80L, 84L, 86P,* 90L, 93P, 96L, 98P, 01L, 05P, 06L
Gambia	66L, 72L, 77L, 82G, 87G, 92G, 96P, 97L, 01P, 02L, 06P, 07L
Georgia	92G, 95G, 99L, 00P, 03L, 04P
German Democratic Republic	*50L, 54L, 58L, 67L, 71L, 76L, 81L, 86L,* 90L

(*continued*)

Table A.1 (*cont.*)

Country	Election year
Ghana	60P, 69L, 79L, 92P, 96G, 00L, 04G
Greece	46L, 50L, 51L, 52L, 56L, 58L, 61L, 63L, 65L, 74L, 77L, 81L, 85L, 89L, 90L, 93L, 96L, 00L, 04L, 07L
Guatemala	47L, 48L, 50P, 53L, *54C*, 55L, 57G, 58G, 59L, 61L, 64C, 66G, 70G, 74G, 78G, 82G, 84C, 85L, 90L, 94L, 95L, 99L, 03L, 07L
Guinea	*61P, 63L, 68G, 74G, 80L, 82P*, 93P, 95L, 98P, 02L, 03P
Guinea-Bissau	94L, 99L, 04L, 05P
Guyana	68L, 73L, 80L, 85L, 92L, 97L, 01L, 06L
Haiti	46G, 50P, 57G, *61L*, 64P, *67L, 73L, 79L, 84L*, 86C, 87G, 88G, 90G, 95P, 97L, 00P, 06G
Honduras	*48G*, 54G, 56C, 57C, 65C, 71G, 80C, 81G, 85G, 89G, 93G, 97G, 01G, 05G
Hungary	47L, *49L, 53L, 58L, 63L, 67L, 71L, 75L, 80L, 85L*, 90L, 94L, 98L, 02L, 06L
India	51L, 57L, 62L, 67L, 71L, 77L, 80L, 84L, 89L, 91L, 96L, 99L, 04L
Indonesia	55L, 71L, 77L, 82L, 87L, 92L, 97L, 99L, 04P
Iran	60L, 61L, *63L, 67G*, 71L, *75L*, 79C, *80P, 81P*, 84L, *85P*, 88L, *89P, 91L, 93P*, 96L, 97P, 98L, 00L, 01P, 04L, 05P
Iraq	47L, 48L, 53L, 54L, *58L*, 80L, 84L, 89L, 95P, 96L, *00L*, 05C
Israel	49L, 51L, 55L, 58L, 61L, 65L, 69L, 73L, 77L, 81L, 84L, 88L, 92L, 96L, 99G, 01P, 03L, 06L
Italy	46C, 48L, 53L, 58L, 63L, 68L, 72L, 76L, 79L, 83L, 87L, 92L, 94L, 96L, 01L, 06L
Jamaica	67L, 72L, 76L, 80L, 83L, 89L, 93L, 97L, 02L, 07L
Jordan	47L, 50L, 51L, 54L, 56L, *61L, 62L, 63L, 67L*, 89L, 93L, 97L, 03L, 07L
Kazakhstan	94L, *95P*, 99P, 04L, 05P, 07L
Kenya	66L, *69G, 74G, 79G, 83G, 88P*, 92G, 94L, 97G, 02G, 07G
Kuwait	*61C, 63L, 67L, 71L, 75L, 81L, 85L*, 90L, 92L, 96L, 99L, *03L*, 06L
Kyrgyz Republic	*91P, 95P*, 00P, 05P, 07L
Laos	55L, 58L, 60L, 65L, 67L, *72L*, 89L, 92L, 97L, 02L, *06L*
Latvia	92L, 95L, 98L, 02L, 06L

Table A.1 (*cont.*)

Country	Election year
Lebanon	47L, 51L, 53L, 57L, 60L, 64L, 68L, 72L, 92L, 96L, 00L, 05L
Lesotho	70L, 93L, 98L, 02L, 07L
Liberia	*51G, 55G, 59G, 63P, 67P, 71P, 75G,* 85G, 97G, 05L
Libya	*52L, 56L, 60L, 64L, 65L*
Lithuania	92L, 93P, 96L, 97P, 00L, 02P, 04P
Macedonia (FRY)	94G, 98L, 99P, 02L, 04P, 06L
Madagascar (Malagasy)	60L, *65P,* 70L, 72P, 77L, *82P, 83L, 89P,* 92P, 93L, 96P, 98L, 01P, 02L, 06P, 07L
Malawi	*78L, 83L, 87L,* 92L, 94G, 99G, 04G
Malaysia	59L, 64L, 69L, 74L, 78L, 82L, 86L, 90L, 95L, 99L, 04L
Mali	*64L, 79G, 82L, 85G, 88L,* 92P, 97P, 02P, 07P
Mauritania	*61P, 65L, 66P, 71G, 76G,* 92P, 96L, 97P, 01L, 03P, 06L, 07P
Mauritius	76L, 82L, 83L, 87L, 91L, 95L, 00L, 05L
Mexico	46G, 49L, 52G, 55L, 58G, 61L, 64G, 67L, 70G, 73L, 76G, 79L, 82G, 85L, 88G, 91L, 94G, 97L, 00G, 03L, 06G
Moldova	*91P,* 94L, 96P, 98L, 01L, 05L
Mongolia	*51L, 54L, 57L, 60L, 63L, 66L, 69L, 73L, 77L, 81L, 86L,* 90L, 92L, 93P, 96L, 97P, 00L, 01P, 04L, 05P
Morocco	63L, 70L, 77L, 84L, 93L, 97L, 02L, 07L
Mozambique	*77L, 86L,* 94G, 99G, 04G
Myanmar	51L, 56L, 60L, *74L, 78L, 81L, 85L,* 90L
Namibia	94G, 99G, 04G
Nepal	59L, *81L, 86L,* 91L, 94L, 99L
Nicaragua	47G, 50G, 57G, 63G, 67G, 72C, 74G, 84G, 90G, 96G, 01G, 06G
Niger	*65P, 70P, 89P,* 93P, 95L, 96P, 99P, 04P
Nigeria	64L, 79P, 83P, 92L, 93P, 98L, 99P, 03P, 07G
North Korea	50L, 52P, 54L, 56P, 58L, 62L, 67L, 72L, 77L, 82L, 86L, 90L, 98L, 03L
Oman	*03L, 07L*
Pakistan	70L, 77L, 85L, 88L, 90L, 93L, 97L, 02L
Panama	48G, 52G, 56G, 60G, 64G, 68G, 72C, 78C, 80C, 84G, 89G, 91L, 94G, 99G, 04G

(*continued*)

Table A.1 (*cont.*)

Country	Election year
Papua New Guinea	77L, 82L, 87L, 92L, 97L, 02L, 07L
Paraguay	*48G, 49G, 50G, 53G, 54P, 58G, 60L, 63G, 68G, 73G,* 78G, 83G, 88G, 89G, 91C, 93G, 98G, 00P, 03G
Peru	*50G, 56G, 62G, 63G, 78C, 80G, 85G, 90L, 92L, 95G,* 00L, 01L, 06L
Philippines	47L, 49G, 51L, 53G, 55G, 57G, 59L, 61G, 63L, 65G, 67L, 69G, 71L, 73P, 77P, 78L, 81P, 84L, 86P, 87L, 92G, 95L, 98G, 01L, 04G, 07L
Poland	47L, *52L, 57L, 61L, 65L, 69L, 72L, 76L, 80L, 85L,* 89L, 90P, 91L, 93L, 95P, 97L, 00P, 01L, 05P, 07L
Portugal	*49P, 51P, 53L, 57L, 58P, 61L, 65L, 69L, 73L, 75C,* 76P, 79L, 80P, 83L, 85L, 86P, 87L, 91P, 95L, 96P, 01P, 02L, 05L, 06P
Rumania	46C, 48C, *52L, 57L, 61L, 65L, 69L, 75L, 80L, 85L,* 90G, 92L, 96L, 00L, 04L, *07P*
Russia (Soviet Union)	*46L, 50L, 54L, 58L, 70L, 74L, 79L, 84L, 89L, 90L,* 91P, 93L, 95L, 96P, 99L, 00P, 03L, 04P, 07L
Rwanda	*65G, 69G, 78P, 81L, 83P, 88P,* 03P
Senegal	*63G, 68G, 73G, 78G, 83G, 88G,* 93P, 98L, 00P, 01L, 07P
Sierra Leone	62L, 67L, 73L, 77L, *82L, 85P, 86L,* 96L, 02G, 07L
Singapore	68L, 72L, 76L, 80L, 84L, 88L, 91L, *93P,* 97L, 01L, 06L
Slovakia	94L, 99P, 02L, 04P, 06L
Slovenia	92G, 96L, 97P, 00L, 02P, 04L, 07P
Somalia	64L, 69L, *79L, 85L, 86L*
South Africa	48L, 53L, 58L, 61L, 66L, 69L, 70L, 74L, 75L, 77L, 81L, 84L, 87L, 89L, 94L, 99L, 04L
South Korea	50L, 52P, 54L, 56P, 58L, 60P, 63P, 67L, 71L, 73L, 78L, 81P, 85L, 87P, 88L, 92P, 96L, 97P, 00L, 02P, 04L, 07P
Spain	77L, 79L, 82L, 86L, 89L, 93L, 96L, 00L, 04L
Sri Lanka	52L, 56L, 60L, 65L, 70L, 77L, 82P, 88P, 89L, 94P, 99P, 00L, 01L, 04L, 05P
Sudan	*58L, 65C, 68C, 71P, 72C, 74L, 77P, 78L, 81L, 83P,* 86L, *96G,* 00G
Swaziland	72L, *93L, 98L, 03L*
Syria	*47L, 49P, 53L, 54L, 71P, 73L, 77L, 78P, 81L, 85P, 86L,* 90L, 91P, 94L, 98L, 99P, 00P, 03L, 07P
Taiwan	*83L, 86L, 89L, 91C, 92L, 95L, 96G, 98L, 00P, 01L, 04P,* 05C

Table A.1 (*cont.*)

Country	Election year
Tajikistan	91P, 94P, 95L, 99P, 00L, 05L, 06P
Tanzania	62P, *65G, 70G, 75G, 80G, 85G, 90G, 95G*, 00G, 05G
Thailand	*46L, 58L, 59L, 52L, 57L*, 69L, 75L, 76L, 79L, 83L, 86L, 88L, 92L, 95L, 96L, 00L, 01L, 05L, 06L, 07L
Togo	*61G, 63G, 79P, 85L, 86P, 90L*, 93P, 94L, 98P, 99L, 02L, 03P, 05P, 07L
Trinidad and Tobago	66L, 71L, 76L, 81L, 86L, 91L, 95L, 00L, 01L, 02L, 07L
Tunisia	*56C, 59G, 64G, 69G, 74G, 79L, 81L, 86L, 89G, 94G, 99G*, 04G
Turkey	46L, 50L, 54L, 57L, 61L, 64L, 65L, 66L, 68L, 69L, 73L, 75L, 77L, 79L, *82P*, 73L, 87L, 91L, 95L, 99L, 02L, 07L
Turkmenistan	*92P, 94L, 98L, 99L, 03L, 04L, 07P*
Uganda	*80L, 94C, 96P, 01P*, 06G
Ukraine	91P, 94P, 98L, 99P, 02L, 04P, 06L, 07L
Uruguay	*46G, 50G, 54G, 58G, 62G, 66G, 71G*, 84G, 89G, 94G, 99L, 04G
Uzbekistan	91P, *94L, 99L, 00P, 04L, 07P*
Venezuela	46C, 47G, 52C, 57P, 58P, 63G, 68G, 73G, 78G, 83G, 88G, 93G, 98P, 99C, 00G, *04P*, 05L, 06P
Vietnam, Dem. Republic	*60L, 64L, 71L, 75L, 76L, 81L, 87L, 92L, 97L, 02L, 07L*
Vietnam, Republic	55P, *56C, 59L*, 61P, *63L*, 66C, 67G, 70L, *71L*, 73L
Yemen, Arab Republic	*71L, 88L*, 93L, 97L, 99P, 03L, 06P
Yemen, People's Republic	*78L, 86L*
Yugoslavia (Serbia)	*50L, 53L, 58L*, 92L, 96L, 00G, 02P, 03P, 04P, 07L
Zambia	68G, 73G, 78G, 83G, *88G*, 91G, 95L, 96G, 01G, 06G
Zimbabwe	70L, 74L, 77L, 79L, 80L, 85L, 90G, 95L, 96P, 00L, 02P, 05L

Note: 2-digit year codes (e.g., 49 = 1949, 02 = 2002). L = Legislative election, P = Presidential, G = General, C = Constitutional convention. *Italic* indicates non-competitive elections. Source: (Hyde and Marinov 2012).

the higher-level election. Thus, if a presidential election was held in the same year as – but separately from – a legislative election, we use the data for the presidential election. Through these steps we reduce NELDA's election-level data set to a country-level data set that can be merged with other country-level data sets containing information on our explanatory and control variables.

In Chapters 3 through 8, we analyze the resulting data set of elections built using the steps described earlier from the original NELDA dataset compiled by Hyde and Marinov (2012). We list these elections later in Table A.1. The table lists the country and year in which the election is held, the type of election, and whether or not the election was competitive according to NELDA.

Summary Statistics for Variables Included in this Book

For more details on coding and sources of the variables listed in the following text, see the discussion of variables in Chapter 4. The number of observations corresponds to the number of elections in both developed and developing countries for which we have observations for that variable.

Glossary of Data Sources

- CGV: Cheibub, Gandhi, and Vreeland (2010)
- CSP: Center for Systemic Peace
- EAC: Ethnic Armed Conflict
- FH: Freedom House
- KA: Kugler-Arbetman
- NELDA: National Elections Across Democracy and Autocracy
- POLCON: Henisz's Political Constraints
- PWT: Penn World Tables
- QOG: Quality of Government
- UCDP: Uppsala Conflict Data Project
- UDS: Unified Democracy Scores
- UN: United Nations
- USAID: United States Agency for International Development
- WBGI: World Bank Governance Indicators
- WDI: World Development Indicators

Table A.2 Summary statistics

Source: Variable	Obs	Mean	Std. dev.	Min	Max
NELDA: Was an election held this year?	2,142	1	0	1	1
NELDA: Competitive?	2,142	.78	.41	0	1
NELDA: Executive election	2,135	.66	.47	0	1
NELDA: Legislative election	2,135	.32	.47	0	1
NELDA: Assembly election	2,142	.02	.15	0	1
NELDA: Competitive executive election	2,135	.57	.5	0	1
NELDA: Competitive legislative election	2,135	.2	.4	0	1
NELDA: Competitive assembly election	2,142	.02	.13	0	1
NELDA: Were there riots/protests after the election?	2,142	.13	.34	0	1
NELDA: Significant violence involving civilian deaths before, during, or after election?	2,142	.18	.38	0	1

(continued)

Table A.2 (*cont.*)

Source: Variable	Obs	Mean	Std. dev.	Min	Max
NELDA: Boycott by some opposition leaders?	2,142	.13	.33	0	1
NELDA: Economic crisis?	2,142	.19	.39	0	1
NELDA: Evidence of gov. harassment of opposition?	2,142	.16	.37	0	1
NELDA: Was the incumbent replaced?	2,142	.28	.45	0	1
NELDA: Were international monitors present?	2,142	.3	.46	0	1
NELDA: Is aid cut off or threatened to be cut off by an outside actor at any point	2,142	.05	.21	0	1
UDS Mean	2,141	.18	.93	−2	2.25
Polity IV: Polity summary score	2,068	2.18	7.23	−10	10
FH PR & CL combined	1,408	6.89	3.85	0	12
FH Political Rights	1,446	4.5	2.09	1	7
FH Civil Liberties	1,446	4.41	1.84	1	7
XPOLITY: Constraints on exec.	2,028	1.14	2.71	−3	4

Table A.2 *(cont.)*

Source: Variable	Obs	Mean	Std. dev.	Min	Max
Polity IV: Competitiveness of executive recruitment	2,092	−.46	14.12	−88	3
Polity IV: Openness of executive recruitment	2,092	1.06	14.39	−88	4
Polity IV: Regulation of chief exec recruitment	2,092	.01	14.18	−88	3
Polity IV: Competitiveness of participation	2,092	.63	14.35	−88	5
Polity IV: Regulation of participation	2,092	1.07	14.4	−88	5
Polity IV: Autocracy	2,068	.27	.44	0	1
Polity IV: Anocracy	2,068	.26	.44	0	1
Polity IV: Democracy	2,068	.47	.5	0	1
XPOLITY: Democracy	2,028	.54	.5	0	1
CGV: Six-fold regime classification	2,031	2.15	1.52	0	5
Colony: Ever colonized?	2,142	.56	.5	0	1
Is this country currently Communist?	2,031	.06	.24	0	1
Dem stock: Based on regime type	2,089	6.04	6.88	0	19
DV: Henisz's political constraints in year 1	52	.2	.21	0	.57

(continued)

Table A.2 (*cont.*)

Source: Variable	Obs	Mean	Std. dev.	Min	Max
PH NELDA: Number of incumbent election losses since 1,946	2,054	1.66	2.57	0	19
PH NELDA: Number of times incumbent has stepped down after election since 1,946	2,054	2.09	2.81	0	14
PH P&T: Number of coups since 1,950	1,965	1.98	3.55	0	23
PH P&T: Number of successful coups since 1,950	1,965	1	1.84	0	11
Natural log of years with executive constraints	2,113	2.25	1.78	0	5.35
PH CGV: Natural log of years as a military dictatorship	2,039	1	1.35	0	4.03
FN Logged tax revenue per capita	1,294	6.65	4.19	−4.4	36.14
High inflation indicator	1,600	.36	.48	0	1
Government effectiveness	557	−.06	.99	−2.04	2.34
Literacy rate	1,267	64.96	30.87	.39	100

Table A.2 (*cont.*)

Source: Variable	Obs	Mean	Std. dev.	Min	Max
Total paved road network (% of total, WDI and IRF)	863	52.58	33.79	.03	313
Kms of road per sq. km (WDI and IRF)	920	.64	.87	0	5.36
Indicator coded 1 if ctry participated in IMF program during any part of year	1,833	.3	.46	0	1
Is there a conflict ongoing?	2,094	.15	.36	0	1
1st 10 years of recovery	2,094	.16	.36	0	1
Country in conflict or 1st 10 yrs of recovery	2,094	.29	.46	0	1
Was there a conflict at war-level in that year?	2,094	.04	.2	0	1
UCDP OSV: One-sided violence in that year?	986	.11	.32	0	1
UCDP OSV: Gov. actor committed violence?	986	.05	.22	0	1
Number of territorial conflicts ongoing in that yr	312	.74	.97	0	5

(*continued*)

Table A.2 (*cont.*)

Source: Variable	Obs	Mean	Std. dev.	Min	Max
Number of control-of-center conflicts in that year	312	.61	.49	0	1
EAC: Ethnic war in this year?	1,895	.1	.3	0	1
EAC: Secessionist war in this year?	1,895	.06	.24	0	1
UCDP: Best estimate of battle deaths	947	120.95	515.63	0	6,377
CSP: Number of IDPs (in 000s) at end of year	1,527	77.59	342.67	0	4,000
Internally Displaced Persons (low estimate)	30	513,439.7	1,051,257	5,000	4,500,000
Democracy aid per capita	663	.35	1.07	0	11.51
UNPKO in that year?	2,142	.07	.26	0	1
UN election monitoring?	2,142	.01	.12	0	1
Logged aid per capita	1,697	1.42	3.69	−5.41	6.86
Natural log of real GDP p.c.	1,863	8.43	1.21	5.37	10.87
Ethnic fractional-ization	2,088	.41	.26	0	.93
Natural log of population	2,023	16.09	1.45	12.35	20.87
Mean Polity 2 score for region	2,094	1.25	5.12	−7.56	9.95
Natural log of state age	2,142	3.84	1.15	0	5.27
Growth in GDP p.c.	1,831	2.39	6.82	−31.12	93.27

Table A.2 (*cont.*)

Source: Variable	Obs	Mean	Std. dev.	Min	Max
GDP p.c. growth below one s.d. below mean	1,831	.07	.26	0	1
Muslim majority	2,139	.2	.4	0	1
Natural log of protests over last 10 years	2,037	1.19	1.13	0	5.42
Natural log of anti-government demonstra-tions	2,026	.27	.54	0	3.64
Colony: ever colonized?	2,142	.56	.5	0	1
Openness to trade, constant prices	1,863	60.94	40.93	1.48	428.95
Dem density score for IGO with highest dem density	1,649	4.07	5.38	−8.62	10
Natural log of oil production value in 2009 dollars	1,890	11.73	10.18	0	26.53
Logged inflation	1,600	3.83	.56	−.13	9.42
Time periods	2,142	1,975.66	16.26	1,940	1,990
Region	2,142	3.66	1.74	1	6

Appendix B
Main Statistical Results

This appendix provides full details for the main statistical results described in the book. Additional results are available in the online appendix. Data and batch files required to estimate all results discussed in the book are available at https://dataverse.harvard.edu/dataverse/irfan.

- Table B.1 reports results discussed in Chapter 4.
- Table B.2 reports results discussed in Chapter 5, 6, and 7.
- Table B.3 reports results discussed in Chapter 8.

Table B.1 Results for Chapter 4

	Electoral legitimacy	Founding election	First 3 elections
Uncompetitive	−0.06		
	(0.05)		
Competitive, no problems	0.03		
	(0.03)		
Founding election		0.11***	
		(0.04)	
First three elections			0.03
			(0.04)
Current democracy	−0.52***	−0.49***	−0.56***
	(0.05)	(0.04)	(0.07)
Per capita income	0.06	0.05	0.00
	(0.05)	(0.05)	(0.06)
Population	−0.23**	−0.21**	−0.14
	(0.10)	(0.10)	(0.16)

Table B.1 (*cont.*)

	Electoral legitimacy	Founding election	First 3 elections
Regional democracy	0.01	0.01	0.01
	(0.01)	(0.01)	(0.02)
State age	−0.02	−0.01	−0.02
	(0.03)	(0.03)	(0.05)
1950s	−0.41***	−0.39***	−0.37***
	(0.09)	(0.09)	(0.11)
1960s	−0.46***	−0.45***	−0.44***
	(0.08)	(0.08)	(0.14)
1970s	−0.30***	−0.29***	−0.28***
	(0.06)	(0.06)	(0.08)
1981–1987	← Reference category →		
Electoral boom	0.11**	0.10**	0.08
	(0.05)	(0.05)	(0.06)
Constant	3.33**	2.99**	2.35
	(1.54)	(1.49)	(2.39)
No. of elections	1,388	1,388	816
R^2	0.28	0.28	0.29

Notes: * < 0.10, ** < 0.05, *** < 0.01. Fixed effects suppressed for space.

Table B.2 Results for Chapters 5, 6, and 7

	Democratic stock	Fiscal space	Conflict
Democratic stock	0.04***		
	(0.01)		
Fiscal Space		0.02	
		(0.02)	
Fiscal Space^2		−0.00	
		(0.00)	
Peace			0.00
			(.)
Recovery: Year 1			−0.06
			(0.06)
Recovery: Year 2			−0.01
			(0.07)
Recovery: Years 3–10			−0.01
			(0.03)
Conflict			−0.10**
			(0.05)
Controls			
Current democracy	−0.25***	−0.61***	−0.52***
	(0.04)	(0.06)	(0.05)
Uncompetitive	−0.02	−0.03	−0.07
	(0.04)	(0.05)	(0.05)
Competitive, no problems	0.05	0.02	0.03
	(0.03)	(0.04)	(0.03)
Per capita income	0.06***	0.02	0.05
	(0.02)	(0.07)	(0.05)
Population	−0.00	−0.14	−0.23**
	(0.01)	(0.16)	(0.10)
Regional democracy	−0.03***	0.01	0.00
	(0.01)	(0.01)	(0.01)
State age	0.01	−0.00	−0.03
	(0.01)	(0.05)	(0.03)
Ethnic fractionalization	−0.07		
	(0.06)		
Hyperinflationary period		−0.05	
		(0.04)	

Table B.2 (*cont.*)

	Democratic stock	Fiscal space	Conflict
Time Periods			
1950s	−0.16***		−0.43***
	(0.06)		(0.09)
1960s	−0.30***	−0.43***	−0.48***
	(0.06)	(0.10)	(0.08)
1970s	−0.26***	−0.21***	−0.31***
	(0.06)	(0.06)	(0.06)
1981–1987	← Reference category →		
Electoral boom	0.02	0.10*	0.12**
	(0.05)	(0.05)	(0.05)
Regions			
Asia/Pacific	0.07		
	(0.05)		
E. Europe	0.11**		
	(0.05)		
Latin America	0.13**		
	(0.06)		
MENA	−0.16***		
	(0.05)		
West	0.36***		
	(0.13)		
Constant	−0.46**	2.13	3.40**
	(0.21)	(2.46)	(1.53)
No. of Elections	1378	988	1,388
R^2		0.34	0.28
Random Effects	Yes		
Fixed Effects	No	Yes	Yes

Notes: $* < 0.10$, $** < 0.05$, $*** < 0.01$. Fixed effects suppressed for space.

Table B.3 Results for Chapter 8

	Monitors	Democracy aid	Aid threats	ODA	UNPKOs	UNPKO w. election
Democratic stock	0.02***	0.04**	0.04***			
	(0.01)	(0.02)	(0.01)			
Election monitors	0.05**					
	(0.02)					
Democratic stock × monitors	−0.01					
	(0.01)					
Democracy aid		0.04***				
		(0.01)				
Democratic stock × democracy aid		−0.02**				
		(0.01)				
Aid threats			0.12*			
			(0.07)			
Democratic stock × aid threats			−0.02			
			(0.03)			
Fiscal space				0.08***		
				(0.02)		
Fiscal space^2				−0.00***		
				(0.00)		

ODA per capita			0.10**		
			(0.04)		
Fiscal space × ODA p.c.			−0.02***		
			(0.01)		
Fiscal space² × ODA p.c.			0.00***		
			(0.00)		
Conflictual				−0.03	−0.26***
				(0.02)	(0.09)
UN PKO				−0.00	
				(0.07)	
Conflictual × UNPKO				−0.03	
				(0.07)	
UNPKO election support					−0.11
					(0.13)
Conflictual × UNPKO election support					0.30***
					(0.09)
No. of elections	1,459	565	1,378	982	1,472	148
R²				0.20	0.13	0.30

Notes: * < 0.10, ** < 0.05, *** < 0.01. Control variables and fixed effects suppressed for space.

227

Notes

Chapter 1 Introduction

1. South Asia is one of the few global bright spots for democracy. Bangladesh returned to democracy in 2008 after a military-dominated caretaker government; Burma's long-ruling military junta initiated political reforms in 2011; 2013 saw opposition party victories in Bhutan (by the People's Democratic Party) and in Nepal (by the Nepali Congress) and a successful second effort at elections in the Maldives; and Sri Lanka's increasingly autocratic Mahinda Rajapaksa was denied a third term by voters in 2015. Perhaps the most surprising democratic victory is Afghanistan, where, in spite of many problems with the electoral process, Hamid Karzai stepped down permitting a peaceful transition of power. Yet, the challenges to the consolidation of these hard-fought victories are very real.

2. See National Democratic Institute for International Affairs (2013).

3. See Jon Boone, "Pakistan Protests: Islamabad Prepares for Anti-Government Demonstration," *The Guardian* (August 10, 2014). Available at www.theguardian.com/world/2014/aug/10/pakistan-protests-islamabad-nawaz-sharif-imran-khan-qadri; accessed August 29, 2014.

4. See Jaffrelot (2002); Jones (2002).

5. See Carlotta Gall, "Runoff will Decide President of Tunisia," *New York Times* (November 25, 2015). Available at http://nyti.ms/1raRtv3; accessed August 28, 2015.

6. For a complete account of Liberia's 1997 elections, see Lyons (1998).

7. Data on elections are from the National Elections across Democracy and Autocracy (NELDA) dataset, collected by Susan Hyde and Nikolay Marinov. We follow their definition of a competitive

executive election as one that determines the head of government (be it a prime minister or president), allows an opposition featuring more than one party, and offers a choice of candidates on the ballots (Hyde and Marinov 2012). We calculate a five-year moving average in order to smooth year-to-year shifts depending on the vagaries of national election calendars.

8. The thirteen states that have yet to hold a national competitive executive election are Bahrain, China, Eritrea, Jordan, Kuwait, Oman, Qatar, Saudi Arabia, Swaziland, Syria, Turkmenistan, the United Arab Emirates, and Vietnam.

9. Emily Beaulieu (2014) provides an excellent analysis of the consequences of electoral protest for democratic reform in the developing world.

10. See Lindberg (2006, 2009a); Teorell (2010).

11. Our measure of democracy is the Polity 2 index from the Polity IV project (Marshall, Gurr, and Jaggers 2014).

12. Our democracy data end in 2012. For this reason, elections from 2008 onward are not included in the calculation of the five-year democratic dividend.

13. See Deutsch (1961); Lipset (1959).

14. See Rustow (1970); O'Donnell and Schmitter (1986).

15. See Schedler (2002); Lindberg (2006, 2009a); Schedler (2009); Teorell (2010).

16. See Brownlee (2007); Gandhi (2010); Levitsky and Way (2010); Slater (2010).

17. See Teorell (2010, 28).

18. See, for example, Meltzer and Richard (1981); Boix (2003); Acemoglu and Robinson (2006).

19. See Lake and Baum (2001); Baum and Lake (2003).

20. See Flores and Nooruddin (2009, 2012).

Chapter 2 Why Have Elections Failed to Deliver? An Answer

1. The World Bank's *World Bank Development Report* (2011) also uses the term "performance legitimacy" to refer to the ability of the state to perform basic duties related to providing security and other public goods. Our development and use of that term are independent of the Bank's but are in the same spirit.

2. See Teorell (2010, 28).

3. See Rustow (1970).
4. See Deutsch (1961).
5. See Lipset (1959); Moore, Jr. (1966).
6. This definition is from Linz and Stepan (1996, 3).
7. See O'Donnell and Schmitter (1986).
8. See Schedler (2002, 2009).
9. See Barkan (2000).
10. See Teorell and Hadenius (2009).
11. See Lindberg (2006).
12. See Hadenius and Teorell (2007); Howard and Roessler (2006); Lindberg (2006, 2009*b*).
13. See Bratton and van de Walle (1997); Lindberg (2009*a*); Teorell and Hadenius (2009); McCoy and Hartlyn (2009); Roessler and Howard (2009).
14. See Brownlee (2009, 145).
15. See Norris (2013*a*); Hyde (2011); Donno (2013).
16. See Norris (2013*a*); Simpser (2013); Schedler (2002); Hyde (2011); Kelley (2012); Gottlieb (2015).
17. See Simpser (2013); Norris (2014); Beaulieu (2014); Donno (2013).
18. See Pop-Eleches and Robertson (2015) for a like-minded argument.
19. Modernization theorists and their intellectual descendants tend not to discuss elections explicitly, focusing instead on expansions of political participation or episodes of democratization. For the purposes of this discussion, however, we consider these equivalent.
20. See, for instance, Przeworski and Limongi (1997); Przeworski et al. (2000).
21. See Moore, Jr. (1966, 418).
22. See Boix (2003); Ross (2001, 2012).
23. See Huntington (1968); Rose and Shin (2001); Fortin (2012); Paris (2004).
24. See Fukuyama (2004, 26).
25. Bratton and van de Walle (1997, 273).
26. See Bratton and van de Walle (1997); Carothers (2006); Rakner and van de Walle (2009); Gibler and Randazzo (2011).
27. Nordlinger (1968, 458).
28. See Weingast (1997); Collier (2009).

29. See, *inter alia*, Mansfield and Snyder (1995, 2002, 2007); Snyder (2000).
30. See Mansfield and Snyder (2007, 10).
31. See O'Donnell (1973).
32. See Levitsky and Way (2010).
33. See Hyde (2011).
34. See Brownlee (2007); Gandhi (2010); Slater (2010).
35. See Levitsky and Way (2010); Brownlee (2007); Slater (2010).
36. Interestingly, Gandhi (2010) does not formally consider elections alongside legislatures and parties as political institutions in dictatorships, since she retains Przeworski et al.'s (2000) definition of dictatorships as regimes not holding competitive elections.
37. For more on these significant recent data collection efforts, see NELDA by Hyde and Marinov (2012); Geddes's (2003) measures of non-democratic regimes; Cheibub, Gandhi, and Vreeland's (2010) Democracy and Development Expanded Dataset, which codes democratic and dictatorial sub-types; the Data on International Election Monitoring and the Quality of Elections Data described by Kelley (2012); and the Electoral Integrity Project described in Norris (2014).
38. See Hyde (2011).
39. See Caroline Wyatt, "Bush and Putin: Best of Friends," *BBC News* (June 2001). Available at http://news.bbc.co.uk/2/hi/europe/1392791.stm; accessed August 23, 2015.
40. On this distinction, see Lave and March (1975).
41. See "Nikita Needles Peking; Hails Ford Methods," *Chicago Tribune* (August 22, 1963). Available at http://archives.chicagotribune.com/1963/08/22/page/14/article/nikita-needles-peking-hails-ford-methods; accessed August 31, 2015. A new line of scholarship, in contrast, argues that the personal background of political leaders meaningfully affects how they govern and how they are perceived by foreign governments. See, for example, Dreher et al. (2009), Kaplan (2013), Flores, Lloyd, and Nooruddin (2014), Gift and Krcmaric (2015), and Horowitz, Stam, and Ellis (2015).
42. See Achen and Bartels (2012). Note, however, that a long line of research problematizes the development of political accountability in democracy (Besley 2007; Gottlieb 2015).
43. Contingent legitimacy is also likely to depend on an election winner's personal characteristics. The first woman or member of an

ethnic minority to win the chief executive's position may enjoy a special form of contingent legitimacy, as might a figure seen as a break from a difficult past. Yet we think of that impact as being essentially random and concentrate instead on the more systemic factors of electoral integrity and founding elections.

44. This, of course, is a probabilistic claim, rather than a deterministic one. We do not deny the possibility of political skills that allow some politicians to perform well, regardless of tough circumstances.

45. See Przeworski (2015) for a detailed analysis of how countries acquire the habit of using elections to change governments peacefully.

46. See Barkan (2000).

47. We leave as an open question whether election winners who inherit deeper stocks of contingent legitimacy also perform in ways that augment democratic change. We return to this question in Chapter 4.

48. See Lake (2010).

49. See Lake (2010).

50. See Flores and Nooruddin (2012).

51. See Meltzer and Richard (1981); Lake and Baum (2001); Acemoglu and Robinson (2006).

52. See Gurr (1970).

53. See Bratton and van de Walle (1997).

54. See Lindberg (2006).

55. See, *inter alia*, Collier (1999); Collier et al. (2003); Kang and Meernik (2005); Flores and Nooruddin (2009); Iqbal (2010).

56. See Flores and Nooruddin (2009, 2012).

57. See Paris (2004).

58. This is an inversion of the standard claim in the grievance literature, which emphasizes that it is horizontal inequality that causes war, not the other way around (Cederman, Gleditsch, and Buhaug 2013).

59. For an account of the FARC's support before drug trafficking, see Flores (2014).

60. See "Uribe Defends Security Policies," *BBC News* (Nov 18, 2004). Available at http://news.bbc.co.uk/2/hi/americas/4021213. stm; accessed August 23, 2015.

Chapter 3 The Third Wave(s) and the Electoral Boom

1. Data on elections again come from NELDA (Hyde and Marinov 2012). Data on democracy come from James Vreeland's XPOLITY correction to Polity IV's coding of regime type (Vreeland 2008).
2. We rely on the Uppsala Conflict Data Program (UCDP) and the Peace Research Institute Oslo's (PRIO) Armed Conflict Dataset to define sovereign states (Gleditsch et al. 2002; Themnér 2013).
3. Data on GDP per capita come from the Penn World Tables. We use data on real per-capita GDP in constant prices at purchasing power parity. Data on elections come from NELDA. Since we take the natural log of GDP per capita, the scale of the y-axis is non-linear.
4. Technically, the whiskers show the position of the largest value of GDP per capita within 1.5 inter-quartile ranges (IQR, or the distance between the 25*th* and 75*th* percentiles) of the 25*th* and 75*th* percentiles.
5. See Collier (2008); Kenny (2012).
6. Data on democracy come from the Polity IV project (Marshall, Gurr, and Jaggers 2014). We use a lowess-smoothed line to diminish yearly variation.
7. These data are for all coups, successful and unsuccessful, and come from Powell and Thyne (2011).
8. Data on taxation come from the World Bank's *World Development Indicators* (http://data.worldbank.org/data-catalog/ world-development-indicators); accessed February 2, 2016, which measures taxation per capita. We convert these data to total taxation in real terms and then calculate the natural log of total taxes per capita. We will discuss this measure in more detail in Chapter 6, but note here that taxation per capita is a reasonable proxy for fiscal space.
9. See Vreeland (2003); Nooruddin and Simmons (2006); Nooruddin (2008).
10. See Williamson (1990).
11. Our definition of Communism relies on two sources: Cheibub, Gandhi, and Vreeland's (2010) comparative data on political systems, which codes whether or not the head of government is also

the leader of the Communist Party in that country, and a measure from La Porta et al. (1999) that codes whether the country's legal origins are socialist. Data from La Porta et al. (1999) are taken from the Quality of Government dataset (http://qog.pol.gu.se/); accessed February 2, 2016.

12. The data on technocrats are our own. We code a leader as a technocrat if she held a graduate degree in a field related to economics (e.g., finance); see Flores, Lloyd, and Nooruddin (2014) for more details.

13. See Huntington (1968).

14. Data on conflict come from the UCDP (Themnér 2013; Themnér and Wallensteen 2013). A civil conflict is defined as featuring the state versus one or more organized groups killing more than twenty-five people per year. We use a lowess-smoothed line to control for yearly variation.

15. See Ball (1996); Ottaway (2003); Paris (2004).

16. See Flores and Nooruddin (2012).

Chapter 4 The Ephemeral Power of Contingent Legitimacy

1. See "As Ethiopia Votes, What's 'Free and Fair' Got To Do With It?" *Washington Post* (May 18, 2015). Available at www.washingtonpost.com/blogs/monkey-cage/wp/2015/05/18/as-ethiopia-votes-whats-free-and-fair-got-to-do-with-it/). See also "Ethiopia's ruling party wins by landslide in general election" *Guardian Online* (June 22, 2015). Available at www.theguardian.com/world/2015/jun/22/ethiopias-ruling-party-win-clean-sweep-general-election accessed February 2, 2016.

2. We thank Thad Dunning for useful conversations about our research design.

3. We use Version 3 of NELDA (Hyde and Marinov 2012), available at http://hyde.research.yale.edu/nelda/; accessed August 29, 2015. We thank Susan Hyde and Niki Marinov for answering questions related to this remarkable public good.

4. That is, we analyze all national elections – legislative and executive, competitive and uncompetitive – in the models discussed throughout the book, though we note that the online appendix provides the results using alternative election lists, such as only

competitive, only executive, or only competitive, executive elections.

5. Appendix A describes in more detail the construction of the dataset and the variables included.

6. We thank Emily Beaulieu for helping us with this definition.

7. The excluded counties are Australia, Austria, Belgium, Canada, Denmark, Finland, France, Germany, Iceland, Ireland, Japan, Luxembourg, the Netherlands, New Zealand, Norway, Sweden, Switzerland, the United Kingdom, and the United States of America.

8. Table A.1 in Appendix A lists the elections analyzed. We check the robustness of our results to including the consolidated democracies in our sample; doing so alters little and, if anything, strengthens our conclusions by sharpening the gulf in resources between these fortunate states and those that aspire to be like them.

9. Pemstein, Meserve, and Melton (2010) describe the Unified Democracy Scores in detail and Marshall, Gurr, and Jaggers (2014) discuss the Polity IV project. Information about the Freedom House project methodology is available at https://freedomhouse.org/sites/default/files/Methodology_FIW_2015.pdf; accessed August 30, 2015.

10. Throughout the book, we discuss the robustness of our results to using alternative dependent variables, including the Polity score. These additional results are made available in the online appendix.

11. It is entirely possible, indeed quite likely, that many countries will experience another election within the five-year window. This makes our specification a generous test of the "democratization-by-elections" thesis. If elections facilitate democratization, then this would be the equivalent of having two doses of medicine but attributing the healing effects to the first dose only. Regardless, we also check our results against a two-year window and a one-year window and the results hold.

12. The sample size is smaller than the 1,755 elections with which we started our investigation due to missing data.

13. Specifically, we estimate a series of ordinary least squares (OLS) regression models of the form $(UDS_{i,t+5} - UDS_{i,t}) = \alpha + \beta * UDS_{i,t} + X_{i,t}\gamma + \ldots + \epsilon$, where $(UDS_{i,t+5} - UDS_{i,t})$ is the democratic

dividend for country i holding an election in year t; α is a constant; β is the coefficient on our democracy measure in the year of the election $UDS_{i,t}$; γ is a vector of coefficients on our covariates $\mathbf{X}$; and ϵ is an error term. Each coefficient captures the impact of the associated independent variable on the democratic dividend for a country holding an election. A positive and statistically coefficient indicates that countries holding an election capture a larger democratic dividend when that independent variable increases. Since countries have multiple elections over the period under study, we estimate standard errors that are corrected for clustering by country. We include country-level fixed effects whenever possible. When the structure of the data requires us to use random effects, we also include region-level fixed effects.

14. See www.correlatesofwar.org/ and www.pcr.uu.se/research/UCDP/ respectively; accessed February 2, 2016.

15. We take the natural log of state age to correct for the variable's extreme skew.

16. We take the natural log of the Penn World Tables measure of real per-capita GDP calculated using a chain series, accessed through the Quality of Government data (available respectively at www.rug.nl/research/ggdc/data/pwt/ and qog.pol.gu.se/data); accessed February 2, 2016. The Penn World Tables offers the benefit of a longer time series, stretching back to 1950.

17. We calculate the mean democracy score for the other countries in the election-holding country's region.

18. We define *time periods* theoretically, rather than strictly by decade. We code five time periods: 1950–1960, 1961–1970, 1971–1980, 1981–1987, and the electoral boom (1988–2010). Replacing this periodization with a more conventional decades variable does not alter our results. For *world region*, we divide our sample into Sub-Saharan Africa, the Middle East and North Africa, Eastern Europe, Asia and the Pacific, Latin America, and Western Europe. The region variable is omitted when we use country fixed effects.

19. Results using this larger set of controls are reported in the online appendix.

20. Norris (2015). See also Norris (2013*a,b*, 2014); Norris, Frank, and Martínez i Coma (2014).

21. See Donno (2013); Norris (2014); Simpser (2013); Sen (2009).
22. See Miller (2015).
23. See the Electoral Integrity Project (EIP) for more detailed measurement strategies. The EIP is available at https://sites.google.com/site/electoralintegrityproject4/home; accessed August 14, 2015.
24. As Hyde and Marinov (2012) cleverly put it, the question is "which elections *can* be lost?" (emphasis ours).
25. Full results are presented in Table B.1 in Appendix B. We focus on the effects of the election variables in the text. Of the control variables, the only ones that are statistically significant consistently are the current level of democracy, population size, and time period effects. Current democracy and population are both negatively signed. For the time periods, the 1980s are the reference category. Prior decades performed worse than the 1980s, while the electoral boom was better for democratic change than the 1980s. In other words, once we control for several key aspects of the environment in which elections took place (e.g., income per capita), elections during the electoral boom actually performed better than those in Wave 3.0 of democracy. We stress that all models also include country fixed effects.
26. Excellent contributions to, as well as surveys of, this vibrant literature can be found in Beaulieu (2014); Donno (2013); Hyde (2011); Norris (2014, 2015); Norris, Frank, and Martínez i Coma (2014); Simpser (2013).
27. Hyde and Marinov (2012) create an indicator for "when a country [that] is newly independent is having its first elections, when a country holds the first multi-party elections after a significant period of non-democratic rule, or when a country transitions from single-party elections to multi-party elections." See http://hyde.research.yale.edu/nelda/NELDA_codebook_2012.pdf; accessed August 14, 2015.
28. We leverage the founding election coding in NELDA to code second and third elections. In this case, however, we lose observations for countries that existed before 1946 and held elections, since we cannot know the sequence of those elections until we know a founding election took place.
29. See also Howard and Roessler (2006).

Chapter 5 Experience Matters: Democratic Stock and Elections

1. See Przeworski (2015).
2. See Dahl (1971).
3. See Carothers (2006) and LeBas (2011) on parties and Gibler and Randazzo (2011) on the role of judiciaries.
4. Teorell and Hadenius (2009, 97) represent an important exception. They show that an authoritarian resurgence after elections is less likely the longer a country's experience of competitive, multiparty elections.
5. Nigeria's latest elections are particularly hopeful given that the incumbent lost and stepped down from power peacefully (Lewis and Kew 2015).
6. Huntington (1968, 12).
7. Huntington (1968, 13–14).
8. See Marshall, Gurr, and Jaggers (2014) for a description of the Polity project. The Polity score ranges from -10 to 10 and classifies as full democracies countries with a score of 6 or over (Jaggers and Gurr 1995).
9. Technically we take the natural logarithm of one plus the number of years that a country has been democratic, since the natural logarithm of 0 is undefined.
10. The measure ranges from 0 (for countries with no previous democratic experience) to roughly 5 (for countries with nearly 200 years of previous democratic experience).
11. The measure is defined as follows: $demstock_t$ $\sum_{i1}^{t-1} (Regime)^{t-i}$. We begin with a measure called *Regime* that is equal to 0 if fully autocratic, .95 if fully democratic and 0.5 if neither autocratic nor democratic (i.e., what Polity IV calls an "anocratic" or "incoherent" regime). Our measure of a country's democratic-institutional stock in year t is equal to the summation of *Regime* raised to the power $t - i$ for all years up to and including year $t - 1$. The measure ranges from 0 for countries with no previous experience of democratic rule to roughly 19 for countries governed without interruption for decades by a democratic regime.
12. See the online appendix for the robustness results.

13. We make one notable change to the baseline model. The baseline is a fixed-effects regression, which effectively introduces an indicator variable for each unit, or country, in our regression. The model therefore only tests whether changes in our independent variables across time within countries affect the democratic dividend. A fixed-effects estimator is both a conceptually and a methodologically poor fit for our analysis of democratic experience, however (Bell and Jones 2014). Democratic experience accumulates slowly even in the best of circumstances; in the sadly numerous cases of countries with no experience of democracy, it exhibits no variance at all. We therefore estimate a random-effects model with regional indicator variables. Clark and Linzer (2015) note that fixed-effects regression may be inappropriate in the case of "sluggish" independent variables, or those that vary mainly across, rather than within, cases. This is precisely the situation in which we find ourselves. Clark and Linzer (2015) use Monte Carlo estimations to show that in the case of a sluggish independent variable and few observations per unit, the choice between random and fixed effects depends on ρ, or the correlation between the unit effects and the unit-level mean of the independent variable of interest. When ρ falls below 0.3 to 0.5, random effects outperforms fixed effects. Our estimate of ρ in our data is 0.56, which is sufficiently low to justify the choice of random effects. We also consider another option, the fixed-effects vector decomposition (FEVD) estimator proposed by Plümper and Troeger (2007). Their technique decomposes fixed effects into two parts, a systematic component driven by time-invariant or slow-moving variables and an error term. This technique yields a positive and statistically significant coefficient on our measure of democratic-institutional stock. Plümper and Troeger's FEVD estimator seems a good fit to our particular estimation challenges, but is also the subject of controversy among methodologists (Breusch et al. 2011; Greene 2011; Bell and Jones 2014).

14. The data confirm these suspicions. The correlation between our measures of democratic experience and democracy in the year of election is 0.68 in our sample. More democratically experienced countries are far more likely to hold competitive elections.

15. We also assess whether this predicted effect is statistically meaningful by examining whether the confidence interval around the prediction includes zero.

16. The full regression results are reported in column 1 of Table B.2.

17. We replicate the analysis in Figure 5.3 using our more complex, decaying measure of democratic experience. Our results are substantively the same and displayed in full in the online appendix.

18. All results described in this paragraph are provided in the online appendix.

19. In a separate test, also reported in the online appendix, we checked to see if the impact of democratic experience is nonlinear. Perhaps the first few years of experience are critically important to successful elections, after which the impact of added experience lessens or even reverses as democratic institutions ossify. We find no evidence of this impact when we insert a quadratic term for democratic experience.

20. This measure is highly correlated with a country's democracy score, since it is an input into that measure.

21. We use POLCON V (Henisz 2000, 2002).

22. The literature on comparative political parties is sprawling, but see Panebianco (1988), Mainwaring (1998, 1999), Chhibber and Kollman (2004), and Nooruddin (2011) for excellent introductions. Carothers (2006) is particularly relevant to our inquiry.

23. These indicators are from the Democracy and Dictatorships dataset collected by Cheibub, Gandhi, and Vreeland (2010). See Braithwaite (2015) for a recent analysis of political party bans. She reports that as many as 121 countries had constitutional party bans in place at some point over the past fifty years. The bulk of these are non-democracies.

24. See Przeworski (2015).

25. See Londregan and Poole (1990). The coup data come from Powell and Thyne (2011). We take the natural log of the number of coups.

26. Full results with control variables are available in the online appendix. Estimating these models jointly using seemingly unrelated regression estimation does not alter the results.

27. We also estimate a model using the Polcon III measure, which excludes judiciaries and sub-federal constraints on policymaking. Our results hold and are available in the online appendix.

28. We double-check one more aspect of these results. Our measure of experience with executive constraints is drawn from Polity IV, as is our systemic measure of democratic experience. This may explain the strong correlation with the democratic dividend. To check this intuition, we also estimate regressions of the impact of a history of competitive political participation, unregulated political participation, open executive recruitment, and competitive executive recruitment. None of these other measures of democratic experience affect the democratic dividend from elections, against suggesting the importance of executive constraints.

29. The coup effect is significant at the 90 percent confidence interval. We also re-estimate our coup models substituting our logged number of coups with an indicator variable equal to 1 if a country has ever experienced either a coup attempt or a successful coup. In this case, neither coefficient is statistically significant, though the coefficient on successful coups comes close (p 0.11). These results are available in the online appendix.

30. We also consider whether the impact of coups depends on their installation of military regimes that deteriorate democratic rule. This does not seem to the case, however. When we add a measure from Cheibub, Gandhi, and Vreeland (2010) on the logged number of years of rule by military junta before an election, the model yields a statistically significant negative coefficient on coup experience and a positive and statistically significant coefficient on length of military rule. This reinforces our notion that it is coups themselves that set the stage for under-performing elections in the future, rather than military rule. These results are available in the online appendix.

31. We make two changes to the analysis. First, we estimate a random-effects logistic regression, instead of a standard regression model, to account for the binary nature of the dependent variables. Second, we substitute our measure of the current democracy score with a measure of the dependent variable in the current election. So, for example, the model of election boycotts in the next election controls for whether there was an election boycott in the

current election. In the coups model, the lagged dependent variable is whether a military coup has occurred since 1950 or the country's birth, whichever comes second.

32. All models control for the core control variables from our main model. Full results are available in the online appendix.

33. These probabilities are calculated for a highly competitive election in a typical Sub-Saharan African country during the electoral boom.

34. On Polity, see Marshall, Gurr, and Jaggers (2014) and www. systemicpeace.org/polityproject.html; accessed February 3, 2016. On Freedom House, see https://freedomhouse.org/ and https:// freedomhouse.org/sites/default/files/Methodology_FIW_2015.pdf; accessed February 3, 2016.

35. Full results are available in the online appendix. We make one change to the baseline model. The lagged dependent variable in each model is the value of itself in the year the election was held. So, for example, we model the five-year change in civil liberties and political rights as a function of democratic experience and civil liberties and political rights in the year the election was held.

36. As before, these predictions are calculated for a highly competitive election in a typical Sub-Saharan African country during the electoral boom.

37. We also separate the Freedom House measures into their two components of civil liberties and political rights. Our results remain the same and are available in the online appendix.

38. See Bueno de Mesquita et al. (2003).

39. For more on the CSES, see www.cses.org/; accessed February 3, 2016.

40. We use the third module of the CSES. Some countries covered by the CSES held more than one election between 2005 and 2010; in these cases, we keep the latter of the two elections, though this does not alter the nature of the plot.

41. A simple bivariate regression analysis supports this intuition, with the coefficient on democratic experience positive and highly statistically significant ($p < 0.001$). We deepen this analysis, also estimating a voter-level model of democratic satisfaction using multilevel modeling techniques. We control for voters' age, gender, marital status, urbanism, religiosity, education, and employment status. The model strongly supports our conclusions

in Figure 5.7: voters in older democracies are far more likely to report satisfaction with the workings of their democracy. Results from the multilevel regression model are available in the online appendix.

42. The regression evidence on this question is mixed. On one hand, removing elections in developed countries from this sample eliminates the positive relationship between democratic satisfaction and democratic experience. On the other hand, when we re-estimate a multilevel model of voter-level democratic satisfaction, democratic experience is once again a strong predictor of voter confidence. Results are available in the online appendix.

Chapter 6 Starved States: Fiscal Space and Elections

1. See Huntington (1968; 1991).
2. See Chandra (2004).
3. For instance, we say little about the interesting literature on the relationship between inequality and democratization. Ansell and Samuels (2014) provide an excellent overview of, and contribution to, that scholarship. Inequality might matter for whether or not countries moved to holding elections, but its relationship to the democratic dividend of those elections is less obvious.
4. See Almond and Verba (1963, 1980); Inglehart (1997); Inglehart and Welzel (2005); Jamal and Nooruddin (2010).
5. See Lipset (1959).
6. See Cutright (1963); Cutright and Wiley (1969).
7. See Huntington (1968, 1971); O'Donnell and Schmitter (1986).
8. See Przeworski et al. (2000).
9. See Acemoglu and Robinson (2006).
10. See Boix and Stokes (2003).
11. See Kennedy (2010).
12. See Miller (2012).
13. See Kapstein and Converse (2008).
14. See Stokes et al. (2013).
15. Nooruddin and Chhibber (2008) apply the concept of fiscal space in their study of anti-incumbency voting and electoral volatility in India's state assembly elections. Their argument is similar in spirit to ours.

16. Comparability of publicly available tax data can be suspect. We utilize data reported by the World Bank in its World Development Indicators dataset, since it covers the largest number of countries and years of any such dataset of which we are aware. We supplement these data with information from the Political Extractive Capacity project headed by Jacek Kugler (Kugler and Tammen 2012). A more recent data collection effort comes from the International Centre for Tax and Development (www.ictd.ac/; accessed February 3, 2016), but these data only go back to 1980, which makes it impractical for our purposes.

17. See Collier (2008).

18. Fortin-Rittberger (2014) provides strong evidence for this claim in the context of the Eastern European states.

19. We use a dichotomous indicator coded "1" if the country's annual inflation rate is greater than fifty. The developing world median inflation rate is 7.37 for our sample. Our results are unaffected if we lower the threshold for what constitutes a high inflation episode to ten, which is the 90th percentile in the estimation sample.

20. The regression estimates are presented in column 2 of Table B.2 in Appendix B. The result for our quadratic term indicates that this is true only to a point, beyond which the positive effect weakens. We can calculate this inflection point using our estimates, and it is $2,115 per capita. And even beyond this point the effect continues to be positive. Recall that the developing country average in 2005 was a little less than $100 – most developing countries are a long way from having to worry about this hypothetical situation of having treasuries that are too flush.

21. Full results for all tests discussed in the remainder of this section are provided in the online appendix to this chapter.

22. Franzese and Jusko (2006) provide a comprehensive overview of the literature on political-economic cycles.

23. See Pevehouse (2005); Donno (2013); Poast and Urpelainen (2015). We thank Daniela Donno for sharing these data with us.

24. On globalization and democracy, see Rudra (2005). The literature on the resource curse is divided but, for our money, Michael Ross has it right (Ross 2001, 2012; Andersen and Ross 2014).

25. More seriously, for an effort to understand how income shocks affect governments' spending decisions, see Beazer, Nooruddin, and Sokhey (2015).
26. The most obvious issue here is that we should also expect better-governed states to be more capable of generating higher tax revenues, since the latter are a function of domestic state capacity. Fully disentangling this relationship is beyond the scope of our book but, for our purposes, showing that the relationship exists represents an adequate test of our argument's posited causal mechanism.
27. For more detail on the World Bank surveys, see Kaufmann, Kraay, and Zoido-Lobatón (2000). See www.govindicators.org (accessed February 3, 2016) for the data and more information on the methodology used.
28. Full regression results are available in the online appendix.
29. The data points in the graph are labeled using their three letter World Bank codes.
30. See Ansell (2010); Nooruddin and Simmons (2006); Stasavage (2005).
31. Results are provided in the online appendix.
32. See Inglehart and Welzel (2005); Jamal and Nooruddin (2010).
33. This positive relationship holds up in a multilevel regression model, the results of which are available in the online appendix. Controlling for a baseline model of individual-level satisfaction with democracy developed by Jamal and Nooruddin (2010), respondents living in countries with greater fiscal space are more likely to state that they are satisfied with democracy in their country.
34. See Levi (1988); Olson (1993); Besley and Persson (2014).

Chapter 7 Violent Votes: Conflict and Elections

1. See Toft (2009).
2. See Ottaway (2003).
3. See Flores and Nooruddin (2009, 2012).
4. See Small and Singer (1976); Russett and Oneal (2001).

5. See Mansfield and Snyder (2007) for the clearest statement of this argument. But see also Daxecker (2007) for a nuanced analysis that takes issue with the broader "democratization leads to interstate conflict" literature.

6. See, *inter alia*, Collier et al. (2003); Collier (2009); Collier, Hoeffler, and Rohner (2009); Braithwaite, Dasandi, and Hudson (2014).

7. See, Cederman, Hug, and Krebs (2010); Cederman, Gleditsch, and Hug (2013).

8. See Ball (1996); Walter (1999); Paris (2004); Mansfield and Snyder (2007).

9. See Flores and Nooruddin (2009).

10. See Flores and Nooruddin (2012).

11. See Brancati and Snyder (2013).

12. See Matanock (2013).

13. See World Bank (2011, 100). Bozzoli, Brück, and Muhumuza (2011) qualify this argument. They conclude that Ugandans exposed to political violence reduced their expectations of their economic prospects.

14. Phillips (2015) shows that civil war even drives up military spending in neighboring countries.

15. See Collier (1999); Collier et al. (2003); Kang and Meernik (2005); Braithwaite, Dasandi, and Hudson (2014).

16. See Ghobarah, Huth, and Russett (2003); Iqbal (2010).

17. See Walter (1999); World Bank (2011); Haggard and Tiede (2014); De Juan and Pierskalla (2014); Hong and Kang (2015).

18. See Daly (2012).

19. See Bar-Tal (2000); Fearon, Humphreys, and Weinstein (2009); Rohner, Thoenig, and Zilibotti (2013); De Juan and Pierskalla (2014); Hong and Kang (2015). Wood (2003) offers an alternative account, in which cooperation between insurgent groups and civilians during El Salvador's long civil war was born of positive changes in political culture that encouraged civilians to defy repression and take pleasure in political agency.

20. See Freedom House, "Sri Lanka," *Freedom in the World* (2011). Available at https://freedomhouse.org/report/freedom-world/2011/sri-lanka; accessed August 30, 2015. See also "Sri Lanka President Wins Re-Election – State TV," *BBC News*

(January 27, 2010). Available at http://news.bbc.co.uk/2/hi/south_asia/8482270.stm; accessed August 29, 2015.

21. See Small and Singer (1982). A full accounting of the differences between various civil war lists is provided by Gleditsch et al. (2002), Fearon and Laitin (2003), Collier and Hoeffler (2004) and Sambanis (2004). Sambanis in particular highlights a series of coding choices that contribute to divergent lists of civil wars in available datasets.

22. See Themnér (2013). The UCDP does differentiate conflicts by their intensity and a related dataset records annual data on battle deaths, yet the main dataset captures lower-intensity organized armed violence excluded by data on war alone (Gleditsch et al. 2002; Themnér and Wallensteen 2013).

23. We do, however, prefer data that focus on organized armed conflict including the central government, as opposed to efforts to code non-state or communal conflict, or organized violence between non-stated armed actors. This preference derives from our focus on how armed violence shifts politicians' attitudes towards electoral competition.

24. For more on the origins of insurgency in Colombia, see Daly (2012); Flores (2014).

25. Countries recovering from civil conflict face a high probability of returning to violence. Our data indicate that two out of five conflict episodes recur within five years and fully half recur with ten. See Flores and Nooruddin (2009, 2012).

26. The full regression results are provided in column 3 of Table B.2 in Appendix B.

27. All results discussed in this section are available in the online appendix.

28. These data come from the UCDP's data on battle deaths (Uppsala Conflict Data Program 2014).

29. These data come from the UCDP's data on one-sided violence (Eck and Hultman 2007).

30. We take the natural log of the UCDP's "best guess" for combatants killed in battle. For countries with multiple conflicts ongoing simultaneously, we combine the estimates for each conflict into one annual measure. The data cover only direct battle deaths and hence likely understate intensity, since they do not capture deaths

of civilians or injuries to surviving combatants that shorten their lives, but do not kill them in battle.

31. This indicator codes whether or not the standing government or organized armed group committed one-sided violence killing over twenty-five civilians in the year the election was held (Eck and Hultman 2007).

32. We therefore reduce our decade dummy variables to only one, which equals 1 if the election took place in 2001 or later and 0 if it occurred between 1989 and 2000. One-sided violence can take place outside of civil war, so we insert three variables: *conflict*, *one-sided violence*, and a multiplicative interaction term of the two variables.

33. The UCDP classifies all civil conflicts as being fought over territory or the control of the central government, so these two indicator variables exhaustively identify all conflicts (Gleditsch et al. 2002; Themnér and Wallensteen 2013).

34. For greater detail, see Wimmer, Cederman, and Min (2009).

35. In each of these cases, we estimate logit models of the probability of a given event in the next election conditional on whether it was in conflict, recovery, or peacetime during this election, the value of the dependent variable in this election, and our baseline set of control variables. The full results are available in the online appendix.

36. No survey was conducted in 1999.

37. The latter question also gives respondents the option to respond that sometimes non-democratic forms of government are preferable to democracy or that the form of government does not matter to "people like me."

38. A commentator on anti-corruption protests in Guatemala puts it well: "Guatemalan society has been maturing, but its political system has remained stagnant. This tension has mobilized the people." See Azam Ahmed, "Guatemala's Corruption Investigations Make Swift Strides," *New York Times* (August 25, 2015). Available at http://nyti.ms/1U4nR01; accessed August 26, 2015.

39. In a remarkable step, a Guatemalan court ruled that former dictator Efraín Ríos Montt must face a genocide trail in spite of his dementia. The trial will be conducted behind closed doors. See

Elizabeth Malkin, "Genocide Retrial Is Set for Guatemalan Former Dictator," *New York Times* (August 25, 2015). Available at
http://nyti.ms/1KLxfLz; accessed August 26, 2015.

40. See David Grann, "A Murder Foretold," *The New Yorker* (April
4, 2011). Available at www.newyorker.com/magazine/2011/04/
04/a-murder-foretold; accessed August 26, 2015.

41. See Human Rights Watch, "World Report 2013". Available at
www.hrw.org/world-report/2013/; accessed August 30, 2015.

42. "El Salvador Gangs Announce Re-launch of 2012 Truce," *BBC
News* (August 30, 2014). Available at www.bbc.com/news/
world-latin-america-29000158; accessed August 29, 2015.

43. See World Bank (2011, 4).

44. See Synge (1997, 112). Mozambique has had regular elections but
no turnover in office. Two decades into Mozambique's history
of holding elections, Azevedo-Harman (2015, 139) describes its
democratic prospects as "cloudy at best."

45. World Bank (2011, 100).

46. We also estimate a model of democratic satisfaction, controlling for age, economic status, and assessment of the national
economy, using our 2010 data. The negative impact of insecurity on democratic satisfaction is robust to these controls. The
results are robust to using the proportion of citizens supporting
democracy over all other forms of government as the dependent variable. These additional results are available in the online
appendix.

Chapter 8 Democracy Promotion for the Twenty-first Century

1. See "Confronting 'Illiberal Democracy,' in Central Europe," *New
York Times* (June 8, 2015). Available at http://nyti.ms/1G6COF7;
accessed August 26, 2015.

2. Miller (2015) makes this point more generally in his analysis of
the democratic benefits of "autocratic" elections.

3. See Hyde (2011).

4. Kelley (2012, 3).

5. See, *inter alia*, Beaulieu and Hyde (2009); Hyde (2011); Kelley
(2012); Norris (2014, 2015).

6. Full results for all models described in this chapter are available in Table B.3 in Appendix B.
7. Carothers (2015) provides an excellent overview of democracy aid's achievements and shortcomings.
8. See Finkel, Pérez-Linan, and Seligson (2007). A different literature, which we review below, reviews the impact of broader official development assistance on democracy and governance.
9. See Dietrich and Wright (2015).
10. These data are from Finkel, Pérez-Linan, and Seligson (2007).
11. See Huntington (1968).
12. This literature is too large for us to review in detail here, but see Mozaffar, Scarritt, and Galaich (2003); Mozaffar and Scarritt (2005); LeBas (2011). Carbone (2007) provides an excellent review.
13. Carothers (2006, 213).
14. Dietrich and Wright (2015) concur.
15. See (Ha and Rogers 2014; Besley and Persson 2014).
16. See Bräutigam and Knack (2004); Bueno de Mesquita and Smith (2012); Easterly (2007); Morrison (2007, 2012).
17. See Arndt, Jones, and Tarp (2014).
18. See Bueno de Mesquita and Smith (2012).
19. See Bräutigam and Knack (2004).
20. See Sachs (2005).
21. See Boulding (2012); Dietrich (2013).
22. See Dietrich and Winters (2015); Dietrich (2015).
23. See Besley and Persson (2014) for a useful summary of this issue.
24. See Walter (1999); Paris (2004); Flores and Nooruddin (2009, 2012); Brancati and Snyder (2013), but also Matanock (2013).
25. See Hultman, Kathman, and Shannon (2014).
26. See Doyle and Sambanis (2006); Fortna (2008); Collier, Hoeffler, and Söderbom (2008); Hultman, Kathman, and Shannon (2015).
27. See Fortna (2008).
28. Data collected from: www.un.org/en/peacekeeping/; accessed August 26, 2015.
29. See Steinert and Grimm (2014).
30. See Hultman, Kathman, and Shannon (2015).
31. Ottaway (2003, 314).
32. Though, on this point, see Dietrich and Wright (2015).

Chapter 9 Conclusions

1. See Fukuyama (1989).
2. See George H. W. Bush, "1991 State of the Union Address" (January 29, 1991). Available at www.presidency.ucsb.edu/ ws/?pid=19253; accessed August 29, 2015. Fukuyama's more recent work is more in line with our analysis and privileges the creation of political order as a pre-condition for building stable societies (2004, 2011, 2014, 2015).
3. See "What's Gone Wrong with Democracy?" *The Economist* (March 1, 2014). Available at www.economist.com/node/2159 7917; accessed August 29, 2015.
4. See Larry Diamond, "Chasing Away the Democracy Blues: Why Democracy is Worth Fighting For – Now More Than Ever," *Foreign Policy* (October 24, 2014). Available at http://foreignpolicy. com/2014/10/24/chasing-away-the-democracy-blues/; accessed August 30, 2015.
5. See Diamond and Plattner (1996, 2015).
6. See Flores and Nooruddin (2009, 2012).
7. See Matanock (2013).
8. See Dietrich and Wright (2015).
9. See Steinert and Grimm (2014) for findings consistent with ours.
10. See Walter (1999); Fortna (2008).
11. See Hultman, Kathman, and Shannon (2014); Hultman, Kathman, and Shannon (2015).
12. See Lloyd (2015).
13. Michael Miller shows that Western countries that limited popular participation in early elections did better at building democracy over the long run. See Miller (2015).
14. See Huntington (1968, 1). Robert Kaplan pays a similar homage to Huntington's intellectual legacy on this topic. See "Huntington on Upheaval," *Forbes* (July 31, 2013). Available at www.forbes.com/sites/stratfor/2013/07/31/huntington-on-upheaval/; accessed August 27, 2015.
15. Huntington (1968, 6).
16. Kaya and Bernhard (2013) examination of democratic change after elections in in thirty-three post-Communist countries represents an important exception.

17. See for example Palfrey (2009) and Woon (2012).
18. For good examples of such research, see Burchard (2015); De Juan and Pierskalla (2014); Dresden (2015); Hong and Kang (2015); Lyons (2005); Matanock (2013).

Bibliography

Acemoglu, Daron and James A. Robinson. 2006. *Economic Origins of Dictatorship and Democracy*. New York: Cambridge University Press.

Achen, Christopher H. and Larry M. Bartels. 2012. "Blind Retrospection: Why Shark Attacks Are Bad For Democracy." Vanderbilt University, Center for the Study of Democratic Institutions, Working paper 5-2013.

Almond, Gabriel A. and Sidney Verba. 1963. *The Civic Culture: Political Attitudes and Democracy in Five Nations*. Princeton, N.J.: Princeton University Press.

Almond, Gabriel A. and Sidney Verba. 1980. *The Civic Culture Revisited*. Beverly Hills, CA: Sage Publications.

Andersen, Jørgen J. and Michael L. Ross. 2014. "The Big Oil Change: A Closer Look at the Haber-Menaldo Analysis." *Comparative Political Studies* 47(7):993–1021.

Ansell, Ben. 2010. *From the Ballot to the Blackboard: The Redistributive Politics of Education*. New York: Cambridge University Press.

Ansell, Ben W. and David J. Samuels. 2014. *Inequality and Democratization: An Elite-Competition Approach*. New York: Cambridge University Press.

Arndt, Channing, Sam Jones, and Finn Tarp. 2014. "What is the Aggregate Economic Rate of Return to Foreign Aid?" WIDER Working Paper 2014/089.

Azevedo-Harman, Elisabete. 2015. "Patching Things Up in Mozambique." *Journal of Democracy* 26(2):139–150.

Ball, Nicole. 1996. *Making Peace Work: The Role of the International Development Community*. Washington, DC: Overseas Development Council.

Bar-Tal, Daniel. 2000. "From Intractable Conflict through Conflict Resolution to Reconciliation: Psychological Analysis." *Political Psychology* 21(2):351–365.

Barkan, Joel D. 2000. "Protracted Transitions among Africa's New Democracies." *Democratization* 7(3):227–243.

Baum, Matthew A. and David A. Lake. 2003. "The Political Economy of Growth: Democracy and Human Capital." *American Journal of Political Science* 47(2):333–347.

Beaulieu, Emily A. 2014. *Electoral Protest and Democracy in the Developing World*. New York: Cambridge University Press.

Beaulieu, Emily A. and Susan D. Hyde. 2009. "In the Shadow of Democracy Promotion: Strategic Manipulation, International Observers, and Election Boycotts." *Comparative Political Studies* 42(3): 392–415.

Beazer, Quintin, Irfan Nooruddin, and Sarah Wilson Sokhey. 2015. "Booms, Busts, and Education Spending." Working paper, Florida State University, Georgetown University, and University of Colorado.

Bell, Andrew and Kelvyn Jones. 2014. "Explaining Fixed Effects: Random Effects Modeling of Time-Series Cross-Sectional and Panel Data." *Political Science Research and Methods* 3(1):133–153.

Besley, Timothy. 2007. *Principled Agents? The Political Economy of Good Government*. New York: Oxford University Press.

Besley, Timothy and Torsten Persson. 2014. "Why Do Developing Countries Tax So Little?" *Journal of Economic Perspectives* 28(4): 99–120.

Boix, Carles. 2003. *Democracy and Redistribution*. Cambridge, UK: Cambridge University Press.

Boix, Carles and Susan C. Stokes. 2003. "Endogenous Democratization." *World Politics* 55(4):517–549.

Boulding, Carew Elizabeth. 2012. "Dilemmas of Information and Accountability: Foreign Aid Donors and Local Development NGOs." In *Credibility and Non-Government Organizations in a Globalizing World: When Virtue is Not Enough*, ed. Peter Gourevitch, David Lake, and Janice Gross Stein. New York: Cambridge University Press pp. 115–136.

Boutros-Ghali, Boutros. 1992. "An Agenda for Peace: Preventive Diplomacy, Peacemaking, and Peace-keeping." *International Relations* 11(3):201–218.

Bozzoli, Carlos, Tilman Brück, and Tony Muhumuza. 2011. "Does War Influence Individual Expectations?" *Economics Letters* 113(3):288–291.

Braithwaite, Alex, Niheer Dasandi, and David Hudson. 2014. "Does Poverty Cause Conflict? Isolating the Causal Origins of the Conflict Trap." *Conflict Management and Peace Science* 33(1):45–66.

Braithwaite, Jessica Maves. 2015. "Fighting for the Right to Party: Political Party Bans and the Onset of Civil Conflict." Working paper, University of Arizona.

Brancati, Dawn M. and Jack L. Snyder. 2013. "Time to Kill: The Impact of Election Timing on Post-conflict Stability." *Journal of Conflict Resolution* 57(5):822–850.

Bratton, Michael and Nicolas van de Walle. 1997. *Democratic Experiments in Africa: Regime Transitions in Comparative Perspective*. New York: Cambridge University Press.

Bräutigam, Deborah A. and Stephen Knack. 2004. "Foreign Aid, Institutions, and Governance in Sub-Saharan Africa." *Economic Development and Cultural Change* 52(2):255–285.

Breusch, Trevor, Michael B. Ward, Hoa Thi Minh Nguyen, and Tom Kompas. 2011. "On the Fixed-Effects Vector Decomposition." *Political Analysis* 19(2):123–134.

Brownlee, Jason. 2007. *Authoritarianism in an Age of Democratization*. New York: Cambridge University Press.

Brownlee, Jason. 2009. "Harbinger of Democracy: Competitive Elections Before the End of Authoritarianism." In *Democratization by Elections: A New Mode of Transition*, ed. Staffan I. Lindberg. Baltimore, MD: Johns Hopkins University Press pp. 128–147.

Bueno de Mesquita, Bruce and Alastair Smith. 2012. "Aid: Blame It All on 'Easy Money'." *Journal of Conflict Resolution* 57(3): 525–537.

Bueno de Mesquita, Bruce, Alastair Smith, Randolph M. Siverson, and James D. Morrow. 2003. *The Logic of Political Survival*. Cambridge, MA: MIT Press.

Burchard, Stephanie M. 2015. *Electoral Violence in Sub-Saharan Africa: Causes and Consequences*. Boulder, CO: Lynne Rienner Publishers.

Carbone, Giovanni M. 2007. "Political Parties and Party Systems in Africa: Themes and Research Perspectives." *World Political Science Review* 3(3):1–29.

Carothers, Thomas. 2006. *Confronting the Weakest Link: Aiding Political Parties in New Democracies*. Washington, DC: Carnegie Endowment for International Peace.

Carothers, Thomas. 2015. "Democracy Aid at 25: Time to Choose." In *Democracy in Decline?*, ed. Larry Diamond and Marc F. Plattner. Baltimore, MD: Johns Hopkins University Press pp. 77–97.

Cederman, Lars-Erik, Kristian Skrede Gleditsch, and Halvard Buhaug. 2013. *Inequality, Grievance, and Civil War*. New York: Cambridge University Press.

Cederman, Lars-Erik, Kristian Skrede Gleditsch, and Simon Hug. 2013. "Elections and Ethnic Civil War." *Comparative Political Studies* 46(3):387–417.

Cederman, Lars-Erik, Simon Hug, and Lutz F. Krebs. 2010. "Democratization and Civil War: Empirical Evidence." *Journal of Peace Research* 47(4):377–394.

Chandra, Kanchan. 2004. *Why Ethnic Parties Succeed: Patronage and Ethnic Head Counts in India*. New York: Cambridge University Press.

Cheibub, José Antonio, Jennifer Gandhi, and James Raymond Vreeland. 2010. "Democracy and Dictatorship Revisited." *Public Choice* 143(1):67–101.

Chhibber, Pradeep and Kenneth Kollman. 2004. *The Formation of National Party Systems*. Princeton, NJ: Princeton University Press.

Clark, Tom S. and Drew A. Linzer. 2015. "Should I Use Fixed or Random Effects?" *Political Science Research and Methods* 3(2):399–408.

Collier, Paul. 1999. "On the Economic Consequences of Civil War." *Oxford Economic Papers* 51(1):168–183.

Collier, Paul. 2008. *The Bottom Billion: Why the Poorest Countries are Failing and What Can Be Done About It*. New York: Oxford University Press.

Collier, Paul. 2009. *Wars, Guns, and Votes: Democracy in Dangerous Places*. New York: HarperCollins.

Collier, Paul and Anke Hoeffler. 2004. "Greed and Grievance in Civil War." *Oxford Economic Papers* 56(4):563–595.

Collier, Paul, Anke Hoeffler, and Dominic Rohner. 2009. "Beyond Greed and Grievance: Feasbility in Civil War." *Oxford Economic Papers* 61(1):1–27.

Collier, Paul, Anke Hoeffler, and Mans Söderbom. 2008. "Post-Conflict Risks." *Journal of Peace* 45(4):461–478.

Collier, Paul, V. L. Elliott, Havard Hegre, Anke Hoeffler, Marta Reynal-Querol, and Nicholas Sambanis. 2003. *Breaking the Conflict Trap: Civil War and Development Policy*. Washington, DC: World Bank.

Cutright, Phillips. 1963. "National Political Development: Measurement and Analysis." *American Sociological Review* 28(2):253–264.

Cutright, Phillips and James A. Wiley. 1969. "Modernization and Political Representation: 1927–1966." *Studies in Comparative International Development* 5(2):23–44.

Dahl, Robert A. 1971. *Polyarchy: Participation and Opposition*. New Haven, CT: Yale University Press.

Daly, Sarah Zukerman. 2012. "Organizational Legacies of Violence: Conditions Favoring Insurgency Onset in Colombia, 1964–1984." *Journal of Peace Research* 49(3):473–491.

Daxecker, Ursula. 2007. "Perilous Polities? An Assessment of the Democratization-Conflict Linkage." *European Journal of International Relations* 13(4):527–533.

De Juan, Alexander and Jan Henryk Pierskalla. 2014. "Civil War Violence and Political Trust: Microlevel Evidence from Nepal." *Conflict Management and Peace Science* 33(1):67–88.

Deutsch, Karl W. 1961. "Social Mobilization and Political Participation." *American Political Science Review* 55(3):493–514.

Diamond, Larry and Marc F. Plattner, eds. 1996. *The Global Resurgence of Democracy*. Baltimore, MD: Johns Hopkins University Press.

Diamond, Larry, and Marc F. Plattner, eds. 2015. *Democracy in Decline?* Baltimore, MD: Johns Hopkins University Press.

Dietrich, Simone. 2013. "Bypass or Engage? Explaining Donor Delivery Tactics in Foreign Aid Allocation." *International Studies Quarterly* 57:698–712.

Dietrich, Simone. 2015. "Donor Political Economies and the Pursuit of Aid Effectiveness." *International Organization* 70(1):65–102.

Dietrich, Simone and Matthew Winters. 2015. "Foreign Aid and Government Legitimacy." *Journal of Experimental Political Science* 2(2):164–171.

Dietrich, Simone and Joseph Wright. 2015. "Foreign Aid Allocation Tactics and Democratic Change in Africa." *Journal of Politics* 77(1):216–234.

Donno, Daniela. 2013. *Defending Democratic Norms: International Actors and the Politics of Electoral Misconduct*. New York: Oxford University Press.

Doyle, Michael W. and Nicholas Sambanis. 2006. *Making War and Building Peace: United Nations Peace Operations*. Princeton, NJ: Princeton University Press.

Dreher, Axel, Michael J. Lamla, Sarah M. Lein, and Frank Somogyi. 2009. "The Impact of Political Leaders Profession and Education on Reforms." *Journal of Comparative Economics* 37:169–193.

Dresden, Jennifer Raymond. 2015. "From Combatants to Candidates: Electoral Competition and the Legacy of Armed Conflict." *Conflict Management and Peace Science*. Advance online publication, doi:10.1177/0738894215593676.

Easterly, William. 2007. "Was Development Assistance a Mistake?" *American Economic Review* 97(2):328–332.

Eck, Kristine and Lisa Hultman. 2007. "One-Sided Violence Against Civilians in War Insights from New Fatality Data." *Journal of Peace Research* 44(2):233–246.

Fearon, James D. and David D. Laitin. 2003. "Ethnicity, Insurgency, and Civil War." *American Political Science Review* 97(1):75–90.

Fearon, James D., Macartan Humphreys, and Jeremy M. Weinstein. 2009. "Can Development Aid Contribute to Social Cohesion after Civil War?

Evidence from a Field Experiment in Post-Conflict Liberia." *American Economic Review* 99(2):287–291.

Finkel, Steven E., Aníbal Pérez-Linan, and Mitchell A. Seligson. 2007. "The Effects of U.S. Foreign Assistance on Democracy Building, 1990–2003." *World Politics* 59:404–439.

Flores, Thomas Edward. 2014. "Vertical Inequality, Land Reform, and Insurgency in Colombia." *Peace Economics, Peace Science and Public Policy* 20(1):5–31.

Flores, Thomas Edward and Irfan Nooruddin. 2009. "Democracy Under the Gun: Understanding Postconflict Economic Recovery." *Journal of Conflict Resolution* 53(1):3–29.

Flores, Thomas Edward and Irfan Nooruddin. 2012. "The Effect of Elections on Postconflict Peace and Reconstruction." *Journal of Politics* 74(2):558–570.

Flores, Thomas Edward, Gabriella E. Lloyd, and Irfan Nooruddin. 2014. "The Technocratic Advantage? Leadership and Sovereign Ratings." Presented at 2014 Annual Conference of the Midwest Political Science Association, Chicago, IL.

Fortin, Jessica. 2012. "Is There a Necessary Condition for Democracy? The Role of State Capacity in Postcommunist Countries." *Comparative Political Studies* 45(7):903–930.

Fortin-Rittberger, Jessica. 2014. "The Role of Infrastructural and Coercive State Capacity in Explaining Different Types of Electoral Fraud." *Democratization* 21(1):95–117.

Fortna, Virginia Page. 2008. *Does Peacekeeping Work? Shaping Belligerents' Choices after Civil War*. Princeton, NJ: Princeton University Press.

Franzese, Jr., Robert J. and Karen Long Jusko. 2006. "Political-economic Cycles." *In Oxford Handbook of Political Economy*, ed. Barry R. Weingast and Donald A. Wittman. New York: Oxford University Press pp. 545–586.

Fukuyama, Francis. 1989. "The End of History?" *The National Interest* (Summer):3–18.

Fukuyama, Francis. 2004. *State-Building: Governance and World Order in the 21st Century*. Ithaca, NY: Cornell University Press.

Fukuyama, Francis. 2011. *The Origins of Political Order: From Prehuman Times to the French Revolution*. New York: Farrar, Straus and Giroux.

Fukuyama, Francis. 2014. *Political Order and Political Decay: From the Industrial Revolution to the Globalization of Democracy*. New York: Farrar, Straus and Giroux.

Fukuyama, Francis. 2015. "Why is Democracy Performing So Poorly?" In *Decline of Democracy?*, ed. Larry Diamond and Marc F. Plattner. Baltimore, MD: Johns Hopkins University Press pp. 11–24.

Gandhi, Jennifer. 2010. *Political Institutions Under Dictatorships*. New York: Cambridge University Press.

Geddes, Barbara. 2003. *Paradigms and Sand Castles: Theory Building and Research Design in Comparative Politics*. Ann Arbor, MI: University of Michigan Press.

Ghobarah, Hazaem Adam, Paul K. Huth, and Bruce Russett. 2003. "Civil wars kill and maim people – Long after the shooting stops." *American Political Science Review* 97(2):189–202.

Gibler, Douglas M. and Kirk A. Randazzo. 2011. "Testing the Effects of Independent Judiciaries on the Likelihood of Democratic Backsliding." *American Journal of Political Science* 55(3):696–709.

Gift, Thomas and Daniel Krcmaric. 2015. "Who Democratizes? Western-Educated Leaders and Regime Transitions." *Journal of Conflict Resolution*. Advance online publication, doi: 10.1177/0022002715590878.

Gleditsch, Nils Petter, Peter Wallensteen, Mikael Eriksson, Margareta Sollenberg, and Håvard Strand. 2002. "Armed Conflict 1946–2001: A New Dataset." *Journal of Peace Research* 39(5):615–637.

Gottlieb, Jessica. 2015. "Greater Expectations: A Field Experiment to Improve Accountability in Mali." *American Journal of Political Science* 60(1):143–157.

Greene, William. 2011. "Fixed Effects Vector Decomposition: A Magical Solution to the Problem of Time-Invariant Variables in Fixed Effects Models?" *Political Analysis* 19(2):135–146.

Gurr, Ted Robert. 1970. *Why Men Rebel*. Princeton, NJ: Princeton University Press.

Ha, Eunyong and Melissa Ziegler Rogers. 2014. "Shifting the Burden in Global Markets: Partisan Effects on Tax Revenue in Less Developed Nations." Working Paper, Claremont Graduate University.

Hadenius, Axel and Jan Teorell. 2007. "Pathways from Authoritarianism." *Journal of Democracy* 18(1):143–157.

Haggard, Stephan and Lydia Tiede. 2014. "The Rule of Law in Post-Conflict Settings: The Empirical Record." *International Studies Quarterly* 58(2):405–417.

Henisz, Witold J. 2000. "The Institutional Environment for Economic Growth." *Economics and Politics* 12(1):1–31.

Henisz, Witold J. 2002. *Politics and International Investment: Measuring Risk and Protecting Profits*. London: Edward Elgar Publishers Ltd.

Hong, Ji Yeon and Woo Chang Kang. 2015. "Trauma and Stigma: The Long-Term Effects of Wartime Violence on Political Attitudes." *Conflict Management and Peace Science*. Advance online publication, doi: 10.1177/0738894215593683.

Horowitz, Michael C., Allan C. Stam, and Cali M. Ellis. 2015. *Why Leaders Fight*. New York: Cambridge University Press.

Howard, Marc Morjé, and Philip G. Roessler. 2006. "Liberalizing Electoral Outcomes in Competitive Authoritarian Regimes." *American Journal of Political Science* 50(2):365–381.

Hultman, Lisa, Jacob D. Kathman, and Megan Shannon. 2014. "Beyond Keeping Peace: United Nations Effectiveness in the Midst of Fighting." *American Political Science Review* 108(4):737–753.

Hultman, Lisa, Jacob D. Kathman, and Megan Shannon. 2015. "United Nations Peacekeeping Dynamics and the Duration of Post-Civil Conflict Peace." *Conflict Management and Peace Science*. Advance online publication, doi:10.1177/0738894215570425.

Huntington, Samuel P. 1968. *Political Order in Changing Societies*. New Haven, CT: Yale University Press.

Huntington, Samuel P. 1971. "The Change to Change: Modernization, Development, and Politics." *Comparative Politics* 3(3):283–322.

Huntington, Samuel P. 1991. *The Third Wave: Democratization in the Late Twentieth Century*. Norman, OK: University of Oklahoma Press.

Hyde, Susan D. 2011. *The Pseudo-Democrat's Dilemma: Why Election Monitoring Became an International Norm*. Ithaca, NY: Cornell University Press.

Hyde, Susan D. and Nikolay Marinov. 2012. "Which Elections can be Lost?" *Political Analysis* 20(2):191–210.

Inglehart, Ronald. 1997. *Modernization and Postmodernization*. Princeton, NJ: Princeton University Press.

Inglehart, Ronald and Christian Welzel. 2005. *Modernization, Cultural Change, and Democracy: The Human Development Sequence*. New York: Cambridge University Press.

Iqbal, Zaryab. 2010. *War and the Health of Nations*. Palo Alto, CA: Stanford University Press.

Jaffrelot, Christophe. 2002. "India and Pakistan: Interpreting the Divergence of Two Political Trajectories." *Cambridge Review of International Affairs* 15(2):251–267.

Jaggers, Keith and Ted Robert Gurr. 1995. "Tracking Democracy's Third Wave with the Polity III Data." *Journal of Peace Research* 32(4):469–482.

Jamal, Amaney and Irfan Nooruddin. 2010. "The Democratic Utility of Trust: A Cross-National Analysis." *Journal of Politics* 72(1):45–59.

Jones, Owen Bennett. 2002. *Pakistan: Eye of the Storm*. New Haven, CT: Yale University Press.

Kang, Seonjou and James Meernik. 2005. "Civil War Destruction and the Prospects for Economic Growth." *Journal of Politics* 67(1):88–109.

Kaplan, Stephen B. 2013. *Globalization and Austerity Politics in Latin America*. New York: Cambridge University Press.

Kapstein, Ethan B. and Nathan Converse. 2008. *The Fate of Young Democracies*. Cambridge: Cambridge University Press.

Kaufmann, Daniel, Aart Kraay, and Pablo Zoido-Lobatón. 2000. "Governance Matters." *Finance & Development* 37(2):10–13.

Kaya, Ruchan and Michael Bernhard. 2013. "Are Elections Mechanisms of Authoritarian Stability or Democratization? Evidence from Postcommunist Eurasia." *Perspectives on Politics* 11(3):734–752.

Kelley, Judith G. 2012. *Monitoring Democracy: When International Election Observation Works, and Why It Often Fails*. Princeton, NJ: Princeton University Press.

Kennedy, Ryan. 2010. "The Contradiction of Modernization: A Conditional Model of Endogenous Democratization." *Journal of Politics* 72(3):785–798.

Kenny, Charles. 2012. *Getting Better: Why Global Development Is Succeeding – And How We Can Improve the World Even More*. New York: Basic Books.

Kugler, Jacek and Ronald Tammen, eds. 2012. *Performance of Nations*. Lanham, MD: Rowman & Littlefield.

La Porta, Rafael, Florencio Lopez-de Silanes, Andrei Shleifer, and Robert Vishney. 1999. "The Quality of Government." *Journal of Law, Economics, and Organization* 15(1):222–282.

Lake, David A. 2010. "Building Legitimate States After Civil Wars." In *Strengthening Peace in Post-Civil War States: Transforming Spoilers Into Stakeholders*, ed. Matthew Hoddie and Caroline A. Hartzell. Chicago, IL: The University of Chicago Press pp. 29–52.

Lake, David A. and Matthew A. Baum. 2001. "The Invisible Hand of Democracy." *Comparative Political Studies* 34(6):587–621.

Lave, Charles A. and James G. March. 1975. *An Introduction to Models in the Social Sciences*. Lanham, MD: University Press of America.

LeBas, Adrienne. 2011. *From Protest to Parties: Party-Building and Democratization in Africa*. New York: Oxford University Press.

Levi, Margaret. 1988. *Of Rule and Revenue*. Berkeley, CA: University of California Press.

Levitsky, Steven and Lucan A. Way. 2010. *Competitive Authoritarianism: Hybrid Regimes After the Cold War*. New York: Cambridge University Press.

Lewis, Peter and Darren Kew. 2015. "Nigeria's Hopeful Election." *Journal of Democracy* 26(3):94–109.

Lindberg, Staffan I. 2006. *Democracy and Elections in Africa*. Baltimore, MD: Johns Hopkins University Press.

Lindberg, Staffan I. 2009*a*. *Democratization by Elections: A New Mode of Transitions*. Baltimore, MD: Johns Hopkins University Press.

Lindberg, Staffan I. 2009*b*. "The Power of Elections in Africa Revisited." In *Democratization by Elections: A New Mode of Transition*, ed. Staffan I. Lindberg. Baltimore, MD: Johns Hopkins University Press pp. 25–46.

Linz, Juan J. and Alfred Stepan. 1996. *Problems of Democratic Transition and Consolidation: Southern Europe, South America, and Post-Communist Europe*. Baltimore, MD: Johns Hopkins University Press.

Lipset, Seymour Martin. 1959. "Some Social Requisites of Democracy: Economic Development and Political Legitimacy." *American Political Science Review* 53(1):69–105.

Lloyd, Gabriella E. 2015. "Security-Building through Peacekeeping? UN Peacekeeping and Police Reform in Post-Civil Conflict States." Working paper, The Ohio State University.

Londregan, John B. and Keith T. Poole. 1990. "Poverty, the Coup Trap, and the Seizure of Executive Power." *World Poltics* 42(2): 151–183.

Lyons, Terrence. 1998. *Voting for Peace: Postconflict Elections in Liberia*. Washington, DC: Brookings Institution Press.

Lyons, Terrence. 2005. *Demilitarizing Politics: Elections on the Uncertain Road to Peace*. Boulder, CO: Lynne Rienner Publishers.

Mainwaring, Scott P. 1998. "Party Systems in the Third Wave." *Journal of Democracy* 9(3):67–81.

Mainwaring, Scott P. 1999. *Rethinking Party Systems in the Third Wave of Democratization: The Case of Brazil*. Palo Alto, CA: Stanford University Press.

Mansfield, Edward D. and Jack L. Snyder. 1995. "Democratization and the Danger of War." *International Sec* 20(1):5–38.

Mansfield, Edward D. and Jack L. Snyder. 2002. "Democratic Transitions, Institutional Strength, and War." *International Organization* 56(2):297–337.

Mansfield, Edward D. and Jack Snyder. 2007. *Electing to Fight: Why Emerging Democracies Go to Wars*. Boston, MA: The MIT Press.

Marshall, Monty G., Ted Robert Gurr, and Keith Jaggers. 2014. "Polity IV Project: Political Regime Characteristics and Transitions, 1800–2013. A Dataset User's Manual." Center for Systemic Peace.

Matanock, Aila M. 2013. "Bullets for Ballots: Electoral Participation Provisions in Peace Agreements and Conflict Recurrence." Working paper, UC Berkeley.

McCoy, Jennifer L. and Jonathan Hartlyn. 2009. "The Relative Powerlessness of Elections in Latin America." In *Democratization by Elections: A New Mode of Transition*, ed. Staffan I. Lindberg. Baltimore, MD: Johns Hopkins University Press pp. 47–76.

Meltzer, Allan H. and Scott F. Richard. 1981. "A Rational Theory of the Size of Government." *Journal of Political Economy* 89(5):914–927.

Miller, Michael K. 2012. "Economic Development, Violent Leader Removal, and Democratization." *American Journal of Political Science* 56(4):1002–1020.

Miller, Michael K. 2015. "Democratic Pieces: Autocratic Elections and Democratic Development Since 1815." *British Journal of Political Science* 45(3):501–530.

Moore, Jr., Barrington. 1966. *Social Origins of Dictatorship and Democracy: Lord and Peasant in the Modern World*. Boston, MA: Beacon Press.

Morrison, Kevin McDonald. 2007. "Natural Resources, Aid, and Democratization: A Best-Case Scenario." *Public Choice* 131(3):365–386.

Morrison, Kevin McDonald. 2012. "What Can We Learn About the Resource Curse from Foreign Aid?" *World Bank Research Observer* 27(1):52–73.

Mozaffar, Shaheen, James R. Scarritt, and Glen Galaich. 2003. "Electoral Institutions, Ethnopolitical Cleavages, and Party Systems in Africa's Emerging Democracies." *American Political Science Review* 97(3):379–390.

Mozaffar, Shaheen and J. R. Scarritt. 2005. "The Puzzle of African Party Systems." *Party Politics* 11(4):399–421.

National Democratic Institute for International Affairs. 2013. "The 2013 National and Provincial Assembly Elections in Pakistan: Final Report." Final Report of the Joint International Election Observation Mission of the National Democratic Institute for International Affairs and the Asian Network for Free Elections.

Nooruddin, Irfan. 2008. "The Political Economy of National Debt Burdens, 1970–2000." *International Interactions* 34(2):156–185.

Nooruddin, Irfan. 2011. Coalition Politics and Economic Development: Credibility and the Strength of Weak Governments. Cambridge, UK: Cambridge University Press.

Nooruddin, Irfan and Pradeep Chhibber. 2008. "Unstable Politics: Electoral Volatility in the Indian State." *Comparative Political Studies* 41(8):1069–1091.

Nooruddin, Irfan and Joel W. Simmons. 2006. "The Politics of Hard Choices: IMF Programs and Government Spending." *International Organization* 60(4):1001–1033.

Nordlinger, Eric A. 1968. "Political Development: Time and Sequence and Rates of Change." *World Politics* 20(3):494–520.

Norris, Pippa. 2013*a*. "Does the World agree about Standards of Electoral Integrity? Evidence for the Diffusion of Global Norms." *Electoral Studies* 32(4):576–588.

Norris, Pippa. 2013*b*. "The New Research Agenda Studying Electoral Integrity." *Electoral Studies* 32(4):563–575.

Norris, Pippa. 2014. *Why Electoral Integrity Matters*. New York: Cambridge University Press.

Norris, Pippa. 2015. *Why Elections Fail*. New York: Cambridge University Press.

Norris, Pippa, Richard W. Frank, and Ferran Martínez i Coma, eds. 2014. *Advancing Electoral Integrity*. New York: Oxford University Press.

O'Donnell, Guillermo A. 1973. *Modernization and Bureaucratic-Authoritarianism: Studies in South American Politics*. Berkeley, CA: University of California Press.

O'Donnell, Guillermo and Phillippe C. Schmitter. 1986. *Transitions from Authoritarian Rule, Vol. 4: Tentative Conclusions about Uncertain Democracies*. Baltimore, MD: Johns Hopkins University Press.

Olson, Mancur. 1993. "Dictatorship, Democracy, and Development." *American Political Science Review* 87(3):567–576.

Ottaway, Marina. 2003. "Promoting Democracy After Conflict: The Difficult Choices." *International Studies Perspectives* 4(3):314–322.

Palfrey, Thomas R. 2009. "Laboratory Experiments in Political Economy." *Annual Review of Political Science* 12(1):379–388.

Panebianco, Angelo. 1988. *Political Parties: Organization and Power*. Cambridge, UK: Cambridge University Press.

Paris, Roland. 2004. *At War's End: Building Peace after Civil Conflict*. Cambridge, UK: Cambridge University Press.

Pemstein, Daniel, Stephen A. Meserve, and James Melton. 2010. "Democratic Compromise: A Latent Variable Analysis of Ten Measures of Regime Type." *Political Analysis* 18(4):426–449.

Pevehouse, Jon C. 2005. *Democracy From Above: Regional Organizations and Democratization*. Cambridge University Press.

Phillips, Brian J. 2015. "Civil War, Spillover, and Neighbors' Military Spending." *Conflict Management and Peace Science* 32(4):425–442.

Plümper, Thomas, and Vera E. Troeger. 2007. "The Estimation of Time-Variant Variables in Panel Analyses with Unit Fixed Effects." *Political Analysis* 15(2):124–139.

Poast, Paul, and Johannes Urpelainen. 2015. "Organizing Democracy: How International Organizations Assist Democratic Consolidation." Book manuscript, University of Chicago and Columbia University.

Pop-Eleches, Grigore, and Graeme B. Robertson. 2015. "Structural Conditions and Democratization." *Journal of Democracy* 26(3):144–156.

Powell, Jonathan M. and Clayton L. Thyne. 2011. "Global Instances of Coups from 1950 to 2010: A New Dataset." *Journal of Peace Research* 48(2):249–259.

Przeworski, Adam. 2015. "Acquiring the Habit of Changing Governments Through Elections." *Comparative Political Studies* 48(1):101–129.

Przeworski, Adam and Fernando Limongi. 1997. "Modernization: Theories and Facts." *World Politics* 49(2):155–183.

Przeworski, Adam, Michael E. Alvarez, Jose A. Cheibub, and Fernando Limongi. 2000. *Democracy and Development: Political Institutions and Well-Being in the World, 1950–1990*. New York: Cambridge University Press.

Rakner, Lise and Nicholas van de Walle. 2009. "Opposition Parties and Incumbent Presidents: The New Dynamics of Electoral Competition in Africa." In *Democratization by Elections: A New Mode of Transitions*, ed. Staffan I. Lindberg. Baltimore, MD: Johns Hopkins University Press pp. 202–225.

Roessler, Philip G. and Marc M. Howard. 2009. "Post-Cold War Political Regimes: When Do Elections Matter?" In *Democratization by Elections: A New Mode of Transition*, ed. Staffan I. Lindberg. Baltimore, MD: Johns Hopkins University Press pp. 101–127.

Rohner, Dominic, Mathias Thoenig, and Fabrizio Zilibotti. 2013. "Seeds of Distrust: Conflict in Uganda." *Journal of Economic Growth* 18(3):217–252.

Rose, Richard and Doh Chull Shin. 2001. "Democratization Backwards: The Problem of Third-Wave Democracies." *British Journal of Political Science* 31(2):331–354.

Ross, Michael L. 2001. "Does Oil Hinder Democracy?" *World Politics* 53(3):325–361.

Ross, Michael L. 2012. *The Oil Curse: How Petroleum Wealth Shapes the Development of Nations*. Princeton, NJ: Princeton University Press.

Rudra, Nita. 2005. "Globalization and the Strengthening of Democracy in the Developing World." *American Journal of Political Science* 49(4):704–730.

Russett, Bruce M. and John Oneal. 2001. *Triangulating Peace: Democracy, Interdependence, and International Organizations*. New York: W. W. Norton.

Rustow, Dankwart A. 1970. "Transitions to Democracy: Toward a Dynamic Model." *Comparative Politics* 2(3):337–363.

Sachs, Jeffrey D. 2005. *The End of Poverty: Economic Possibilities for Our Time.* New York: Penguin Press.

Sambanis, Nicholas. 2004. "What Is Civil War? Conceptual and Empirical Complexities of an Operational Definition." *The Journal of Conflict Resolution* 48(6):814–858.

Schedler, Andreas. 2002. "The Menu of Manipulation." *Journal of Democracy* 13(2):36–50.

Schedler, Andreas. 2009. "The Contingent Power of Authoritarian Elections." In *Democratization by Elections: A New Mode of Transition,* ed. Staffan I. Lindberg. Baltimore, MD: Johns Hopkins University Press pp. 291–313.

Sen, Ronojoy. 2009. "The Problem of Corruption." *Journal of Democracy* 20(4):89–92.

Simpser, Alberto. 2013. *Why Governments and Parties Manipulate Elections: Theory, Practice, and Implications.* New York: Cambridge University Press.

Slater, Dan. 2010. *Ordering Power: Contentious Politics and Authoritarian Leviathans in Southeast Asia.* New York: Cambridge University Press.

Small, Melvin and J. David Singer. 1976. "The War-Proneness of Democratic Regimes." *Jerusalem Journal of International Relations* 1(1):50–69.

Small, Melvin and J. David Singer. 1982. *Resort to Arms: International and Civil Wars, 1816–1980.* Beverly Hills, CA: Sage Publications.

Snyder, Jack L. 2000. *From Voting to Violence: Democratization and Nationalist Conflict.* New York: W. W. Norton & Company.

Stasavage, David. 2005. "Democracy and Education Spending In Africa." *American Journal of Political Science* 49(2):343–358.

Steinert, Janina Isabel and Sonja Grimm. 2014. "Too Good to be True? United Nations Peacebuilding and the Democratization of War-torn States." *Conflict Management and Peace Science.* Advance online publication, doi:10.1177/0738894214559671.

Stokes, Susan C., Thad Dunning, Marcelo Nazareno, and Valeria Brusco. 2013. *Brokers, Voters, and Clientelism: The Puzzle of Distributive Politics.* New York: Cambridge University Press.

Synge, Richard. 1997. *Mozambique: UN Peacekeeping in Action, 1992–94.* Washington, DC: United States Institute of Peace.

Teorell, Jan. 2010. *Determinants of Democratization: Explaining Regime Change in the World, 1972–2006.* Cambridge, UK: Cambridge University Press.

Teorell, Jan and Axel Hadenius. 2009. "Elections as Levers of Democratization: A Global Inquiry." In *Democratization by Elections: A New Mode of Transition*, ed. Staffan I. Lindberg. Baltimore, MD: Johns Hopkins University Press pp. 77–100.

Themnér, Lotta. 2013. "UCDP/PRIO Armed Conflict Dataset Codebook." Version 4-2013. Uppsala Conflict Data Program.

Themnér, Lotta and Peter Wallensteen. 2013. "Armed Conflict, 1946–2012." *Journal of Peace Research* 50(4):509–521.

Toft, Monica Duffy. 2009. *Securing the Peace: The Durable Settlement of Civil Wars*. Princeton, NJ: Princeton University Press.

Uppsala Conflict Data Program. 2014. "UCDP Battle-Related Deaths Dataset v.5–2014." Available at: www.pcr.uu.se/research/UCDP/; accessed February 14, 2016.

Vreeland, James Raymond. 2003. *The IMF and Economic Development*. New York: Cambridge University Press.

Vreeland, James Raymond. 2008. "The Effect of Political Regime on Civil War: Unpacking Anocracy." *Journal of Conflict Resolution* 52(3):401–425.

Walter, Barbara F. 1999. "Designing Transitions from Civil War: Demobilization, Democratization, and Commitments to Peace." *International Security* 24(1):127–155.

Weingast, Barry. 1997. "The Political Foundations of Democracy and the Rule of Law." *American Political Science Review* 91(2):245–263.

Williamson, John. 1990. "What Washington Means by Policy Reform." In *Latin American Readjustment: How Much has Happened*, ed. John Williamson. Washington, DC: Institute for International Economics.

Wimmer, Andreas, Lars-Erik Cederman, and Brian Min. 2009. "Ethnic Politics and Armed Conflict. A Configurational Analysis of a New Global Dataset." *American Sociological Review* 74(2):316–337.

Wood, Elisabeth J. 2003. *Insurgent Collective Action and Civil War in El Salvador*. Cambridge, UK: Cambridge University Press.

Woon, Jonathan. 2012. "Democratic Accountability and Retrospective Voting: A Laboratory Experiment." *American Journal of Political Science* 56(4):913–930.

World Bank. 2011. *World Development Report 2011: Conflict, Security, and Development*. Washington, DC: The World Bank.

Index